Spanish
Workbook

by Gail Stein

for dummies®
A Wiley Brand

Spanish Workbook For Dummies®

Published by: **John Wiley & Sons, Inc.,** 111 River Street, Hoboken, NJ 07030-5774, www.wiley.com

For general information on our other products and services, please contact our Customer Care Department within the U.S. at 877-762-2974, outside the U.S. at 317-572-3993, or fax 317-572-4002. For technical support, please visit https://hub.wiley.com/community/support/dummies.

Wiley publishes in a variety of print and electronic formats and by print-on-demand. Some material included with standard print versions of this book may not be included in e-books or in print-on-demand. If this book refers to media such as a CD or DVD that is not included in the version you purchased, you may download this material at http://booksupport.wiley.com. For more information about Wiley products, visit www.wiley.com.

ISBN: 978-1-119-91025-1 (pbk); 978-1-119-91026-8 (ebk); 978-1-119-91027-5 (ebk)

SKY10044342_031123

Contents at a Glance

Table of Contents

PART 3: GIVING AND OBTAINING INFORMATION 163

Introduction

You've picked up this book because your goal is to learn and communicate in Spanish. That's fantastic! Knowledge of a foreign language will open up a world of opportunities for you. So here you are, eager to jump in and acquire a new skill. Whether you're planning a trip, engaging in business with Spanish speakers, or just a lover of languages, *Spanish Workbook For Dummies* will help you achieve your goals quickly, painlessly and effortlessly. Turn the page and enter a world that will provide you with endless opportunities, intriguing experiences, and exciting challenges. Embark on a journey that will open the door to a different culture, a unique lifestyle, and a distinctive outlook on life. Immerse yourself in all things Spanish-related and perfect your foreign language skills. Therein lies the main goal of this book.

Spanish Workbook For Dummies not only presents you with all the grammar you need to know to communicate on a beginning level but also provides you with clear examples and interesting and meaningful theme-based exercises that will help you hone your skills. I give you the opportunity to put what you've learned to work and to express your thoughts and ideas fluidly. If you can finish the exercises in a flash, you know you've mastered the material well. Some exercises, of course, present more of a challenge and require additional attention and focus. That's to be expected. Just keep in mind that after you finish all the chapters, you'll be a full-fledged beginning graduate! Feel free to give yourself a pat on the back!

About This Book

This book is for anyone who wants to have a basic, working knowledge of Spanish. It's a reference book and a workbook for people who strive to communicate and improve their proficiency in a language that is popular worldwide. If you want to get "up to speed" with language structures so you can understand, speak, read, and write in Spanish, this book is for you.

Each chapter in this book covers a different topic that affords you the opportunity to practice your skills by completing exercises designed to increase your vocabulary and develop your grammar skills. I reinforce nuances of style, usage, and grammar rules every step of the way so that you understand and practice how native speakers and writers use the language. I also include plenty of examples to guide you through the rules and exercises and to expose you to colloquial, everyday, correct Spanish that native speakers expect to hear from someone using Spanish.

Each section covers a different topic. Rest assured that basic elementary Spanish is fully covered. Each chapter includes exercises that allow you to practice and master what you've learned. More specifically, I make sure that each chapter contains the following:

>> An introduction to the material being presented

>> An explanation of how the grammar works

» Sample questions and answers that show you how to complete the exercises

» Exercises that help you perfect your skills

» An answer key with detailed explanations for each exercise

Before you move on, I must reiterate an important point: This is a workbook! Don't be afraid to write in it. Use your favorite colored highlighter or your trusty red pen to underline the points you want to remember. Complete an exercise, commit to your answers, then flip to the end of the chapter where the answer key will provide you not only with the correct answers but also a detailed explanation of how to get to that answer.

One final thought — don't feel compelled to follow this book strictly from beginning to end. Feel free to skip around to whatever section interests you the most. Don't be shy about consulting the Thematic Vocabulary lists located at the end of the book. They will certainly be extremely useful in helping you quickly build your vocabulary skills.

Foolish Assumptions

When writing this book, I made the following assumptions about you. If they apply, you've come to the right place:

» You have limited experience with and knowledge of the fundamentals of Spanish grammar. You're looking for the opportunity to use what you already know and intend to move forward to new areas of knowledge.

» You want to perfect your Spanish because you're planning a trip, conducting business, or are a foreign-language student.

» You want to speak and write Spanish colloquially, like a native does, and you want to use Spanish in practical, everyday situations.

» You want a book that's complete but isn't so advanced that you get lost in the rules. I try to explain the rules as clearly as possible without using too many grammatical terms. I've left out advanced grammar because you simply don't need it to be understood in everyday situations. Keep it clean and simple and you'll do just fine, and others will appreciate your honest attempts at communicating in another language.

Icons Used in This Book

Icons are those cute little drawings on the left side of the page that call out for your attention. They signal a particularly valuable piece of information, a rule that you should consider if you want to avoid making an unnecessary error, or a list of exercises that you can complete. Here's a list of the icons in this book:

Remember icons call your attention to important information about the language — something you shouldn't neglect or something that's out of the ordinary. Don't ignore these paragraphs.

Tip icons are there to show you explicitly how to execute a task. Tips present time-saving tidbits that make communication quick and effective. If you want to know the proper way to do things, check out the Tip icons first.

Warning icons alert you to irregularities within the language that can lead you astray and cause you to make mistakes that identify you as a non-native speaker.

The Practice icons flag exercises, which is where you need to go to put the grammar rules you read about into action. Language theory is grand, but if you can't apply it properly, it really isn't worth very much. The practice exercises are your golden opportunity to perfect your Spanish skills.

Beyond the Book

In addition to the material in this book or ebook, be sure to look for the free Cheat Sheet for additional quick reference notes pertaining to the most useful Spanish grammar topics. To get this Cheat Sheet, simply go to www.dummies.com and search for "Spanish Workbook" in the Search box.

Where to Go from Here

One great thing about this book (and all *For Dummies* books) is that you don't have to follow it chapter by chapter from the very beginning to the (not-so) bitter end. You can start where you like and jump all over the place if that is your pleasure. Each chapter stands on its own and doesn't require that you complete any of the other chapters in the book. This saves you a lot of time if you've mastered certain topics but feel a bit insecure or hesitant about others.

So go ahead and jump right in. Get your feet wet. If you're not sure exactly where to begin, take a good look at the table of contents and select the topic that seems to best fit your abilities and needs. If you're concerned and are new to the Spanish language, you can start at the very beginning and slowly work your way through the book. If you feel confident and self-assured, skip right to the practice exercises and see how well you do. Because each lesson is an entity unto itself, you can hop around from the middle to the front to the back without missing a beat.

An important thing to keep in mind is that this isn't a race, and it isn't a contest. Work at a pace that best suits your needs. Don't hesitate to read a chapter a second or third or even a fourth time several days later. You may even want to repeat some exercises. This is a book that you can easily adapt to your learning abilities. Remember, too, that you need to have a positive, confident attitude. Yes, you'll make mistakes. Everyone does — as a matter of fact, many native Spanish speakers do all the time. Your main goal should be to do the best you can; if you do trip up, it isn't the end of the world. If you can make yourself understood, you've won the greatest part of the battle.

1

Getting Started
with the Basics

Chapter **1**

Getting a Jump Start in Spanish

Whether you're a student, a traveler, a businessperson, or simply someone who wants to learn another language, you'll need and, indeed, *want* to know certain foreign language basics for most everyday situations. For example, it's essential that you address your peers, acquaintances, as well as total strangers in a socially acceptable manner. Can you greet those around you in a casual manner, or is being more formal the appropriate way to proceed? Some social interactions require that you arrange appointments and meetings, plan trips, consult schedules, or discuss financial transactions where numbers, dates, and telling time are crucial basics to know.

This chapter provides you not only with those Spanish basics but also with communicative exercises that will enable you to confidently express greetings and salutations, numbers, days of the week, months of the year, seasons, dates, and time for speaking and writing in Spanish.

Expressing Greetings and Salutations

The Spanish language clearly recognizes and requires that you use different levels of formality depending on whom you're addressing. You certainly wouldn't speak or write to a stranger, teacher, business acquaintance, customer, boss, or any person in a position of authority in the same way as you would to a family member, friend, or child. It's not just your tone of voice that matters; it's the words you use that make the difference. And in today's rapidly changing world, being inclusive and respectful of others is of paramount importance.

Use the following formal phrases when you want to meet and greet a stranger, someone you don't know very well, someone in a position of authority, or someone to whom you should show respect.

Buenos días.	Hello. Good morning.
Buenas tardes.	Good afternoon.
Buenas noches	Good evening.
Señor	Mister, sir.
Señorita	Miss, young woman.
Señora	Mrs. (or older unmarried woman)
Me llamo . . .	My name is . . .
¿Cómo se llama?	What is your name?
¿Cómo está?	How are you?
Muy bien.	Very well.
Así así.	So-so.
Regular.	Fair.
Mucho gusto.	Nice to meet you.
Es un placer.	It's a pleasure.
El gusto es mío.	The pleasure is mine.
Adiós.	Goodbye.
Hasta luego.	See you later.
Hasta mañana.	See you tomorrow.

Use the following informal phrases when you want to meet and greet a single friend, relative, child, and, of course, your beloved pet.

¡Hola!	Hi.
Me llamo . . .	My name is . . .
¿Cómo te llamas?	What's your name?
¿Cómo estás?	How are you?
¿Cómo te va?	How's it going?
¿Qué tal?	How are things?
¿Qué pasa?	What's going on?
¿Qué hay de nuevo?	What's new?
Nada de particular.	Nothing much.
Nos vemos.	See you later.
Hasta (muy) pronto.	See you (very) soon.
Hasta la vista.	Till the next time.
Que te vaya bien.	Have a good day.
Que tengas un buen día.	Have a good day.
Adiós./Chau.	Bye.

PRACTICE

Should you be formal or more informal? Express what you would say to the people in the following circumstances. Sometimes, more than one response may be correct.

Q. You are walking home from school and meet a friend you haven't seen in a while. You greet this friend by saying . . .

_____

A. ¿Cómo te va? or ¿Qué tal? or ¿Qué pasa? or ¿Qué hay de nuevo? These particular friendly questions (all four of them) inquire about what your friend has been up to lately.

Now try the following, remembering to be polite or casual depending on whom you're addressing.

_____

1. There's a new student in your class whom you want to get to know better. But first you have to find out more information, such as the person's name. You would ask . . .

_____

2. A new neighbor has moved in across the street. When you see him leaving for work in the morning, you would greet him by saying . . .

_____

3. You just came back from a long day away from home and your dog comes to greet you at the door. You would respond to her by saying . . .

_____

4. You are the new person on a job and you want to introduce yourself to your coworkers. You would say . . .

_____

5. You have an afternoon appointment at the doctor. When you enter the office, you would say . . .

_____

6. Recently, life has been pretty boring. When a friend asks you what's new, you would answer . . .

_____

7. It's the end of the workday and you see your boss, Mr. López, as you are leaving. As you walk out the door, you would say . . .

_____

8. Your friend has been sneezing and coughing. You would say . . .

_____

9. After meeting a new colleague and exchanging initial pleasantries, you would say . . .

_____

10. You want to express to a certain friend that you are looking forward to seeing them again soon. You would say . . .

_____

Referring to Others Using Subject Pronouns

A pronoun is a part of speech used in place of a noun. Subject pronouns are followed by the verb expressing the main action in the sentence. (See Chapter 6 for more on verb conjugation.)

In English, you use subject pronouns all the time in place of, or to avoid, repeating subject nouns. It's much simpler to write, "They left," rather than "Mr. Anthony Bolavolunta and Miss Cleopatra Johnson left." The subject pronouns *I, you, he, she, we,* and *they* enable you to write clear, concise sentences. Subject nouns and pronouns alike are followed by the appropriate forms of the verbs expressing particular actions.

TIP

You don't use Spanish subject pronouns as frequently as their English counterparts, because a Spanish verb ending generally indicates the subject. You use Spanish subject pronouns, therefore, mainly to be polite, to emphasize or stress the subject, or to be perfectly clear as to who (or what) is acting as the subject of the sentence.

Meeting the subject pronouns

Just like in English, Spanish subject pronouns have a person (first, second, or third) and a number (singular or plural), as you can see in Table 1-1.

Table 1-1   Spanish Subject Pronouns

Person	Singular	Meaning	Plural	Meaning
1st person	yo	*I*	nosotros (nosotras)	*we*
2nd person informal (familiar)	tú	*you*	vosotros (vosotras)	*you*
2nd person formal (polite)	usted (Ud.)	*you*	ustedes (Uds.)	*you*
3rd person	él	*he*	ellos	*they*
	ella	*she*	ellas	*they*

You don't express the English pronoun *it* as a subject in Spanish; it can be understood from the meaning of the sentence:

¿Qué es? (*What is it?*)

Es una herramienta. (*It's a tool.*)

Unlike the English subject pronoun *I*, which is always capitalized, the Spanish pronoun **yo** is capitalized only at the beginning of a sentence. You always write the abbreviations **Ud.** and **Uds.** with capital letters, even though you write the English equivalent *you* with a lowercase letter, unless it appears at the beginning of a sentence. When **usted** and **ustedes** aren't abbreviated, they're capitalized only at the beginning of a sentence. Here are some examples:

Yo me voy. (*I'm leaving.*)

Eduardo y yo salimos. (*Edward and I are going out.*)

¿Busca Ud. (usted) algo? (*Are you looking for something?*)

¿Uds. (Ustedes) necesitan ayuda? (*Do you need help?*)

Applying subject pronouns

The use of certain subject pronouns can be confusing because two different Spanish pronouns may have the same English meaning. Other Spanish subject pronouns are used either primarily in Spain or in Latin America. Finally, some Spanish subject pronouns refer only to females while others refer to males or to a mixed group of males and females. The following section helps you select the correct subject pronoun for all circumstances in all parts of the Spanish-speaking world.

Tú versus Ud.

You use the informal (familiar) subject pronoun **tú** to address one friend, relative, child, or pet, because it is the informal, singular form of *you*. You use **tú** to express *you* when you enjoy a close relationship with a person, when you are in a familiar or informal situation, or when you are speaking to a pet:

Tú eres mi mejor amigo. (*You're my best friend.*)

You use **Ud.** to show respect to an older person or when speaking to a stranger or someone you don't know well, because **Ud.** is the formal, singular form of *you*. You may also use **Ud.** when you want to get to know the person better:

¿Es Ud. español? (*Are you Spanish?*)

Vosotros (Vosotras) versus Uds.

Vosotros and **vosotras** are informal (familiar) plural subject pronouns expressing *you*. The **vosotros** (**vosotras**) form is used primarily in Spain to address more than one friend, relative, child, or pet — the informal, plural form of *you*. You use **vosotros** when speaking to a group of males or to a combined group of males and females. You use **vosotras** only when speaking to a group of females. You use **vosotros** (**vosotras**) only in Spain when speaking to a group of people in a familiar or informal situation.

¿Vosotros me comprendéis? (*Do you understand me?*)

Uds. is a plural subject pronoun that also expresses *you.* **Uds.** is used throughout the Spanish-speaking world to show respect to more than one older person or when speaking to multiple strangers or people you don't know well. **Uds.** is the formal, plural form of *you* (but is also used as the informal plural) and is used instead of **vosotros** (**vosotras**) in Latin American countries. You're playing it safe if you use **Uds.** when speaking to a group of people:

Uds. son muy simpáticos. (*You are very nice.*)

Él versus ella

Él refers to one male person (*he*); **ella** (*she*) refers to one female person:

Él toca la guitarra mientras ella baila. (*He plays the guitar while she dances.*)

Ellos versus ellas

Ellos (*they*) refers to more than one male or to a combined group of males and females, no matter the number of each gender present. **Ellas** refers to a group of females only:

Juan y Jorge (Ellos) escuchan. (*Juan and Jorge [They] listen.*)

Luz y Susana (Ellas) escuchan. (*Luz and Susana [They] listen.*)

Juan y Luz (Ellos) escuchan. (*Juan and Luz [They] listen.*)

El niño y mil niñas (Ellos) escuchan. (*The boy and 1,000 girls [They] listen.*)

Nosotros (Nosotras)

When you're talking about someone else and yourself at the same time, you must use the *we* form (**nosotros/nosotras**) of the verb. **Nosotros** refers to more than one male or to a combined group of males and females, no matter the number of each gender present. **Nosotras** refers to a group of females only:

Jorge y yo (Nosotros) jugamos al tenis. (*George and I [We] play tennis.*)

Luz y yo (Nosotras) jugamos al tenis. (*Luz and I [We] play tennis.*)

Gender neutral pronoun

Although not readily used in everyday Spanish conversation, and not included in the dictionary of the Royal Academy of the Spanish Language (Real Academia Española), the gender neutral pronouns **elle** (instead of **él** or **ella**) and **elles** (instead of **ellos** or **ellas**) are being used in progressive and academic circles as an option for trans and nonbinary individuals in Spanish-speaking countries. The English equivalent of **elle** (EH-jeh) and **elles** (EH-jehs) is *they* or *their.*

Elle habla español. (*They speak Spanish.*)

Elles trabajan bien. (*They work well.*)

PRACTICE

If you choose to use a pronoun when forming a sentence, which would you use to speak about the following people?

Q. Roberto and yourself? _____

Two female friends? _____

You (a person you know well) _____

_____

A. nosotros. Use **nosotros** (*we*) when the subject is you and another person.

ellas. Use **ellas** (*they*) when referring to two females.

tú. Use **tu** (*you*) when referring to someone you know well.

Now that you've had some practice, select the pronoun you'd use to address the following people:

11 you (your doctor) _____

12 you and your best (male) friend _____

13 Alicia _____

14 the girls and the boys _____

15 yourself _____

16 you (an unfamiliar group of people) _____

17 Miguel _____

18 your pet _____

Focusing on Numbers

You need numbers to express dates and tell time. And when I talk numbers, I'm talking cardinal and ordinal numbers. You use *cardinal numbers* (the more popular of the two) to count, to bargain with a merchant about a price, to express the temperature, or to write a check. You use *ordinal numbers* to express the number of a floor, the act of a play, or the order of a person in a race or competition.

Cardinal numbers

You use cardinal numbers many times during the average day, probably without even realizing it. As a matter of fact, you probably use them at least once an hour in the course of normal conversation or in writing. The Spanish cardinal numbers are as follows:

Number	Spanish	Number	Spanish
0	cero	24	veinticuatro
1	uno	25	veinticinco
2	dos	26	veintiséis
3	tres	27	veintisiete
4	cuatro	28	veintiocho
5	cinco	29	veintinueve
6	seis	30	treinta
7	siete	40	cuarenta
8	ocho	50	cincuenta
9	nueve	60	sesenta
10	diez	70	setenta
11	once	80	ochenta
12	doce	90	noventa
13	trece	100	cien
14	catorce	101	ciento uno
15	quince	200	doscientos
16	dieciséis	500	quinientos
17	diecisiete	1.000	mil
18	dieciocho	2.000	dos mil
19	diecinueve	100.000	cien mil
20	veinte	1.000.000	un millón
21	veintiuno	2.000.000	dos millones
22	veintidós	1.000.000.000	mil millones
23	veintitrés	2.000.000.000	dos mil millones

In most instances, people simply write numerals when they need to express numbers. However, when you write checks, the transactions won't take place unless you write out the amounts of the checks in words.

For this exercise, fill in the incomplete checks with the written Spanish numbers:

PRACTICE

Juan Gómez	Banco Nacional de España	**101**
1000 Calle Cruz	1111 Avenida Cristóbal Colón	00-000/000
Madrid, España	Madrid, España	(Fecha) _____ 20 __

Páguese a
la orden de ___Geraldo Nuñez_____ ____79____ €

_____ EUROS

MEMORÁNDUM _____   _____
                                                              FIRMA AUTORIZADA

A. **setenta y nueve.** The numbers for *70* and *nine* are written separately and are joined by **y** (*and*).

Now try your hand at filling in the incomplete checks with the written Spanish numbers.

19

Juan Gómez	Banco Nacional de España	**102**
1000 Calle Cruz	1111 Avenida Cristóbal Colón	00-000/000
Madrid, España	Madrid, España	(Fecha) _____ 20 __

Páguese a
la orden de ___José Martín_____ ___621___ €

_____ EUROS

MEMORÁNDUM _____   _____
                                                              FIRMA AUTORIZADA

20

Juan Gómez	Banco Nacional de España	**103**
1000 Calle Cruz	1111 Avenida Cristóbal Colón	00-000/000
Madrid, España	Madrid, España	(Fecha) _____ 20 __

Páguese a
la orden de ___Julia López_____ ___1,595___ €

_____ EUROS

MEMORÁNDUM _____   _____
                                                              FIRMA AUTORIZADA

21

Juan Gómez
1000 Calle Cruz
Madrid, España

Banco Nacional de España
1111 Avenida Cristóbal Colón
Madrid, España

104
00-000/000

(Fecha) _____ 20 ___

Páguese a
la orden de ___Luz Cabral_____   42,717 €

_____ EUROS

MEMORÁNDUM _____   _____
                                    FIRMA AUTORIZADA

22

Juan Gómez
1000 Calle Cruz
Madrid, España

Banco Nacional de España
1111 Avenida Cristóbal Colón
Madrid, España

105
00-000/000

(Fecha) _____ 20 ___

Páguese a
la orden de ___Roberto Cádiz_____   170,733 €

_____ EUROS

MEMORÁNDUM _____   _____
                                    FIRMA AUTORIZADA

23

Juan Gómez
1000 Calle Cruz
Madrid, España

Banco Nacional de España
1111 Avenida Cristóbal Colón
Madrid, España

106
00-000/000

(Fecha) _____ 20 ___

Páguese a
la orden de ___Roberto Cádiz_____   416,149 €

_____ EUROS

MEMORÁNDUM _____   _____
                                    FIRMA AUTORIZADA

English speakers generally write the number 1 in one short, downward stroke. In the Spanish-speaking world, however, the number 1 has a little hook on top, which makes it look like a 7. So to distinguish a 1 from a 7, you put a line through the 7, which makes it look like this: 1.

TIP

Keep the following rules in mind when using cardinal numbers in Spanish:

>> **Uno** (*one*), used only when counting, becomes **un** before a masculine noun and **una** before a feminine noun, whether the noun is singular or plural:

- **uno, dos, tres** (*one, two, three*)
- **un niño y una niña** (*a boy and a girl*)
- **sesenta y un dólares** (*61 dollars*)
- **veintiuna personas** (*21 people*)

>> You use the conjunction **y** (*and*) only for numbers between 31 and 99. You don't use it directly after hundreds:

- **ochenta y ocho** (*88*)
- **doscientos treinta y siete** (*237*)

>> You generally write the numbers 16–19 and 21–29 as one word. The numbers 16, 22, 23, and 26 have accents on the last syllable:

- 16: **dieciséis**
- 22: **veintidós**
- 23: **veintitrés**
- 26: **veintiséis**

>> When used before a masculine noun, **veintiún** (*21*) has an accent on the last syllable:

- **veintiún días** (*21 days*)
- **veintiuna semanas** (*21 weeks*) **Veintiún** (21) becomes **veintiuna** (note the dropped accent) before a feminine noun.

>> **Cien** (100) is used before nouns of either gender and before the numbers **mil** and **millones**. **Cien** becomes **ciento** between 100-199. **Un** is not used before **cien** or **mil** but precedes **millón**. When a noun follows **millón,** you put the preposition **de** between **millón** and the noun:

- **cien sombreros** (*100 hats*)
- **cien blusas** (*100 blouses*)
- **cien mil millas** (*100,000 miles*)
- **cien millones de euros** (*100 million euros*)
- **ciento noventa acres** (*190 acres*)
- **mil posibilidades** (*1,000 possibilities*)
- **un millón de razones** (*1,000,000 reasons*)

>> In compounds of **ciento** (**doscientos, trescientos**), there must be agreement with a feminine noun:

- **cuatrocientos pesos** (*400 pesos*)
- **seiscientas pesetas** (*600 pesetas*)

When it comes to numerals and decimals, Spanish uses commas where English uses periods, and vice versa:

English	Spanish
6,000	6.000
0.75	0,75
$14.99	$14,99

Imagine that you are doing a report on Mexico and have to give its population.

Q How would you write 129 million people?

A. **ciento veintinueve millones de personas. Ciento** is the number for one hundred before another number. You generally write 29 as one number — the final **-e** of **veinte** becomes an **-i** before **nueve.** The word **millón** must be made plural by adding **-es.** Because **millón** ends in a consonant, the accent is dropped to maintain the proper stress in the plural. Add **de** after **millones** when it's followed by a noun, in this case, **personas.**

Now use the situations that follow to give yourself additional practice in using Spanish numbers.

24 You are in a bank in Spain and would like to change your dollars into euros. Say that you would like to change $575 dollars.

Quisiera cambiar _____ dólares a euros.

25 You are looking for your room in a Colombian hotel. Ask for room 1782.

¿Dónde está la habitación _____?

26 You make a new acquaintance who asks for your cell number. Express that your number is (813) 555-1161.

Mi número de móvil es _____.

27 You are doing a math problem in Spanish. Express the following: 219 + 392 = 611.

_____ y _____ son _____.

28 A Spanish-speaking friend asks you for the population of the United States. Give the approximate answer: 332 million.

Hay _____ de personas.

Ordinal numbers

You use *ordinal numbers* — those used to express numbers in a series — far less frequently than cardinal numbers, but they still have some very important applications in everyday life. Perhaps when you go to work, you must ask for your floor in an elevator. During a job interview or on a college application, you may have to express where you placed in your class standings. The following chart presents the Spanish ordinal numbers:

Ordinal	Spanish
1st	**primero**
2nd	**segundo**
3rd	**tercero**
4th	**cuarto**
5th	**quinto**
6th	**sexto**
7th	**séptimo**
8th	**octavo**
9th	**noveno**
10th	**décimo**

The following list outlines everything you need to know when using ordinal numbers in Spanish:

>> Spanish speakers rarely use ordinal numbers after 10th. After that, they usually use cardinal numbers in both the spoken and written language:

- **el séptimo mes** (*the seventh month*)

- **el siglo quince** (*the 15th century*)

>> Ordinal numbers must agree in gender (masculine or feminine) with the nouns they modify. You can make ordinal numbers feminine by changing the final **-o** of the masculine form to **-a**:

- **el cuarto día** (*the fourth day*)

- **la cuarta vez** (*the fourth time*)

>> **Primero** and **tercero** drop the final **-o** before a masculine singular noun:

- **el primer muchacho** (*the first boy*)

- **el tercer hombre** (*the third man*)

>> A cardinal number that replaces an ordinal number above 10th is always masculine, because the masculine word **número** (*number*) is understood:

- **la calle (número) doscientos dos** (*202nd Street*)

≫ In dates, **primero** is the only ordinal number you use. All other dates call for the cardinal numbers:

- **el primero de mayo** (*May 1st*)

- **el doce de enero** (*January 12th*)

≫ In Spanish, cardinal numbers precede ordinal numbers:

- **las dos primeras escenas** (*the first two scenes*)

≫ You use cardinal numbers when expressing the first part of an address:

- **mil seiscientos Avenida Pennsylvania** (*1600 Pennsylvania Avenue*)

You are taking a friend to a restaurant you like.

PRACTICE

Q   **He asks how many times you've eaten there. Tell him it's the fifth time.**

Es la _____ vez.

A.   **quinta.** The word for *the time*, **la vez,** is singular and feminine. Change the **-o** for the masculine form of **quinto,** to **-a** to get the feminine form of *fifth*, **quinta.**

Your friend is visiting from Spain and needs some help. Respond to her email by telling her which floor of the building she can get the assistance she may need. Write out the ordinal numbers in the email you write after consulting the following directory of offices:

Edificio Cabeza de Vaca	
Restaurante El Marino	10
Banco de Madrid	9
Juan López, Doctor	8
Nina Hernández, Dentista	7
Santiago López, reparaciones de computadoras	6
Cibercafé de la Ciudad	5
Cine Rodrigo	4
María Rodrigo, salón de belleza	3
Farmacia	2
Supermercado	1

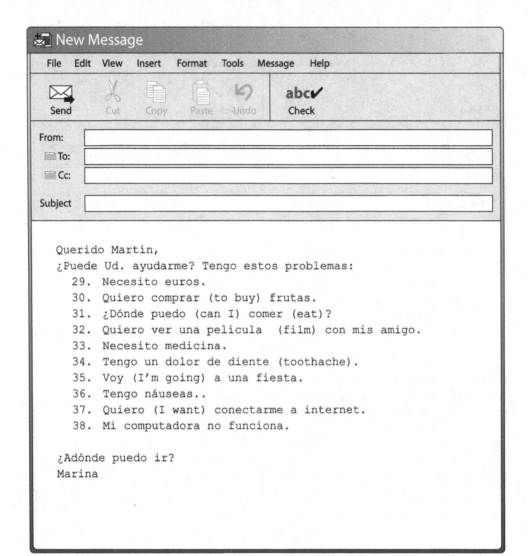

New Message

File   Edit   View   Insert   Format   Tools   Message   Help

Send   Cut   Copy   Paste   Undo   abc✔ Check

From:

To:

Cc:

Subject

Querido Martín,
¿Puede Ud. ayudarme? Tengo estos problemas:
29. Necesito euros.
30. Quiero comprar (to buy) frutas.
31. ¿Dónde puedo (can I) comer (eat)?
32. Quiero ver una película (film) con mis amigo.
33. Necesito medicina.
34. Tengo un dolor de diente (toothache).
35. Voy (I'm going) a una fiesta.
36. Tengo náuseas..
37. Quiero (I want) conectarme a internet.
38. Mi computadora no funciona.

¿Adónde puedo ir?
Marina

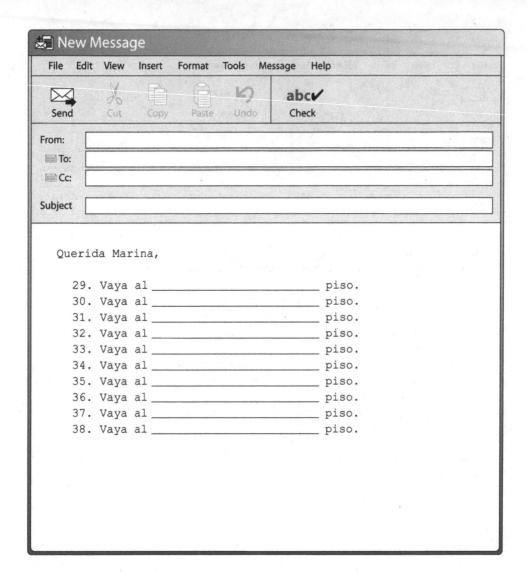

New Message

File   Edit   View   Insert   Format   Tools   Message   Help

Send   Cut   Copy   Paste   Undo   **abc✔** Check

From:

To:

Cc:

Subject

Querida Marina,

29. Vaya al _____ piso.
30. Vaya al _____ piso.
31. Vaya al _____ piso.
32. Vaya al _____ piso.
33. Vaya al _____ piso.
34. Vaya al _____ piso.
35. Vaya al _____ piso.
36. Vaya al _____ piso.
37. Vaya al _____ piso.
38. Vaya al _____ piso.

Making Dates

Dates are important parts of everyday life (in more ways than one!). If you're writing a paper with a strict due date, leaving on vacation and need flight confirmations, or scheduling appointments for your clients and customers, you need to know how to express dates. To write out dates in Spanish, you have to practice the days of the week, the months of the year, and numbers (see the previous section).

Days

If you hear **¿Qué día es hoy?** someone must have forgotten what day of the week it is. You should respond with **Hoy es . . .** (*Today is . . .*) and then provide the name of one of the days listed here:

English	Spanish
Monday	**lunes**
Tuesday	**martes**
Wednesday	**miércoles**
Thursday	**jueves**
Friday	**viernes**
Saturday	**sábado**
Sunday	**domingo**

Unlike the English calendar, the Spanish calendar starts with Monday.

REMEMBER Here are two more guidelines for talking about days of the week in Spanish:

>> Unless you use them at the beginning of a sentence, you don't capitalize the days of the week in Spanish:

- **Lunes es un día de vacaciones.** (*Monday is a vacation day.*)
- **Lunes y martes son días de vacaciones.** (*Monday and Tuesday are vacation days.*)

>> You use **el** when referring to a single instance of a particular day of the week and **los** to get the idea across that an action repeats every week:

- **No trabajo el sábado.** (*I'm not working on Saturday.*)
- **No trabajo los sábados.** (*I don't work on Saturdays.*)

With the exception of **sábado** and **domingo,** the plural forms of the days of the week are the same as the singular forms:

REMEMBER

Singular	Plural
lunes	**lunes**
martes	**martes**
miércoles	**miércoles**
jueves	**jueves**
viernes	**viernes**
sábado	**sábados**
domingo	**domingos**

Months

If you hear **¿En qué mes . . . ?** someone is asking you in what month a certain event takes place. Maybe they want to know when the school year begins or ends, when a special holiday celebration occurs, when the next business meeting will take place, or when you're planning to take your next family vacation. Here are the names of the months so that you can stay on top of all those important social and business obligations:

English	Spanish
January	enero
February	febrero
March	marzo
April	abril
May	mayo
June	junio
July	julio
August	agosto
September	septiembre (or setiembre)
October	octubre
November	noviembre
December	diciembre

REMEMBER

Like days of the week, the months aren't capitalized in Spanish.

Junio es un mes agradable. (*June is a nice month.*)

Junio y julio son meses agradables. (*June and July are nice months.*)

In Spanish, the seasons are masculine except for **la primavera** (*the spring*):

el invierno (*the winter*)

la primavera (*the spring*)

el verano (*the summer*)

el otoño (*the autumn [fall]*)

Writing dates

If you want to ask a passerby or an acquaintance about the date, politely inquire **¿Cuál es la fecha de hoy?** (*What is today's date?*) The person should respond with **Hoy es . . .** (*Today is . . .*) and then use the following formula to express the correct date:

day + (**el**) + cardinal number (except for **primero**) + **de** + month + **de** + year

The following is an example translation, using this formula:

Sunday, April 15, 2021: **Hoy es domingo, el quince de abril de dos mil veintiuno.**

Now that you have a handy formula, you need to know a few more details about writing dates in Spanish:

>> You express the first day of each month with primero. You use cardinal numbers for all other days:

● **el primero de enero** (*January 1st*)

- **el treinta y uno de diciembre** (*December 31st*)

>> Use **el** to express *on* with Spanish dates:

- **Partimos el once de octubre.** (*We are leaving on October 11th.*)

>> In Spanish, you express years in thousands and hundreds:

- **mil cuatrocientos noventa y dos** (*1492: fourteen hundred ninety-two*)

WARNING

In Spanish, when dates are written as numbers, they follow the sequence day/month/year, which may prove confusing to English speakers — especially for dates below the 12th of the month:

You write February 9th as 2/9 in English, but in Spanish it's 9/2.

When speaking of dates in everyday language, the words and expressions that follow may come in handy:

English	Spanish
a day	**un día**
a month	**un mes**
a week	**una semana**
a year	**un año**
ago	**hace**
day after tomorrow	**pasado mañana**
day before yesterday	**anteayer**
during	**durante**
from	**desde**
in	**en**
last (in a series)	**último (-a)**
last	**pasado (-a)**
next	**próximo (-a)**
today	**hoy**
tomorrow afternoon	**mañana por la tarde**
tomorrow morning	**mañana por la mañana**
tomorrow night	**mañana por la noche**
tomorrow	**mañana**
yesterday	**ayer**

PRACTICE

You're writing a paper for your Spanish class on famous Hispanic men who fought for the independence of their country.

Q. **Fill in the dates in Spanish for the birth and death of Bernardo O'Higgins:**

(August 20, 1778_____–October 24, 1842_____)
Bernardo O'Higgins, hombre que luchó (*fought*) **por la independencia de Chile, nació**
_____**y murió** _____.

A. **el veinte de agosto de mil setecientos setenta y ocho; el veinticuatro de octubre de mil ochocientos cuarenta y dos.** For the date of birth, use the definite article before the cardinal number for 20, **veinte.** Use the preposition **de** to express *of*. Write the name of the month, remembering to use lowercase for the first letter. Use **de** before the number of the year. Because hundreds are not be used to express the date, start with **mil.** Use the irregular form, **setecientos** to express 700. Join **setenta** (70) and **ocho** (8) with **y.**

Then for the date of death, use the definite article before the cardinal number for 24, **veinticuatro.** Use the preposition **de** to express *of*. Write the name of the month, remembering to use lowercase for the first letter. Use **de** before the number of the year. Because hundreds are not be used to express the date, start with **mil.** Combine **ocho y cientos** to express 800. Join **cuarenta** (40) and **dos** (2) with **y.**

Now fill in the dates for the following:

39 (May 8, 1753_____–July 30, 1811_____)
Miguel Hidalgo, iniciador de la revolución mexicana, nació _____y murió _____.

40 (July 24, 1783_____–December 17, 1830_____)
Simón Bolívar, libertador y figura destacada(leading) de la independencia de Sudamérica nació _____y murió _____.

41 (January 28, 1853_____–May 19, 1895_____)
José Martí, espíritu de la lucha (fight) por la independencia de Cuba, nació _____y murió _____.

Telling Time

If you're anything like me, you consult your watch or a clock on a nearby wall several times a day. Knowing how to understand, speak, and write time-related words and phrases is a must for anyone who's studying a foreign language and planning to put their studies to use (to do some traveling one day, for instance).

If you hear **¿Qué hora es?** someone wants to know the time. You should start by responding with the following:

> **Es la una** or **Son las** + any time after 1

To express the time after the hour (but before half past the hour), use **y** (*and*) and the number of minutes. Use **menos** (*less*) + the number of the following hour to express the time before the next hour (after half past the hour).

You can also express time numerically (as shown in the third example below):

> **Es la una y media.** (*It's 1:30.*)

Son las cinco menos veinte. (*It's 4:40.*)

Son las cuatro y cuarenta. (*It's 4:40.*)

If you want to discuss "at" what time a particular event will occur, you can use a question — **¿A qué hora . . . ?** — or answer with **A la una** or **A las** + any time after 1:

¿A qué hora vienen? (*At what time are they coming?*)

A la una. (*At 1.*)

A las tres y cuarto. (*At 3:15.*)

The following chart puts the previous information to use by presenting many different ways to discuss time:

Time	Spanish
1:00	la una
2:05	las dos y cinco
3:10	las tres y diez
4:15	las cuatro y cuarto or las cuatro y quince
5:20	las cinco y veinte
6:25	las seis y veinticinco
7:30	las siete y media or las siete y treinta
7:35	las ocho menos veinticinco or las siete y treinta y cinco
8:40	las nueve menos veinte or las ocho y cuarenta
9:45	las diez menos cuarto or las nueve y cuarenta y cinco
10:50	las once menos diez or las diez y cincuenta
11:55	las doce menos cinco or las once y cincuenta y cinco
noon	el mediodía
midnight	la medianoche

When expressing time, the words and expressions below may come in handy:

English Phrase	Spanish Equivalent	English Phrase	Spanish Equivalent
a second	un segundo	in an hour	en una hora
a minute	un minuto	in a while	dentro de un rato
a quarter of an hour	un cuarto de hora	until ten o'clock	hasta las diez
an hour	una hora	before nine o'clock	antes de las nueve
a half hour	una media hora	after seven o'clock	después de las siete
in the morning (a.m.)	por la mañana	since what time?	¿desde qué hora?
in the afternoon (p.m.)	por la tarde	since eight o'clock	desde las ocho
in the evening (p.m.)	por la noche	one hour ago	hace una hora
at what time?	¿a qué hora?	early	temprano
at exactly nine o'clock	a las nueve en punto	late	tarde
at about two o'clock	a eso de las dos	late (in arriving)	de retraso

You are in Spain and you want to see a classic Spanish movie, one that one prizes and that critics acclaimed as excellent. You call your Spanish-speaking friend to tell at what times the films start. Give him the information.

Q. Ciné Doré – Y tu mamá también – 2:15, 5:20, 8:50

A. **Y tu mamá también empieza a las dos y cuarto (quince), a las cinco y veinte, y a las nueve menos diez.**

Use the preposition **a** + the definite article **las** before each time after 1 o'clock to express "*at.*" Use **las dos** to express *2 o'clock.* Use **y** to join the hour and time expression or the number of minutes, **cuarto (quince).** Use **cinco** to express *5 o'clock.* After **y** add **veinte** to express 20 minutes after the hour. Use **nueve** to express *9 o'clock.* Use **menos** to express before the hour and **diez** to express 10 minutes before the hour.

42 Cine Capitol – Roma – 1:10, 4:35, 7:40

_____
_____
_____.

43 Teatro Español – Volver – 1:50, 3:30, 6:05

_____
_____
_____.

44 Sala Triángulo – Los lunes al sol – 11:15, 3:20, 6:40

_____
_____
_____.

Answers to "Getting a Jump Start" Practice Questions

The following are the answers to the practice questions presented in this chapter.

1. **¿Cómo te llamas?** This is the informal question used to ask a person's name.

2. **Buenos días.** You want to be friendly but polite, and **buenos días** is used during the day, especially the early hours of the day.

3. **¡Hola!** Your dog is your friend! So, say *"hi."*

4. **Me llamo . . .** (Literally, *"I call myself . . ."*) followed by your name.

5. **Buenas tardes** is used to greet people in the afternoon.

6. **Nada de particular** if nothing very exciting has happened.

7. **Buenas noches** is said in the evening and is a very polite way of speaking.

8. **¿Cómo estás?** is the friendly way of asking someone how they are feeling.

9. **Mucho gusto** or **Es un placer** to indicate that you are happy to make that person's acquaintance.

10. **Hasta la vista** or **Hasta muy pronto** to show that you anticipate seeing your friend again soon.

11. **Ud.** is the formal pronoun used to express *you.*

12. **Nosotros** is the pronoun to use to express *we* when at least one person is male.

13. **Ella** is the pronoun used to express *she.*

14. **Ellos** is the pronoun used to express *they* when there is at least one male.

15. Use the pronoun **yo** (*I*) when speaking about yourself.

16. **Uds.** is the pronoun used to express the plural *you,* especially when the people are unfamiliar.

17. **Él** is the pronoun used to express *he.*

18. Use the familiar **tú** when speaking to your pet, who is, after all, your friend.

19. **seiscientos veintiuno.** Use **seiscientos** to express 600, remembering to add **-s** to show that 600 is plural. Immediately follow **seiscientos** with **veintiuno** (21).

20. **mil quinientos noventa y cinco. Mil** (1,000) doesn't need to be pluralized. Add the irregular form **quinientos** to express 500. The word for 90 is **noventa,** to which you must add **cinco** (5). The two numbers are joined by **y.**

21. **cuarenta y dos mil setecientos diecisiete.** Use **cuarenta y dos** (42) before **mil** (1,000), which doesn't need to be pluralized. Add the irregular form **setecientos** to express 700. Use **diecisiete** to express 17.

(22) **ciento setenta mil setecientos treinta y tres.** Use **ciento** to express 100 before **setenta** (70) and then add the word **mil** (1,000). Add the irregular form **setecientos** to express 700. The word for 30 is **treinta**. Join it to **tres** (3) with **y.**

(23) **cuatrocientos dieciséis mil ciento cuarenta y nueve.** Use **cuatrocientos** to express 400 and **dieciséis** to express 16, remembering to put an accent on the final **-e**. Then add the word **mil** (1,000). Use **ciento** to express 100, **cuarenta** to express 40, and join it to **nueve** (9) by adding **y.**

(24) **quinientos setenta y cinco.** Use the irregular form **quinientos** to express 500. Use **setenta** to express 70, and join it to **cinco** (5) with **y.**

(25) **mil setecientos ochenta y dos.** Use **mil** to express 1,000 and the irregular form **setecientos** to express 700. Use **ochenta** to express 80, and join it to **dos** (2) with **y.**

(26) **ochocientos trece, quinientos cincuenta y cinco, mil novecientos sesenta y cinco.** Use **ochocientos** to express 800, remembering to add **-s** to **ciento** to show the plural. Use **trece** to express 13. Use the irregular form **quinientos** to express 500. Use **cincuenta** for 50 and join it to **cinco** using **y**. Use **mil** to express 1,000 and **ciento** to express 100. Use **sesenta** to express 60 and join it to **uno** (1) with **y.**

(27) **doscientos diecisiete** y **trescientos noventa y dos** son **seiscientos nueve.** Use **doscientos** to express 200 and **diecinueve** to express 19. Use **trescientos** to express 300. Join it with **noventa** for 90 that is attached to **dos** with **y**. Use **seiscientos** to express 600 and once to express 11.

(28) **trescientos treinta y dos millones.** Use **trescientos** to express 300. Add **treinta** (30) that is joined to **dos** (2) with **y**. Drop the accent on **millón** and add **-es** to form the plural **millones.**

(29) **noveno.** The bank is on the ninth floor.

(30) **primer.** Drop the final **-o** from **primero** before the noun, **piso.** You would buy fruit in the supermarket on the first floor.

(31) **decimo.** You would eat in the restaurant on the tenth floor.

(32) **cuarto.** You would see a film in the movie theater on the fourth floor.

(33) **segundo.** You would go to the pharmacy to buy medicine on the second floor.

(34) **séptimo.** You would go to the dentist on the seventh floor if you had a toothache.

(35) **tercer.** You would go to a beauty salon on the third floor if you were going to a party. Drop the final **-o** from **tercero** before a noun.

(36) **octavo.** You would go to the doctor on the eighth floor if you were nauseous.

(37) **quinto.** You would go to a cybercafe on the fifth floor if you wanted to connect to the internet.

(38) **sexto.** You would go to the sixth floor if your computer was broken.

(39) **el ocho de mayo de mil setecientos cincuenta y tres; el treinta de julio de mil ochocientos once.** For the date of birth, use the definite article before the cardinal number for 8, **ocho.** Use the preposition **de** to express *of*. Write the name of the month, remembering to use lowercase for the first letter. Use **de** before the number of the year. Because hundreds are not

used to express the date, start with **mil.** Use the irregular form, **setecientos** to express 700. Join **cincuenta** (50) and **tres** (3) with **y.**

For the date of death, use the definite article before the cardinal number for 30, **treinta.** Use the preposition **de** to express *of.* Write the name of the month, remembering to use lowercase for the first letter. Use **de** before the number of the year. Because hundreds are not used to express the date, start with **mil.** Use **ochocientos** to express 800. Use **once** to express 11.

40 **el veinticuatro de julio de mil setecientos ochenta y tres; el diecisiete de diciembre de mil ochocientos treinta.** For the first date, use the definite article before the cardinal number for 24, **veinticuatro.** Use the preposition **de** to express *of.* Write the name of the month, remembering to use lowercase for the first letter. Use **de** before the number of the year. Because hundreds are not used to express the date, start with **mil.** Use the irregular form, **setecientos** to express 700. Join **ochenta** (80) and **tres** (3) with y.

For the second date, use the definite article before the cardinal number for 17, **diecisiete.** Use the preposition **de** to express *of.* Write the name of the month, remembering to use lowercase for the first letter. Use **de** before the number of the year. Because hundreds are not used to express the date, start with **mil.** Use **ochocientos** to express 800. Use **treinta** to express 30.

41 **el veintiocho de enero de mil ochocientos cincuenta y tres; el diecinueve de mayo de mil ochocientos noventa y cinco.** For the date of birth, use the definite article before the cardinal number for 28, **veintiocho.** Use the preposition **de** to express *of.* Write the name of the month, remembering to use lowercase for the first letter. Use **de** before the number of the year. Because hundreds are not used to express the date, start with **mil.** Use **ochocientos** to express 800. Join **cincuenta** (50) and **tres** (3) with **y.**

For the date of death, use the definite article before the cardinal number for 19, **diecinueve.** Use the preposition **de** to express *of.* Write the name of the month, remembering to use lowercase for the first letter. Use **de** before the number of the year. Because hundreds are not used to express the date, start with **mil.** Use **ochocientos** to express 800. Join **noventa** (90) and **cinco** (5) with **y.**

42 **Roma empieza a la una y diez, a las cinco menos veinticinco, y a las ocho menos veinte.** Use the preposition **a** + the definite article **la** before 1 *o'clock* to express "*at.*" Use **una** to express 1 *o'clock.* Use **y** to join the hour and the number of minutes, **diez** (10). Use **cinco** to express 5 *o'clock.* Use **menos** to express before the hour and **veinticinco** to express 25 minutes before the hour. Use **ocho** to express 8 *o'clock.* Use **menos** to express before the hour and **veinte** to express 20 minutes before the hour.

43 **Volver empieza a las dos menos diez, a las tres y media, y a las seis y cinco.** Use the preposition **a** + the definite article **las** before 2 *o'clock.* Use **dos** to express 2 *o'clock.* Use **menos** to express before the hour and **diez** to express 10 minutes before the hour. Use the preposition **a** + the definite article **las** before 3 *o'clock.* Use **y** to join the hour and the time expression **media** (*half past*). Use the preposition **a** + the definite article **las** to express "*at.*" Use **seis** to express 6 *o'clock.* After **y** add **cinco** to express 5 minutes after the hour.

44 **Los lunes al sol empieza a las once y cuarto, a las tres y veinte y a las siete menos veinte.** Use the preposition **a** + the definite article **las** before 11 *o'clock.* Use **once** to express 11 *o'clock.* Use **y** to join the hour and the time expression **cuarto** (*a quarter*). Use **a** + the definite article **las** to express 3 *o'clock.* Use **y** to join the hour and the number of minutes **veinte** (20). Use the preposition **a** + the definite article **las** to express "*at.*" Use **siete** to express 7 *o'clock.* Use **menos** to express before the hour and **veinte** to express 20 minutes before the hour.

Chapter **2**

Selecting the Proper Part of Speech

Years ago, diagramming sentences was an essential topic covered in English grammar class. Most students preferred to read the steamy, famous novel *du jour*, but they were forced to sit in class, pen (and sometimes ruler) in hand, figuring out where to place a noun, a verb, or an elusive direct or indirect object.

Many old-timers, such as myself, still remember this experience with a certain amount of distaste. Those tedious exercises, however, have served many of us very well in our careers; we're now tempted to mark up the grammar errors we see on signs, menus, and correspondences. For those who want to transfer that ability — the ability to understand, write, speak, and correct the "Queen's Spanish" — this chapter is essential for you.

In this chapter, I provide a quick course on identifying and using the parts of speech that make Spanish sentences grammatically correct. Specifically, you discover how to recognize verbs, nouns, adjectives, adverbs, and pronouns, and you get some practice in using them properly. Also, finding the correct word in a bilingual dictionary can be a tricky task. Don't worry; help is here! I show you how to navigate both sides of the vocabulary lists so that you don't make a mistake.

Identifying and Using Parts of Speech

You may be questioning why it's so important to know your Spanish grammar. Can't you just grab a dictionary when you want to find a word and move on? The answer would be "yes" if it were that simple a task. What many people fail to realize is that a Spanish word may have many applications depending on its usage in the sentence.

In addition, many idiomatic phrases, when used properly, will distinguish a native speaker from someone who's unfamiliar with the language. (An *idiomatic phrase* is a phrase used in a particular language and whose meaning can't easily be understood by a literal translation of its component words. An English example would be: "It's raining cats and dogs.") As you browse through the following sections and do the exercises, you'll certainly realize the need to muscle up your grammar skills.

Nouns

A *noun* is the part of speech that refers to a person, place, thing, quality, idea, or action. Here are some examples of nouns in action:

>> Person: *The **boy** is friendly.* (**El *muchacho* es amable.**)

>> Place: *I want to go **home**.* (**Quiero ir a *casa*.**)

>> Thing: *I would like to see that **book**.* (**Quisiera ver ese *libro*.**)

>> Quality: *I admire her **courage**.* (**Admiro su *coraje*.**)

>> Idea: ***Communism** is a political theory.* (**El *comunismo* es una teoría politica.**)

>> Action: *The plane's **departure** is imminent.* (**La *salida* del avión es inminente.**)

In everyday speaking/writing, you'll use nouns most often in the following forms:

>> As the subject of a verb: ***Mary** speaks Spanish.* (***María* habla español.**)

>> As the direct object of a verb: *I see **Mary**.* (**Yo veo a *María*.**)

>> As the indirect object of a verb: *I speak to **Mary**.* (**Yo le hablo a *María*.**)

>> As the object of a preposition: *I went out with **Mary**.* (**Yo salí con *María*.**)

TIP

Unlike English nouns, all Spanish nouns have a gender: masculine or feminine. All words you use to qualify or describe a noun must agree with the noun with respect to gender. I discuss this in more detail in Chapter 3, but for now, keep in mind that **el** (*the*) indicates a masculine noun, and **la** (*the*) indicates a feminine noun.

The Spanish language classifies nouns as common or proper but also as collective, concrete, or abstract. A *common noun* refers to a general class of persons, things, places, and so on:

El *hombre* es grande. (*The **man** is tall.*)

Los *edificios* son modernos. (*The **buildings** are modern.*)

Me gustan los *deportes*. (*I like **sports**.*)

A *proper noun* is the specific name of a person, thing, place, and so on:

George Washington fue un presidente. (*George Washington was a president.*)

Guernica es una pintura de Picasso. (*Guernica is a painting by Picasso.*)

España es un país en Europa. (*Spain is a country in Europe.*)

A *collective noun* is used singularly and refers to a group:

Mi *familia* es pequeña. (*My **family** is small.*)

A *concrete noun* refers to something that you can perceive with your senses; an *abstract noun* refers to an idea:

Concrete: **El *agua* es azul.** (*The **water** is blue.*)

Abstract: **El *odio* es un vicio.** (*Hate is a vice.*)

Pronouns

A *pronoun* is a part of speech used in place of a noun. The following list outlines the pronouns I discuss in this book:

>> Subject pronouns (see Chapter 1) are followed by the verb expressing the main action in the sentence (*I, you, he, she, it, we, they*):

- *You are nice.* (**Ud. es simpático.**)

>> Interrogative pronouns (see Chapter 8) ask a question (*who, which, what,* and so on):

- *Who is that?* (**¿Quién es?**)

>> Direct object pronouns (see Chapter 9) replace direct object nouns; they answer whom or what the subject is acting upon. The direct object pronouns are **me, te, lo, la** (**le** in Spain), **nos, os, los,** and **las** (**les** in Spain):

- *I'll be seeing you.* (**Te veo.**)

>> Indirect object pronouns (see Chapter 9) replace indirect object nouns; they explain to or for whom something is done. They include **me, te, le, nos, os,** and **les:**

- *He wrote to me.* (**Me escribió.**)

>> Reflexive pronouns (see Chapter 10) show that the subject is acting upon itself (**me, te, se, nos, os**):

- *Juan bought himself a car.* (**Juan se compró un coche.**)

>> Prepositional pronouns (see Chapter 12) are used after prepositions (**mí, ti, él, ella, Ud., nosotros, vosotros, ellos, ellas, Uds.**):

- *They're going to the movies without me.* (**Van al cine sin mí.**)

Adjectives

An *adjective* is a part of speech that describes a noun:

> *The house is* **white.** (**La casa es *blanca.***)

In addition to being descriptive, a Spanish adjective can also have other applications, as outlined in the following list:

» A possessive adjective tells to whom the noun belongs:

- *It's* **my** *book.* (**Es *mi* libro.**)

» A demonstrative adjective shows *this, that, these,* or *those:*

- ***That*** *film is good.* (***Esa* película es buena.**)

» An interrogative adjective asks the question *whose, which,* or *what:*

- **Whose** *car is that?* (**¿*De quién* es ese coche?**)

» An indefinite adjective shows an indefinite amount:

- *He has* **many** *friends.* (**Él tiene *muchos* amigos.**)

» A number (cardinal or ordinal; see Chapter 1) is an adjective that gives a specific amount:

- *I need* **one** *piece of paper.* (**Necesito una hoja de papel.**)
- *It's his* **tenth** *birthday.* (**Es su *décimo* aniversario.**)

Verbs

A *verb* is a part of speech that shows an action or a state of being. In Spanish, as in English, verbs change from their infinitive form (they're conjugated, in other words) in the following situations:

» To agree with the person performing the action (*I, you, he, she, you, it, we, they*)

» To agree with the time when the action was performed (past, present, future)

» To agree with the mood (indicative, imperative, subjunctive) of the action

The *infinitive* of the verb is its "raw" form — its *to* form before it's conjugated. (Think Hamlet's "To be or not to be . . .") Infinitives in Spanish have three different endings, and you conjugate them according to these endings: **-ar, -er,** and **-ir** when a subject is present or implied.

> **Me gusta nadar.** (*I like to swim.*) The infinitive is used.

> **Yo nado todos los días.** (*I swim every day.*) The verb **nadar** is conjugated to agree with the subject.

> **Nadamos bien.** (*We swim well.*) The subject, **nosotros,** is implied.

Adverbs

An *adverb* is a part of speech that modifies a verb, an adjective, or another adverb:

> Modifying a verb: *You **speak** quickly.* (**Ud. *habla* rápidamente.**)
>
> Modifying an adjective: *Her grandmother is very old.* (**Su abuela es muy *vieja*.**)
>
> Modifying an adverb: *They eat **too** slowly.* (**Ellos comen *demasiado* despacio.**)

In English, many adverbs end in -*ly*: *calmly, certainly,* and so on. In Spanish, many adverbs end in -**mente: tranquilamente** (*calmly*), **ciertamente** (*certainly*), and so on.

To be able to express your English thoughts in Spanish, you must know the part of speech you need, because many words can be tricky. For example, **la obra** is a noun that means *the work,* as in a work of art; **trabajar** is a verb that means *to work,* as in doing some type of labor. With that in mind, read each Spanish word and determine whether it's a noun, verb, adjective, or adverb. This exercise will help you navigate the next section of this chapter.

Q. mucho

A. Adjective. **Mucho** means "much" and is an adjective that precedes a noun.

1. el hospital_____

2. ¿Cómo? _____

3. grande _____

4. completamente _____

5. decidir _____

6. segundo _____

7. responder _____

8. muy _____

9. yo _____

10. pasar _____

Using a Bilingual Dictionary

A *bilingual* Spanish dictionary is one with a Spanish-to-English section and an English-to-Spanish section (complete with idiomatic words and expressions). A good dictionary also will have Spanish pronunciation and spelling rules. Using a bilingual Spanish dictionary may sound easy, but it requires a lot of finesse and patience. Finding the exact word you want to use forces you to read carefully, to know your parts of speech, and to double-check your findings.

TIP

In the front of every bilingual dictionary, you'll find a list of abbreviations, identifying the parts of speech and gender of a noun. This list is invaluable in determining whether the word you're looking for is a noun, pronoun, verb, adjective, adverb, and so on. Table 2-1 gives you a quick look at the most useful abbreviations you can expect to find.

Table 2-1   Useful Abbreviations

Abbreviation	Full Word	Abbreviation	Full Word
adj	adjective	*nm* (sometimes *sm*)	masculine noun
adv	adverb	*neg*	negative
conj	conjunction		
EEUU	United States	*pl*	plural
excl	exclamation	*pp*	past participle
f	feminine	*pref*	prefix
infin	infinitive	*prep*	preposition
inv	invariable	*pron*	Pronoun
irr	irregular	*sing*	Singular
liter	literary	*v* (sometimes *vb*)	Verb
m	masculine	*vi*	intransitive verb
mf	masculine and feminine	*vr*	reflexive verb
n (or sometimes *s for substantive*)	noun	*vt*	transitive verb
nf (sometimes *sf*)	feminine noun		

To understand how a person may be confused by what they find in a bilingual dictionary, it helps to look at an example of a dictionary entry. Focusing on the word *well*, here's what you should find:

well	
n	**pozo m.**
vi (*to well up*)	**brotar, manar**
adv (*in a good way*)	**bien**
adj (*healthy*)	**bien**
excl	**bueno, pues**

Perhaps you can see how confusing an entry can be — one word has five different applications. When looking at the Spanish equivalents for the English word *well*, you have to make sure you select the proper word.

PRACTICE

Here are some sample sentences to give you some practice. In the following blanks, add the word that you think fits:

1 *I am well, thank you.* **Estoy _____ gracias.**

2 *There is no water in the well.* **No hay agua en _____.**

3 *You speak Spanish well.* **Ud. habla _____ el español.**

4 *Tears will well up in my eyes.* **Las lágrimas van a _____ en mis ojos.**

5 *Well, that story is interesting!* **_____, esa historia es interesante!**

TIP

How do you check yourself to make sure you chose properly? It takes your left hand. That's right! You must always keep fingers from both hands on both sides of the dictionary. Search for the word using your right hand, and then check the Spanish section with your left hand to make sure you used the correct part of speech. Generally, the dictionary will contain examples to help you. So if you picked **pozo** for the first sample sentence, for instance, when you look on the Spanish side, you'll see *n* (or *s*) and [**de agua**] after the word **pozo,** which indicates that you've made a mistake. This method may be tricky and time-consuming, but it certainly helps you select the word you need.

So, how did you do? Check your answers:

1. **bien** 2. **el pozo** 3. **bien** 4. **brotar** 5. **bueno**

Now on to some more intensive practice.

PRACTICE

Using your dictionary, try your hand at the following sentences to see how many you can complete properly.

11 *He has a cold.* **Él tiene _____.**

I'm cold. **Yo tengo _____.**

12 *What was the end result?* **¿Cuál fue el resultado _____?**

The match is going to end at 10 o'clock. **El partido va a _____ a las diez.**

13 *She is going to play the piano.* **Ella va a _____ el piano.**

He likes to play golf. **Le gusta _____ al golf.**

14 *Is that book good?* **¿Es _____ ese libro?**

He works for the common good. **Él trabaja por _____ común.**

15 *Please hand a towel to Julia.* **Favor de _____ una toalla a Julia.**

I hurt my hand. **Me lastimé la _____.**

16. Are they going to fire many workers? **¿Van a** _____ **a muchos obreros?**

Did you see the fire? **¿Ha visto** _____ **?**

17. You aren't going to miss the train. **Ud. no va a** _____ **el tren.**

Excuse me, miss. **Perdón,** _____ **.**

18. It's one of a kind. **Es** _____ **.**

You are very kind. **Ud. es muy** _____ **.**

19. Our plane is going to land. **Nuestro avión va a** _____ **.**

They live off the land. **Ellos viven de** _____ **.**

20. At what time are you going to leave the house? **¿A qué hora va a** _____ **de casa?**

You must leave the keys in the office. **Ud. tiene que** _____ **las llaves en la oficina.**

21. What is your net profit? **¿Cuál es su beneficio** _____ **?**

The fish is in the net. **El pez està en** _____ **.**

22. Let's go to the park. **Vamos al** _____ **.**

She is going to park the car. **Ella va a** _____ **el coche.**

23. Are you going to pass the test? **¿Tú vas a** _____ **el examen?**

Are they going to pass by your house? **¿Van a** _____ **por su casa?**

24. It's not a question of money. **No es** _____ **de dinero.**

I have a question. **Yo tengo** _____ **.**

25. Who won the race? **¿Quién ganó** _____ **?**

Race is not a factor in hiring. **La** _____ **no es un factor en la contatación.**

26. Is the child safe? **¿Está** _____ **el niño?**

Put your money in the safe. **Ponga su dinero en** _____ **.**

27. They are going to train their dog. **Ellos van a** _____ **a su perro.**

I missed the train. **Yo perdí** _____ **.**

28. Let's go for a walk. **Nosotros vamos a dar** _____ **.**

We are going to walk through the park. **Nosotros vamos a** _____ **por el parque.**

Recognizing Cognates

So what exactly is a cognate? First, a bit of philological history. Many English and Spanish words have the same or almost the same spelling and meaning because they come from the same Latin or Greek root. These "look-alike" words are called cognates. Take a look at the following Spanish words that are spelled exactly as they are in English and have the same meaning:

Perfect Cognates

actor	conductor	idea	pefume
admirable	director	individual	piano
agenda	doctor	invisible	popular
cable	error	motor	probable
central	festival	musical	radio
cereal	general	natural	sociable
chocolate	horrible	normal	terrible
club	hospital	original	total
color	hotel	patio	violin

Many other cognates are easily recognizable by adhering to the following rule:

Many English words that end in *-tion* can be converted to Spanish by changing *-tion* to **-ción**.

Here are some examples:

Near Perfect Cognates

English	Spanish
action	**acción**
attention	**atención**
celebration	**celebración**
combination	**combinación**
condition	**condición**
nation	**nación**
pronunciation	**pronunciación**

WARNING

Although spellings may be identical or nearly identical in both languages, the pronunciations are different.

For the following cognates, some English words that end in *-y* can be converted to Spanish by changing *-y* to **-ario:**

English	Spanish
commentary	**comentario**
salary	**salario**
solitary	**solitario**
temporary	**temporario**
vocabulary	**vocabulario**

Some English words that end in *-ty* can be converted to Spanish by dropping *-ty* and adding **-dad**, as follows:

English	Spanish
curiosity	**curiosidad**
electricity	**electricidad**
generosity	**generosidad**
society	**sociedad**
university	**universidad**

Some near perfect adjectives add an accent to the preceding vowel and an **-o** to an English *-ic* ending:

English	Spanish
automatic	**automático**
basic	**básico**
domestic	**doméstico**
dramatic	**dramático**
ironic	**irónico**
public	**público**
tragic	**trágico**

The following English words that end in *-ct* add **-o** to form a Spanish cognate:

English	Spanish
conflict	**conflicto**
correct	**correcto**
exact	**exacto**
insect	**insecto**
perfect	**perfecto**
product	**producto**

Finally, some English words that end in *-y* end in **-ia**, **-ía**, or **-io** in Spanish:

English	Spanish
history	**historia**
photography	**fotografía**
remedy	**remedio**

Cognates make learning a foreign language quite easy and gives you a rather large number of words that are easily recognizable.

Can you guess the meaning of the words that follow? They shouldn't present much of a problem at all.

Q. variedad

A. *Variety.* Spanish **-dad** replaces English *-ty.*

29 admiración _____

30 memoria _____

31 concentración _____

32 realidad _____

33 capacidad _____

34 abstracto _____

35 mágico _____

36 contrario _____

TIP

You'll be able to guess the meaning of many Spanish words that begin with **-es** simply by dropping the initial **-e**: **especial** (*special*), **estudiar** (*to study*).

Some almost perfect cognates don't follow any rules, but their spelling makes them easy to guess:

English	Spanish
bank	**banco**
bicycle	**bicicleta**
comfortable	**confortable**
computer	**computadora**
different	**diferente**
difficult	**difícil**
famous	**famoso**
group	**grupo**
magnificent	**magnífico**
park	**parque**
restaurant	**restaurante**
telephone	**teléfono**

You are well on your way to developing a very basic proficiency in Spanish simply by focusing on cognates.

PRACTICE

See how much you can understand by giving the meaning of the sentences that follow. The articles **el** and **la** (discussed in Chapter 3) mean *the*, and the Spanish word **es** means *is*. Now full speed ahead!

Q. El hospital es moderno.

A. *The hospital is modern.*

37. El actor es famoso. _____

38. La hamburguesa es deliciosa. _____

39. El estudiante es tímido. _____

40. El programa es interesante. _____

41. La communicación es importante. _____

42. El aeropuerto es grande. _____

43. La familia es sociable. _____

44. El hotel es moderno. _____

45. El parque es popular. _____

46. La universidad es espléndida. _____

WARNING

Watch out! You don't want to be too sure of yourself! Avoid the trap of assuming that all Spanish words that resemble ones in English have the same meaning. *False friends* are words that are spelled exactly the same or almost the same in Spanish and English but have different meanings and may even be different parts of speech.

Spanish	English
actual	*current*
adecuado	*appropriate*
asistir	*to attend*
avisar	*notify, warn*
bombero	*firefighter*
carpeta	*folder*
casualidad	*coincidence, chance*
codo	*elbow*
colegio	*high school*
compromiso	*commitment*
constipado	*having a cold*

Spanish	English
contestar	to answer
decepción	disappointment
delito	crime
dormitorio	bedroom
embarazada	pregnant
empresa	enterprise
enviar	to send
fábrica	factory
ganga	bargain
injuria	insult
introducir	to insert
largo	long
lectura	reading
librería	bookstore
mantel	tablecloth
miseria	poverty
molestar	to bother, annoy
nudo	knot
parada	stop (bus stop)
pariente	relative
pie	foot
preocupado	worried
preservativo	condom
presumir	to show off
pretender	to try
realizar	to carry out, perform, achieve
recordar	to remember
regalo	present
ropa	clothing
sensible	sensitive
simpático	likable, pleasant, agreeable
sopa	soup
soportar	to stand
suceso	event
tener éxito	to succeed
tópico	commonplace, trivial
últimamente	recently
vaso	glass

Answers to "Selecting the Proper Part of Speech" Practice Questions

The following are the answers to the practice questions presented in this chapter.

(1) **Noun. El** is used to express *the* before the masculine noun, **hospital**.

(2) **Pronoun. ¿Cómo**? is an interrogative pronoun expressing "how."

(3) **Adjective. Grande** is an adjective showing how big something is.

(4) **Adverb. Completamente** means "completely." The Spanish adverbial ending –**mente** replaces the adverbial English ending –**ly**.

(5) **Verb. Decidir** (*to decide*) can be recognized as a verb by its –**ir** ending.

(6) **Adjective. Segundo** (*second*) is an adjective that gives a specific amount.

(7) **Verb. Responder** (*to respond*) can be recognized as a verb by its –**re** ending.

(8) **Adverb.** Although it doesn't end in –**mente, muy** is an adverb that means *very* and can be used to modify an adjective or another adverb.

(9) **Pronoun. Yo** (*I*) is a subject pronoun.

(10) **Verb. Pasar** (*to pass, spend [time]*) can be recognized as a verb by its –**ar** ending.

(11) **un resfriado; frío.** Use the noun **un resfriado,** which refers to an illness. Use the noun **frío** in this idiomatic expression, which refers to body temperature.

(12) **final; terminar.** Use **final** as an adjective. Use **terminar** as a verb.

(13) **tocar; jugar. Tocar** means "to play an instrument." **Jugar** means "to play a sport."

(14) **bueno; el bien; Bueno** is used as an adjective describing the book. **El bien** is used as a noun.

(15) **pasar; la mano.** Use **pasar** as a verb meaning "to pass something over." **La mano** is a noun.

(16) **despedir; el fuego. Despedir** is the verb you use to fire someone. **El fuego** refers to the noun.

(17) **perder; señorita. Perder** is the verb meaning "to miss a train." **Señorita** is a noun.

(18) **único; amable.** Use **único** as an adverb to represent something unique. Use **amable** as an adjective to describe someone who's nice.

(19) **atterizar; la tierra. Aterrizar** is a verb. **La tierra** is a noun.

(20) **salir; dejar. Salir** is a verb that means "to leave a place." **Dejar** is a verb that means "to leave something behind."

(21) **neto; la red.** You use **neto** as an adjective. **La red** is a noun.

(22) **parque; aparcar. Parque** is a noun. **Aparcar** is a verb.

(23) **aprobar; pasar. Aprobar** is the verb that means "to pass an exam." **Pasar** is the verb that means "to pass by a place."

(24) **cuestión; una pregunta. Cuestión** is the noun you use when referring to a question. Use **una pregunta** when the subject is asking a specific question.

(25) **la carrera; raza. La carrera** is the noun for a race that's a contest. **Raza** is the noun for ethnicity.

(26) **seguro; la caja fuerte. Seguro** is an adjective. **La caja fuerte** is a noun.

(27) **adiestrar; el tren. Adiestrar** is the verb that means "to train an animal." **El tren** is a noun.

(28) **un paseo; andar. Un paseo** is a noun. **Andar** is a verb.

(29) *admiration.* Spanish –**ción** replaces English –*tion.*

(30) *memory.* Spanish –**ia** replaces English *y.*

(31) *concentration.* Spanish –**ción** replaces English –*tion.*

(32) *reality.* Spanish –**dad** replaces English –*ty.*

(33) *capacity.* Spanish –**dad** replaces English –*ty.*

(34) *abstract.* Some English words drop the final –**o** from their Spanish equivalent.

(35) *magic.* Some English words drop the accent and the final –**o** from their Spanish equivalents.

(36) *contrary.* Spanish –**io** replaces English *y.*

(37) *The actor is famous.*

(38) *The hamburger is delicious.*

(39) *The student is shy.*

(40) *The program is interesting.*

(41) *Communication is important.*

(42) *The airport is big.*

(43) *The family is sociable.*

(44) *The hotel is modern.*

(45) *The park is popular.*

(46) *The university is splendid.*

2
The Here and Now

IN THIS PART . . .

Master gender differences

Handle agreement in gender and number

Work with definite and indefinite articles

Get acquainted with demonstrative and possessive adjectives

Form the plural of nouns

Make comparisons

Chapter **3**

Sorting Out Word Gender

Let the battle of the sexes begin! Gender is a battle that English speakers don't fight. In English, a noun is a simply a noun; you don't have to worry about a noun having a gender (a masculine or feminine designation). In Spanish, a noun has a gender, and the gender of a noun often determines the spelling of other words in the sentence. What determines this gender? Certainly not what we perceive to be masculine or feminine. Don't assume anything. For instance, a tie (**una corbata**) is feminine in Spanish, while lipstick (**un lápiz de labios**) is masculine! Don't ask me why. I can't explain it. Gender in language is one of those things you have to accept. Take heart, though, because in Spanish, many word endings will help you determine the gender of certain nouns.

In this chapter, I help you correctly mark the gender of a noun by using definite articles (which express *the*), indefinite articles (which express *a, an,* or *some*), or demonstrative adjectives (which express *this, that, these,* or *those*). I demystify the gender of nouns by showing you noun endings that tend to be masculine or feminine. You discover the tricks to making nouns plural. And, finally, I show you how to express possession.

Marking Gender with Definite Articles

A *definite article* expresses the English word *the* and indicates a specific person or thing, such as *the boy* or *the book*. If you know whether a noun is masculine or feminine in Spanish (or singular or plural), you must choose the correct definite article to mark that noun to say *the*. Using definite articles is easy after you determine the noun's gender (see the sections on gender later in this chapter).

Identifying the definite articles

Spanish features four distinct definite articles that correspond to *the* in English. The following table lists these articles:

	Masculine	Feminine
Singular	el	la
Plural	los	las

REMEMBER

The definite article precedes the noun it modifies and agrees with that noun in number and gender. For example, **El muchacho es rubio y las muchachas son morenas.** (*The boy is blond and the girls are brunette.*)

Here are some examples of these definite articles in action:

El muchacho es grande. (*The boy is big.*)

Los libros son interesantes. (*The books are interesting.*)

La muchacha es alta. (*The girl is tall.*)

Las casas son blancas. (*The houses are white.*)

Using the definite articles

You'll come across many instances in Spanish where you'll use the definite article, even though you may or may not use it in English. Study the rules in the following list; they show how to use the definite articles in Spanish in many different situations:

» With nouns in a general or abstract sense:

- **El amor es divino.** (*Love is divine.*)

» With nouns in a specific sense:

- **María trae el postre.** (*Maria is bringing dessert.*)

» With names of languages (except after the verb **hablar** and after the prepositions **de** and **en**):

- **Me gusta el español.** (*I like Spanish.*)

- **¿Dónde está mi libro de español?** (*Where's my Spanish book?*)

- **Escríbame en español.** (*Write to me in Spanish.*)

» With parts of the body (when the possessor is clear) in place of the possessive adjective:

- **Me duelen los pies.** (*My feet hurt.*)

» With titles and ranks when you aren't addressing the person:

- **La señora Rivera está aquí.** (*Mrs. Rivera is here.*)

- **Siéntase, señora Rivera.** (*Have a seat, Mrs. Rivera.*)

>> With last names:

- **Los Gómez viven en Colombia.** (*The Gómez's live in Colombia.*)

>> With days of the week (except after the verb **ser**):

- **El domingo voy a México.** (*On Sunday, I'm going to Mexico.*)

- **Hoy es miércoles.** (*Today is Wednesday.*)

>> With seasons (you may omit the article after **en**):

- **No trabajo en (el) verano.** (*I don't work in the summer.*)

>> With dates:

- **Es el cinco de mayo.** (*It's May 5th.*)

>> With the hour of the day and other time expressions:

- **Son las once y media.** (*It's 11:30.*)

- **Salgo por la tarde.** (*I'm going out in the afternoon.*)

>> With the names of many cities and countries (although there's a tendency to omit the article in current usage):

- **Visitamos (el) Brasil.** (*We visited Brazil.*)

- **Vivo en los Estados Unidos.** (*I live in the United States.*)

>> With rivers, seas, and other geographical locations:

- **El Orinoco es un río.** (*The Orinoco is a river.*)

>> With the names of boats or ships:

- **El Titanic se hundió.** (*The Titanic sank.*)

>> With clothing used in a general sense:

- **Al entrar él se quitó el sombrero.** (*Upon entering, he removed his hat.*)

WARNING

Capitalized articles are actually parts of the names of the countries, whereas articles in lower-case aren't. For example, **Yo nací en El Salvador pero pasé muchos años en la Argentina.** (*I was born in El Salvador, but I spent many years in Argentina.*)

Omission of the definite articles

You omit the definite articles in the following situations in Spanish:

>> Before nouns in apposition (when one noun explains another):

- **Madrid, capital de España, es una ciudad popular.** (*Madrid, the capital of Spain, is a popular city.*)

>> Before numerals that express the title of rulers:

- **Carlos Quinto** (*Charles the Fifth*)

Contractions with the definite articles

A contraction is a way to combine two words to make them shorter. (An English example is *I'm* for *I am* or *you're* for *you are*.) Spanish features only two contractions. They occur when the definite article **el** is joined with the preposition **a** (**a** + **el** = **al**) or **de** (**de** + **el** = **del**). The only exception to the rule is when the definite article is part of the title or name. Here are some examples of this construction:

> **Vamos al Uruguay.** (*I'm going to Uruguay.*) **Voy a El Salvador.** (*I'm going to El Salvador.*)
>
> **Soy del Uruguay.** (*I'm from Uruguay.*) **Soy de El Salvador.** (*I'm from El Salvador.*)

PRACTICE

Complete the paragraph about this person's day by using the correct form of the definite article — **el, la, los, las** — when needed.

Q. Miro _____ horario de autobuses.

A. **el.** Use the definite article **el** before masculine word **horario** (*schedule*).

No voy a (1) _____ escuela hoy. Mi familia y yo estamos de vacaciones. Tenemos una habitación grande en (2) _____ hotel moderno, Alfonso (3) _____ Quinto en (4)_____ Ciudad de México. Me despierto tarde por (5) _____ mañana, a (6) _____ once. No tomo (7) _____ desayuno porque no tengo (8) _____ hambre. Es (9) _____ primavera y hace buen tiempo. Me pongo (10) _____ suéter y (11) _____ gorra y salgo. Tengo ganas de pasar toda (12) _____ tarde visitando (13) _____ pirámides construídas por (14) _____ aztecas. Tomo (15) _____ autobús en (16) _____ Calle (17) _____ Sexto. Según (18) _____ director de (19) _____ universidad de México, es importante visitar Teotihuacán, uno de (20)_____ mayores complejos arqueológicos de México.

Marking Gender with Indefinite Articles

An *indefinite article*, which expresses the English words *a*, *an*, or *some*, refers to persons or objects not specifically identified (such as *a boy* or *some books*). Just like with definite articles, when you know whether a noun is masculine or feminine (and singular or plural), you can choose the correct indefinite article to mark that noun.

REMEMBER

As with definite articles, the indefinite article precedes the noun it modifies and agrees with that noun in number and gender.

Identifying the indefinite articles

Four Spanish indefinite articles correspond to *a*, *an*, and *one* in the singular and to *some* in the plural. The following table presents these articles:

	Masculine	Feminine
Singular	un	una
Plural	unos	unas

Here are some examples of the indefinite articles in action:

Compró un abrigo. (*She bought an [one] overcoat.*)

Es una mujer muy astuta. (*She is a very astute woman.*)

Necesito unos limones y unas limas. (*I need some lemons and some limes.*)

Omission of the indefinite article

You omit the indefinite article from your Spanish constructions in the following situations:

WARNING

>> Before unmodified nouns that express nationality, profession, or religious or political affiliation:

- **El señor Robles es profesor.** (*Mr. Robles is a teacher.*)

When the noun is modified with the help of an adjective or adverb, you use the indefinite article:

- **El señor Robles es un profesor popular.** (*Mr. Robles is a popular teacher.*)

>> Before nouns in apposition:

- **Cervantes, escritor español, escribió Don Quijote.** (*Cervantes, a Spanish writer, wrote Don Quixote.*)

>> Before the following words:

- **cien** (*one hundred*): **cien niños** (*a hundred children*)

- **cierto** (*certain*): **cierto día** (*a certain day*)

- **mil** (*a thousand*): **mil dólares** (*a thousand dollars*)

- **otro** (*other*): **otra clase** (*another class*)

- **qué** (*what a*): **qué lástima** (*what a pity*)

- **tal** (*such a*): **tal cosa** (*such a thing*)

PRACTICE

It's a rainy day in paradise! You're on a cruise, and you've finally found the time to write a letter to your pen pal in Grenada. Complete the letter by filling in the correct definite article, indefinite article, or nothing at all. Use one of the following choices: **el, la, los, las, al, del, un, una, unos,** or **unas.**

Q. Son _____ nueve de la mañana.

A. **las.** Use the feminine plural definite article before a number indicating time.

Querido Juan,

Hoy es (21)_____ lunes pero no trabajo en (22)_____

oficina. Estoy de (23)_____ vacaciones con mi primo, Ernesto, y

con (24)_____ compañero mío, Carlos. Ernesto es (25)_____

programador y Carlos es (26)_____ artista serio. Nos llevamos bien.

Mis amigos y yo hacemos (27)_____ crucero. Tenemos

(28)_____ camarote magnífico a bordo (29)_____ barco

grande que se llama (30)_____ Reina María (31)_____

Sexta. Nos levantamos temprano por (32)_____ mañana porque

hay (33)_____ mil cosas que hacer. (34)_____ Primero

tomamos (35)_____ desayuno enorme. Comemos mucho

más posible porque todo es muy delicioso. Entonces siempre queremos

participar en todas (36)_____ actividades a bordo

(37)_____ barco. Vamos (38)_____ gimnasio todos

(39)_____ días. Nadamos en (40)_____ piscina.

Jugamos (41)_____ golf miniatura, (42)_____ volíbol, y a

(43)_____ naipes. Generalmente tomamos (44)_____

almuerzo a (45)_____ una con tres muchahas inglesas y nos

divertimos muchísimo. Durante (46)_____ día, cuando llega

(47)_____ barco a (48)_____ puerto interesante,

salimos para hacer (49)_____ visita (50)_____ país o de

(51)_____ isla. (52)_____ semana pasada Ernesto

compró (53)_____ discos compactos para sus hermanos y Carlos

compró (54)_____ camisetas. Yo tuve (55)_____ mucha

suerte. Yo compré (56)_____ reloj de oro en (57)_____

tienda libre de impuestos. Yo pagué solamente (58)_____ cien

dólares. ¡Qué ganga! Por (59)_____ noche, siempre hay

(60)_____ bailes y (61)_____ espectáculos. De vez en

cuando pasan (62)_____ película reciente. Una vez vimos

(63)_____ desfile de modas. Ernesto y Carlos piensan que

(64)_____ crucero es estupendo.

Su amigo,

José

Being Demonstrative with Demonstrative Adjectives

I'm afraid I'm not content with just anything or anyone, and I make my requirements and needs known by specifically referring to *this, that, these,* or *those* things or people. If you're like me, you'll need to make use of the Spanish demonstrative adjectives that enable you to express exactly what or who you're seeking.

Demonstrative adjectives indicate or point out the person, place, or thing that a speaker is referring to — for instance, "this shirt" or "that pair of pants." Demonstrative adjectives precede and agree in number and gender with the nouns they modify. In Spanish, you select the demonstrative adjective according to the distance of the noun from the speaker. Table 3-1 presents demonstrative adjectives and addresses this distance issue.

Table 3-1   Demonstrative Adjectives

	Masculine	Feminine	Meaning	Distance
Singular	**este**	**esta**	*this*	Near to or directly concerned with speaker
Plural	**estos**	**estas**	*these*	
Singular	**ese**	**esa**	*that*	Not near to or directly concerned with speaker
Plural	**esos**	**esas**	*those*	
Singular	**aquel**	**aquella**	*that*	Rather far from and not directly concerned with speaker
Plural	**aquellos**	**aquellas**	*those*	

Here are some examples of demonstrative adjectives in action:

> **Estos pantalones son cortos y esta camisa es larga.** (*These pants are short and this shirt is long.*)

> **Tengo que hablar con esa muchacha y esos muchachos ahí.** (*I have to speak to that girl and those boys over there.*)

> **Aquellos países son grandes y aquellas ciudades son pequeñas.** (*Those countries are large and those cities are small.*)

Use **es** to express *is* and **son** to express *are*.

TIP

Here's what you need to know about demonstrative adjectives in Spanish:

>> You use them before each noun:

   ● **este abogado y ese cliente** (*this lawyer and that client*)

>> You can use adverbs to reinforce location:

   ● **esta casa aquí** (*this house here*)

   ● **esas casas ahí** (*those houses there*)

   ● **aquella casa allá** (*that house over there*)

PRACTICE

You're walking through your place of business with your boss while hastily taking notes about the attitudes of the workers. Write out full sentences from your notes. Use the appropriate demonstrative adjective to describe the noun. Then combine the elements of the sentence by using the correct form of the verb **ser** (*to be*).

Q. abogado/aquí/fiel

A. **Este abogado aquí es fiel. Aquí** indicates that the lawyer is "here" (nearby). Use the masculine, singular demonstrative adjective **este** (*this*). Use the singular **es** (*is*), and follow it with the adjective **fiel** (*proud*).

Q. vendedoras/ahí/habladoras

A. **Esas vendedoras ahí son habladoras. Ahí** indicates that the lawyer is "there" (a distance from speaker). Use the feminine plural demonstrative adjective **esas** (*those*). Use the plural **son** (*are*), and follow it with the feminine, plural adjective **habladoras** (*talkative*).

65 ingeniero/allá/razonable

_____

66 técnicos/aquí/simpáticos

_____

67 banqueros/ahí/honrados

_____

68 secretarias/ahí/amables

_____

69 obreros/allá/ambiciosos

_____

70 directora/allá/sincera

_____

71 científicas/aquí/serias

_____

72 hombre de negocios/aquí/optimista

_____

73 empleadas/allá/agresivas

_____

74 investigador/ahí/trabajador

_____

75 traductora/aquí/concienzuda

_____

Identifying the Gender of Singular Spanish Nouns

Spanish nouns are either masculine or feminine. Nouns that refer to males are always masculine, and nouns that refer to females are feminine, no matter their endings. You can't always be sure when it comes to places or things, though. So this section explores how to determine the gender of singular Spanish nouns.

In Spanish, certain endings are good indications as to the gender (masculine or feminine designation) of nouns. For instance, singular nouns that end in **-o** are generally, but not always, masculine. Singular nouns that end in **–a**, **-ad** (**la ciudad** [*city*]), **-ie** (**la serie** [*the series*]), **-ción** (**la canción** [*the song*]), **-sión** (**la discusión** [*discussion*]), **-ud** (**la salud** [*health*]), and **-umbre** (**la costumbre** [*custom*]) are generally feminine. And nouns that end in **-s** are generally plural.

Here are more rules that deal with gender in Spanish:

>> Certain nouns belonging to a theme are masculine. These include

- Numbers (**el cuatro** [*four*])

- Days of the week (**el jueves** [*Thursday*])

- Compass points (**el norte** [*north*])

- Names of trees (**el manzano** [*apple tree*])

- Compound nouns (**el mediodía** [*noon*])

- Names of rivers, lakes, mountains, straits, and seas (**el Mediterraneo** [*the Mediterranean*])

>> Certain nouns belonging to a theme are feminine. These include

- Many illnesses (**la gripe** [*the flu*])

- Certain geographical names (**la India** [*India*])

The following sections dive in to more detail with respect to noun gender in Spanish, including some special cases you must consider.

Exploring reverse-gender nouns

Some nouns are tricky because they end in **-a** but are masculine while others end in **-o** but are feminine. These nouns may be referred to as reverse-gender nouns.

Some nouns that end in **-ma** and **-eta** (words that are derived from the Greek language) are masculine, as are the words **el día** (*the day*) and **el mapa** (*the map*). The following table outlines these masculine words:

-ma	-eta
el clima (*the climate*)	**el atleta** (*the athlete*)
el drama (*the drama*)	**el planeta** (*the planet*)
el idioma (*the language*)	**el poeta** (*the poet*)
el poema (*the poem*)	**el cometa** (*the comet*)
el problema (*the problem*)	
el programa (*the program*)	
el sistema (*the system*)	
el telegrama (*the telegram*)	
el tema (*the theme*)	

A couple of nouns ending in **-o** are feminine:

>> **la mano** (*the hand*)

>> **la radio** (*the radio*)

WARNING

Don't get confused by abbreviations that end in **-o**, like **la foto** (abbreviation for **la fotografía** [*the photgraph*]) and **la moto** (abbreviation for **la motocicleta** [*the motorcycle*]).

Recognizing nouns that are the same for both genders

Some nouns have the same spelling for both genders. For these nouns, all you have to do is change the definitive article to reflect whether the person in question is male or female. Here are some high-frequency examples that might prove useful:

el artista	la artista	*the artist*
el dentista	la dentista	*the dentist*
el periodista	la periodista	*the journalist*
el modelo	la modelo	*the model*
el joven	la joven	*the youth*
el estudiante	la estudiante	*the student*

The following nouns always remain feminine regardless of the gender of the person being described:

REMEMBER

la persona (*the person*)

la víctima (*the victim*)

PRACTICE

You're studying for a vocabulary test in your Spanish class. Use the following words to complete the definitions described by the clues. You must add the appropriate definite article.

Q. un hombre que escribe poemas

A. **el poeta.** Some nouns that end in **-eta** are masculine.

cine	ciudad	día
gripe	jueves	mano
nación	noche	norte
oficina	ojo	persona
planeta	problema	serie

76 cuarto día de la semana _____

77 una dirección _____

78 órgano de visión _____

79 situación difícil de resolver _____

80 enfermedad contagiosa _____

81 local donde se trabaja _____

82 lugar como New York _____

83 un individuo _____

84 territorio geográfico _____

85 conjunto de cosas relacionadas _____

86 veinticuatro horas _____

87 cuando las personas duermen _____

88 edificio donde se pueden ver películas _____

89 parte del cuerpo _____

90 cuerpo celeste _____

Adding to Your Knowledge with Noun Plurals

You use *noun plurals* to refer to more than one person, place, thing, quality, idea, or action. Not surprisingly, just as you do in English, you use the letters **-s** and **-es** to form the plurals of Spanish nouns. The following list outlines the many plural variations you see in Spanish nouns and the rules for forming plurals.

>> You add **-s** to form the plural of nouns ending in a vowel:

- **el mango** (*the mango*); **los mangos** (*the mangoes*)

- **la manzana** (*the apple*); **las manzanas** (*the apples*)

>> You add **-es** to form the plural of nouns ending in a consonant (including **-y**):

- **el emperador** (*the emperor*); **los emperadores** (*the emperors*)

- **el rey** (*the king*); **los reyes** (*the kings*)

>> You add or delete an accent mark in some nouns ending in **-n** or **-s** to maintain the original stress:

- **el joven; los jóvenes** (*the youths*)

- **el examen; los exámenes** (*the tests*)

- **la canción; las canciones** (*the songs*)

- **el francés; los franceses** (*the Frenchmen*)

- **el inglés; los ingleses** (*the Englishmen*)

- **el interés; los intereses** (*the interests*)

- **el autobús; los autobuses** (*the buses*)

- **el limón; los limones** (*the lemons*)

- **el melón; los melones** (*the melons*)

- **el melocotón; los melocotones** (*the peaches*)

>> Nouns that end in **-z** change **z** to **-c** before you add **-es**:

- **la luz** (*the light*); **las luces** (*the lights*)

>> Nouns that end in **-es, -is, or -us** (except for those mentioned above) don't change in the plural, except for **el mes** (*the month*), which becomes **los meses** and **el país** (*the country*), which becomes **los países**:

- **el lunes** (*Monday*); **los lunes** (*Mondays*)

- **la crisis** (*the crisis*); **las crisis** (*the crises*)

- **el virus** (*the virus*); **los virus** (*the viruses*)

>> Compound nouns (nouns composed of two nouns that are joined to make one) don't change in the plural:

- **el abrelatas** (*can opener*); **los abrelatas** (*can openers*)

>> You express the plural of nouns of different genders (where one noun is masculine and the other[s] is feminine) with the masculine plural:

- **el rey y la reina** (*the king and queen*); **los reyes**

- **el muchacho y la muchacha** (*the boy and the girl*); **los muchachos**

REMEMBER

Some nouns are always plural, such as

las gafas/los espejuelos (*eyeglasses*)

las matemáticas (*mathematics*)

las vacaciones (*vacation*)

PRACTICE

You're looking out your hotel window into the street. Note your observations of the street scene in your travel journal. Write all the English words in parentheses in their Spanish plural equivalents.

Q. Dos _____ tocan _____ (*people, guitars*)

A. Dos <u>personas</u> tocan <u>guitarras</u>.

91. Dos_____ hablan de sus _____ . (Frenchmen, vacation)	
92. Dos_____ venden _____ , _____	
_____ y _____ . (men, peaches, lemons, melons)	
93. Dos_____ cantan bellas _____ . (young people, songs)	
94. Dos_____ tienen dos _____ en las _____ .	
(boys, fish, hands)	
95. Dos_____ buscan sus _____ . (women, eyeglasses)	
96. Dos_____ miran los _____ . (tourists, skyscrapers)	
97. Dos_____ hablan de las _____ . (judges, laws)	
98. Dos_____ indican que hay dos_____ de f~~ú~~tbol los	
_____ . (signs, matches, Mondays)	
99. Dos_____ llevan _____ . (Germans, umbrellas)	
100. Dos_____ hablan de los _____ españoles.	
(students, kings)	

What's Mine Is Mine: Expressing Possession

All of us, at some time in our lives, are possessive of our loved ones and of our things. You can express possession in Spanish in several ways: by using the preposition **de** (*of*) or by using possessive adjectives before the person or thing belonging to you. The sections that follow guide you through the ways you can stake your claims.

Using de

Expressing possession by using the preposition **de** (*of*) is quite unlike what people are accustomed to in English. English speakers put an apostrophe + *s* after the noun representing the possessor: John's family. Spanish nouns have no apostrophe + *s*; you must use a reverse word order joined by the preposition **de**. The following list presents the rules of using **de**:

>> You use the preposition **de** (*of*) between the noun that's possessed and the proper noun representing the possessor:

  ● **Es el coche de Julio.** (*It's Julio's car.*)

>> You use the preposition **de** + a definite article between the noun that's possessed and a common noun representing the possessor:

  ● **Tengo el abrigo de la muchacha.** (*I have the girl's coat.*)

REMEMBER

>> **De** contracts with the definite article **el** to form **del** (*of the*) before a masculine singular common noun:

  ● **Necesito el libro del profesor.** (*I need the teacher's book.*)

>> If the sentence contains more than one possessor, you need to repeat **de** before each noun:

  ● **Voy a la casa de Roberto y de Marta.** (*I'm going to Robert and Marta's house.*)

TIP

>> You use a construction that's the reverse of English to answer the question "**¿De quién es . . . ?** (*Whose*)":

  ● **¿De quién es la idea?** (*Whose idea is it?*)

  ● **Es la idea de Julia.** (*It is Julia's idea.*)

PRACTICE

It's the end of the school year, and many items still remain in the lost and found. Identify the owner of each thing by following the example:

Q. bolígrafo/Juan

A. Es el bolígrafo de Juan. Use **es** to express *it is*. Because **bolígrafo** is masculine and singular, use the definite article **el** to express *the*. Use **de** to express *of* before the proper name **Juan.**

Q. libros/profesores

A. Son los libros de los profesores. Use **son** to express *they are*. Because **libros** is masculine and plural, use the definite article **los** to express *the*. Use **de** to express *of* and add the masculine, plural definite article **los** before the noun **profesores.**

(101) mochila/Julio _____

(102) pupitre/alumno _____

(103) cuadernos/Marta y Ana _____

(104) mapa/profesora de historia _____

(105) plumas/consejeros _____

(106) diccionarios/muchachas _____

Using possessive adjectives

You use *possessive adjectives* before the noun that's possessed to express *my, your, his, her, its, our,* and *their*. Possessive adjectives must agree in gender and number (singular or plural) with the object that's possessed; they never agree with the possessor. Check out the Spanish possessive adjectives in Table 3-2 with examples that follow.

Table 3-2   Possessive Adjectives

English word	Masculine singular	Masculine plural	Feminine singular	Feminine plural
my	mi	mis	mi	mis
your	tu	tus	tu	tus
his/her/your	su	sus	su	sus
our	nuestro	nuestros	nuestra	nuestras
your	vuestro	vuestros	vuestra	vuestras
their/your	su	sus	su	sus

REMEMBER

All forms of **vuestro** (**vuestra, vuestros, vuestras**) are used informally only in Spain. **Su** and **sus** are used formally and informally in Latin America.

Julia les escribe a sus amigas. (*Julia writes to her friends.*)

Yo perdí mis gafas. (*I lost my glasses.*)

Nosotros escuchamos a nuestro profesor. (*We listen to our teacher.*)

TIP

Because **su** can mean *his, her,* or *their,* you can clarify whom the possessor really is by replacing the possessive adjective (*su*) with the corresponding definite article (**el, la, los, or las**) + **de** + **él** (**ellos, ella, ellas, Ud., Uds.**):

I need his (her) help.

Necesito su ayuda.

Necesito la ayuda de ella (él).

With parts of the body or clothing, when the possessor is clear, you replace the possessive adjective with the correct definite article:

Me cepillo los dientes dos veces al día. (*I brush my teeth twice a day.*)

Having good communication with your family members is very important. Express with whom each of the following interact.

Q. Él expresa _____ opiniones a _____ esposa.

A. **sus, su.** Possessive adjectives agree with the noun possessed, not with the possessor. Use the plural possessive adjective **sus** to express *his* before the plural noun **opiniones**. Use the singular possessive adjective **su** to express *his* before the singular noun **esposa**.

107 Ella revela _____ esperanzas (*hopes*) a _____ padre.

108 Nosotros hablamos de _____ problemas a _____ hermana.

109 Yo escribo _____ pensamientos (*thoughts*) a _____ tía.

110 Él verbaliza _____ sentimientos a _____ esposa.

111 Vosotros explicáis _____ ideas a _____ primo.

112 Uds. declaran _____ aerofobia (*fear of flying*) a _____ padres.

113 Tú describes _____ ambiciones a _____ madre.

114 Javier y Isabel mencionan _____ inseguridades a _____ abuelo.

Answers to "Sorting Out Word Gender" Practice Questions

The following are the answers to the practice questions presented in this chapter.

1. **la**. Use the feminine singular definite article before the feminine singular noun escuela.

2. **el**. Use the masculine singular definite article before the masculine singular noun **hotel.**

3. No definite article is required before the ordinal number **quinto.**

4. **el**. Use the masculine singular definite article before the masculine singular noun **hotel.**

5. **la**. Use the feminine singular definite article before the feminine singular noun **mañana.**

6. **las**. Use the feminine plural definite article before the number **once.**

7. **el**. Use the masculine singular definite article before the masculine singular noun **desayuno.**

8. No definite article is required before **hambre.** The expression **tengo hambre** means to be hungry.

9. **la**. Use the feminine singular definite article before the feminine singular noun **primavera.**

10. **el**. Use the masculine singular definite article before the masculine singular noun **suéter.**

11. **la**. Use the feminine singular definite article before the feminine singular noun **gorra.**

12. **la**. Use the feminine singular definite article before the feminine singular noun **tarde.**

13. **las**. Use the feminine plural definite article before the feminine plural noun **pirámides.**

14. **los**. The noun **aztecas** is masculine plural; therefore, the masculine plural definite article **los** is used.

15. **el**. Use the masculine singular definite article before the masculine singular noun **autobús.**

16. **la**. Use the feminine singular definite article before the feminine singular noun **calle.**

17. No definite article is required before the ordinal number **sexto.**

18. **el**. Use the masculine singular definite article before the masculine singular noun **director.**

19. **la**. Use the feminine singular definite article before the feminine singular noun **universidad.**

20. **los**. Use the masculine plural definite article before the masculine plural noun **complejos.**

21. The definite article is generally not used before the name of the day of the week.

22. **la**. Use the definite article before the feminine singular noun **oficina.**

23. The definite article isn't needed after the preposition **de** and before the noun **vacaciones.**

24. **un**. Use the masculine singular indefinite article before **compañero** to express *a.*

25. The indefinite article is omitted before an unmodified profession.

(26) **un.** Use the masculine singular indefinite article to express *a* before a modified profession.

(27) **un.** Use the masculine singular indefinite article before **crucero** to express *a*.

(28) **un.** Use the masculine singular indefinite article before **camarote** to express *a*.

(29) **un.** Use the masculine singular indefinite article before **barco** to express *a*.

(30) **la.** The feminine definite article is used before the feminine name of a boat.

(31) The definite article is omitted before numerals expressing the titles of rulers.

(32) **la.** Use the feminine singular definite article **la** before the feminine noun **tripulación** to express *the*.

(33) The indefinite article is omitted before the number **mil.**

(34) The definite article isn't used before the **primero.**

(35) **un.** Use the masculine singular indefinite article before **desayuno** to express *a*.

(36) **las.** Use the feminine plural definite article **las** before the feminine noun **actividades** to express *the*.

(37) **del.** Contract the masculine singular definite article **el** with **de** after **a bordo.**

(38) **al.** Contract the masculine singular definite article **el** with **a** before **gimnasio.**

(39) **los.** Use the masculine plural definite article before **días,** which is a masculine noun.

(40) **la.** Use the feminine singular definite article **la** before the feminine noun **piscina** to express *the*.

(41) **al.** Contract the masculine singular definite article **el** with **a** before **golf.**

(42) **al.** Contract the masculine singular definite article **el** with **a** before **volíbol.**

(43) **los.** Use the masculine plural definite article before **naipes,** which is a masculine noun.

(44) **el.** Use the definite article before the masculine singular noun **almuerzo.**

(45) **la.** Use the feminine definite article before a time.

(46) **el.** Use the masculine singular definite article before the masculine singular noun **día.**

(47) **el.** Use the masculine singular definite article before the masculine singular noun **barco.**

(48) **un.** Use the masculine singular indefinite article before the masculine singular noun **puerto.**

(49) **una.** Use the feminine singular indefinite article before the feminine singular noun **visita.**

(50) **del.** Contract the masculine singular definite article **el** with **de** before **país.**

(51) **la.** Use the feminine singular definite article **la** before the feminine noun **isla.**

(52) **la.** Use the feminine singular definite article **la** before the feminine noun **semana.**

(53) **unos.** Use the masculine plural indefinite article before **discos** to express *some*.

(54) **unas.** Use the feminine plural indefinite article before **camisetas** to express *some*.

(55) No article is needed in the idiomatic expression **tener suerte.**

(56) **un.** Use the masculine singular indefinite article before the masculine singular noun **reloj.**

(57) **una.** Use the feminine singular indefinite article before the feminine singular noun **visita.**

(58) The indefinite article is omitted before the number **cien.**

(59) **la.** Use the feminine singular definite article **la** before the feminine noun **noche.**

(60) No article is needed after the word **hay** (*there is/are*).

(61) No article is needed after the word **hay** (*there is/are*).

(62) **una.** Use the feminine singular indefinite article before the feminine singular noun **película.**

(63) **un.** Use the masculine singular indefinite article before the masculine singular noun **desfile.**

(64) **el.** Use the masculine singular definite article before the masculine singular noun **crucero.**

(65) **Aquel ingeniero allá es razonable.** Use the masculine singular demonstrative adjective indicated by the adverb **allá.**

(66) **Estos técnicos aquí son simpáticos.** Use the masculine plural demonstrative adjective indicated by the adverb **aquí.**

(67) **Esos banqueros ahí son honrados.** Use the masculine plural demonstrative adjective indicated by the adverb **ahí.**

(68) **Esas secretarias ahí son amables.** Use the feminine singular demonstrative adjective indicated by the adverb **ahí.**

(69) **Aquellos obreros allá son ambiciosos.** Use the masculine plural demonstrative adjective indicated by the adverb **allá.**

(70) **Aquella directora allá es sincera.** Use the feminine singular demonstrative adjective indicated by the adverb **allá.**

(71) **Estas científicas aquí son serias.** Use the feminine plural demonstrative adjective indicated by the adverb **aquí.**

(72) **Este hombre de negocios aquí es optimista.** Use the masculine singular demonstrative adjective indicated by the adverb **aquí.**

(73) **Aquellas empleadas allá son agresivas.** Use the feminine plural demonstrative adjective indicated by the adverb **allá.**

(74) **Ese investigador ahí es trabajador.** Use the masculine singular demonstrative adjective and pronoun indicated by the adverb **ahí.**

(75) **Esta traductora aquí es concienzuda.** Use the feminine singular demonstrative adjective indicated by the adverb **aquí.**

(76) **el jueves.** The names of the days of the week are masculine.

(77) **el norte.** Compass points are masculine.

(78) **el ojo** Nouns that end in **-o** are generally masculine.

(79) **el problema.** Some nouns that end in **-ma** are masculine.

(80) **la gripe.** The names of many illnesses are feminine.

(81) **la oficina.** Nouns that end in **-a** are generally feminine.

(82) **la ciudad.** Nouns that end in **-dad** are generally feminine.

(83) **la persona.** The word for *person* is always feminine.

(84) **la nación.** Nouns that end in **-ción** are generally feminine.

(85) **la serie.** Nouns that end in **-ie** are generally feminine.

(86) **El día.** Some nouns that end in **-a** are masculine.

(87) **la noche.** Some nouns that end in **-e** are feminine.

(88) **el cine.** Some nouns that end in **-e** are masculine.

(89) **la mano.** Some nouns that end in **-o** are feminine.

(90) **el planeta.** Some nouns that end in **-eta** are masculine.

(91) **franceses/vacaciones.** The masculine singular noun **francés** (*French man*) is made plural by adding an **-es** because it ends in a consonant. The accented **é** is replaced by **e** in the plural to maintain the proper stress. The Spanish word for *vacation* is always plural: **vacaciones.**

(92) **hombres, melocotones, limones, melones.** The masculine singular noun **hombre** (*man*) is made plural by adding an **-s** because the noun ends in a vowel. The three masculine singular nouns (**melocotón, limón,** and **melón**) are made plural by adding an **-es** because they end in a consonant. The unaccented singular **-o** is changed to **-ó** in the plural to maintain the proper stress.

(93) **jóvenes/canciones.** Add **-es** to **joven** (*youth*) to form the plural because it ends in a consonant. Add an accent on the **-o** to preserve the proper stress. The feminine singular noun **canción** (*song*) is made plural by adding an **-es** because it ends in a consonant. The accented singular **-ó** is changed to **-o** in the plural to maintain the proper stress.

(94) **muchachos/peces/manos.** The masculine singular noun **muchacho** (*boy*) is made plural by adding an **-s** because the noun ends in a vowel. Change **pez** (*fish*) to **peces.** Nouns ending in **-z** change **-z** to **-c** before adding the plural **-es** ending. The masculine singular noun **mano** (*hand*) is made plural by adding an **-s** because the noun ends in a vowel.

(95) **mujeres/gafas.** Add **-es** to **mujer** (*woman*) to form the plural because it ends in a consonant. The Spanish word for eyeglasses is always plural: **gafas.**

(96) **turistas/rascacielos.** The masculine singular noun **turista** (*tourist*) is made plural by adding an **-s** because the noun ends in a vowel. The Spanish word for the compound noun *skyscraper* is always plural: **rascacielos.**

(97) **jueces/leyes.** Change **juez** (*judge*) to **jueces.** Nouns ending in **-z** change **-z** to **-c** before adding the plural **-es** ending. Add **-es** to **ley** (*law*) because it ends in **-y.**

(98) **carteles (letreros)/partidos/lunes.** Add **-es** to **cartel** (*sign*) because it ends in a consonant. The masculine singular noun **partido** (*match*) is made plural by adding an **-s** because the noun ends in a vowel. The Spanish word for *Monday,* **lunes,** doesn't change in the plural.

(99) **alemanes/paraguas.** Add **-es** to **alemán** (*German*) to form the plural because it ends in a consonant. Remove the accent on the **-á** to preserve the proper stress. The masculine plural noun **paraguas** (*umbrella*) remains unchanged in the plural because it ends in **-s.**

(100) **estudiantes/reyes.** The masculine singular noun **estudiante** (*student*) is made plural by adding an **-s** because the noun ends in a vowel. Add **-es** to **rey** (*king*) because it ends in **-y.**

(101) **Es la mochila de Juan.** Use **es** to express *it is.* Because **mochila** is feminine and singular, use the definite article **la** to express *the.* Use **de** to express *of* and then add the name **Juan.**

(102) **Es el pupitre del alumno.** Use **es** to express *it is.* Because **pupitre** is masculine and singular, use the definite article **el** to express *the.* Use the contraction **del** (**de + el**) to express *of the* before the masculine singular noun **alumno.**

(103) **Son los cuadernos de Marta y de Ana.** Use **son** to express *they are.* Because **cuadernos** is masculine and plural, use the definite article **los** to express *the.* Use **de** to express *of* before each proper name.

(104) **Es el mapa de la profesora de historia.** Use **es** to express *it is.* Because **mapa** is masculine and singular (an exception to the rule), use the definite article **el** to express *the.* Use **de** to express *of* and **la** to express *the* before the feminine singular noun **profesora.**

(105) **Son las plumas de los consejeros.** Use son to express *they are.* Because **plumas** is feminine and plural, use the definite article **las** to express *the.* Use **de** to express *of* and **los** to express *the* before the masculine plural noun **consejeros.**

(106) **Son los diccionarios de las muchachas.** Use **son** to express *they are.* Because **diccionarios** is masculine and plural, use the definite article **los** to express *the.* Use **de** to express *of* and **las** to express *the* before the feminine plural noun **muchachas.**

(107) **sus, su.** Possessive adjectives agree with the noun possessed, not with the possessor. Use the plural possessive adjective **sus** to express *her* before the plural noun **esperanzas.** Use the singular possessive adjective **su** to express *her* before the singular noun **padre.**

(108) **nuestros, nuestra.** Use the plural possessive adjective **nuestros** to express *our* before the masculine plural noun **problemas.** (Some nouns ending in **-ema** are masculine.) Use the singular possessive adjective **nuestra** to express *our* before the feminine singular noun **hermana.**

(109) **mis, mi.** Use the plural possessive adjective **mis** to express *my* before the plural noun **pensamientos.** Use the singular possessive adjective **mi** to express *my* before the singular noun **tía.**

(110) **sus, su.** Use the plural possessive adjective **sus** to express *his* before the plural noun **sentimientos.** Use the singular possessive adjective **su** to express *his* before the singular noun **esposa.**

(111) **vuestras, vuestro.** Use the feminine plural possessive adjective **vuestras** to express *your* before the feminine plural noun **ideas.** Use the singular possessive adjective **vuestro** to express *your* before the singular noun **primo.**

(112) **su, sus.** Use the singular possessive adjective **su** to express *your* before the singular noun **aerofobia.** Use the plural possessive adjective **sus** to express *your* before the plural noun **padres.**

(113) **tus, tu.** Use the plural possessive adjective **tus** to express *your* before the plural noun **ambiciones.** Use the singular possessive adjective **tu** to express *your* before the singular noun **madre.**

(114) **sus, su.** Use the plural possessive adjective **sus** to express *their* before the plural noun **inseguridades.** Use the singular possessive adjective **su** to express *their* before the singular noun **abuelo.**

Chapter **4**

Coloring Your Sentences with Adjectives

To be a good writer, you need to be descriptive. And to be descriptive, you must have a good command of adjectives. Your writing will be far more interesting if you can zero in on the physical qualities or personality traits of the person you're portraying or the characteristics of the place or thing you want to discuss. The bottom line is that writing well means being able to go beyond a simple, declarative sentence by adding color and excitement to your thoughts. And, yes, you can certainly do this in Spanish with only a small amount of effort.

This chapter illustrates how adjectives in Spanish are different from adjectives in English and presents all that you need to know to use them properly. It also discusses the two Spanish verbs equivalent to English *to be*. By the end of this chapter, you'll be able to describe everything you want.

Describing People and Things with Adjectives

The function of an adjective is to describe a noun or pronoun so that your audience gains a better understanding of what that noun or pronoun is like. Is the house *big*? Are the trees *green*? You should use adjectives frequently when you write so that readers have the most information about, and the best possible understanding of, what you're describing. The following sections show you how to use adjectives by discussing their agreement and positioning in sentences.

Agreement of adjectives

Unlike in English, where adjectives have only one form, Spanish adjectives agree with the gender (masculine or feminine) and number (singular or plural) of the nouns they describe. When the noun or pronoun is feminine, the adjective describing it must also be feminine. When the noun or pronoun is singular, its verb and any adjectives describing it must also be singular.

REMEMBER

Over the course of this chapter, I present some high-frequency Spanish adjectives that will come in handy in most everyday learning, traveling, and business situations.

The gender of adjectives

Most Spanish adjectives end in **-o** or **-a**. Adjectives that end in **-o**, like most nouns, are masculine. (In some instances, however, masculine adjectives end in another vowel and maybe even in a consonant; see the following section.) As you may expect, a masculine, singular adjective ending in **-o** forms its feminine counterpart by changing **-o** to **-a**.

Here are some common Spanish adjectives:

Masculine	Feminine	Meaning
aburrido	aburrida	*boring*
afortunado	afortunada	*fortunate*
alto	alta	*tall*
atractivo	atractiva	*attractive*
bajo	baja	*short*
bonito	bonita	*pretty*
bueno	buena	*good*
delgado	delgada	*thin*
delicioso	deliciosa	*delicious*
divertido	divertida	*fun*
enfermo	enferma	*sick*
enojado	enojada	*angry*
famoso	famosa	*famous*
feo	fea	*ugly*
flaco	flaca	*thin*
generoso	generosa	*generous*
gordo	gorda	*fat*
guapo	guapa	*pretty, good-looking*
listo	lista	*ready (smart)*
magnífico	magnífica	*magnificent*
malo	mala	*bad*
moderno	moderna	*modern*
moreno	morena	*dark-haired*

Masculine	Feminine	Meaning
necesario	necesaria	*necessary*
negro	negra	*black*
nuevo	nueva	*new*
ordinario	ordinaria	*ordinary*
orgulloso	orgullosa	*proud*
pardo	parda	*brown*
peligroso	peligrosa	*dangerous*
pequeño	pequeña	*small*
perezoso	perezosa	*lazy*
perfecto	perfecta	*perfect*
rico	rica	*rich*
romántico	romántica	*romantic*
rubio	rubia	*blond*
serio	seria	*serious*
simpático	simpática	*nice*
sincero	sincera	*sincere*
tímido	tímida	*shy*
todo	toda	*all*
viejo	vieja	*old*

TIP

Listo (lista) means *ready* when used with the verb **estar** and *smart* when used with **ser**.

Ella está lista. (*She is ready.*)

Ella es lista. (*She is smart.*)

Here's an example of an adjective in action:

Mi primo Jaime es tímido y mi prima Francisca es tímida también. (*My cousin James is shy, and my cousin Francisca is shy, too.*)

PRACTICE

The people within a family have different ideas, opinions, physical characteristics and personality traits. Describe the members of the Rojas family by filling in the blank with the appropriate adjective.

Q. La Señora Rojas tiene ochenta años. Ella es _____.

A. **vieja.** If she is 80 years old, then she is old. Use the feminine form of the adjective, which ends in **-a**.

1. Carolina recibe buenas notas en la escuela. Trabaja mucho. No es _____.

2. Paco no habla mucho. Es _____.

3 Ricardo no es alto. Es _____.

4 Isabel gana mucho dinero. Es _____.

5 Alicia no es fea. Es _____.

6 Juan no tiene pelo moreno. Es _____.

Exceptions to the rules

Of course, there are some exceptions to every rule. In Spanish, there are some masculine, singular adjectives that end in **-a**, **-e**, or a consonant (other than **-or**). The adjectives that follow don't change in their feminine form, for instance.

Masculine	Feminine	Meaning
egoísta	egoísta	selfish
materialista	materialista	materialistic
optimista	optimista	optimistic
pesimista	pesimista	pessimistic
realista	realista	realistic
alegre	alegre	happy
amable	amable	nice
eficiente	eficiente	efficient
elegante	elegante	elegant
excelente	excelente	excellent
grande	grande	big
horrible	horrible	horrible
importante	importante	important
inteligente	inteligente	intelligent
interesante	interesante	interesting
pobre	pobre	poor
responsable	responsable	responsible
sociable	sociable	sociable
triste	triste	sad
valiente	valiente	brave

Here's an example of how this works:

Ricardo es optimista pero su hermana es pesimista. (*Ricardo is optimistic, but his sister is pessimistic.*)

The following adjectives end in consonants and also undergo no change for gender.

Masculine	Feminine	Meaning
cortés	cortés	*courteous*
azul	azul	*blue*
débil	débil	*weak*
fácil	fácil	*easy*
fiel	fiel	*loyal*
genial	genial	*great, awesome*
leal	leal	*loyal*
puntual	puntual	*punctual*
tropical	tropical	*tropical*
joven	joven	*young*
popular	popular	*popular*
feroz	feroz	*ferocious*
sagaz	sagaz	*astute*
suspicaz	suspicaz	*suspicious*

Here's an example of one of these adjectives at work:

> **Mi padre es joven y mi madre es joven también.** (*My father is young, and my mother is young, too.*)

In Spanish, some adjectives of nationality with a masculine form ending in a consonant add **-a** to form the feminine. The adjectives **inglés** (and other adjectives of nationality that end in **-és**) and **alemán** also drop the accent on their final vowel to maintain their original stresses:

Masculine	Feminine	Meaning
español	española	*Spanish*
inglés	inglesa	*English*
alemán	alemana	*German*

And some adjectives with a masculine form ending in **-or** add **-a** to form the feminine:

Masculine	Feminine	Meaning
encantador	encantadora	*enchanting*
hablador	habladora	*talkative*
trabajador	trabajadora	*hardworking*

Here are some examples:

> **Fritz es alemán y Heidi es alemana también.** (*Fritz is German, and Heidi is German, too.*)

> **Carlota es trabajadora pero su hermano no es trabajador.** (*Carlota is hardworking, but her brother isn't hardworking.*)

Now describe the people in your neighborhood using the correct form of the adjective.

Q. El señor Rafael es de Berlin. El es _____.

A. alemán. If he is from Berlin, he is German. The masculine adjective has an accent.

7 El señor Robles habla constantemente. Él es _____.

8 Jorge tiene muchos amigos. Él es _____.

9 Marta es de Londres. Ella es _____.

10 La señora Molina es juez. Ella debe ser _____.

11 Patricia siempre dice "por favor" y "muchas gracias." Ella es _____.

12 Alberto siempre llega temprano. Él es _____.

Gender sensitivity

Today, most people are very attuned to respecting an individual's gender choice. Because Spanish grammar is based on a gendering system, accommodations are being made to accept gender neutrality. The **-x** and **-e** gender-neutral endings are generally considered to be the most popular choices. To date, however, these options are not considered grammatically correct nor have they been accepted by the Royal Academy of the Spanish Language (Real Academia Española).

The letter **x** may be used to replace the typical **-o** and **-a** gender endings that most people are familiar with. The problem is that **x** isn't a common sound in most Spanish dialects. So, although writing **latinx** doesn't pose much of a problem, pronouncing **latinx** (*lah-tee-nehks*) may be quite difficult for some Spanish speakers. The **-x** ending works as follows:

> **Alto/alta** becomes **altx.**

> **Hablador/habladora** becomes **habladorx.**

Another alternative, one that already exists as gender-neutral in Spanish, is the final **-e** ending. This option is slowly becoming popular in Spain and some South American countries. Here's how this works:

> **Alto/alta** becomes **alte.**

> **Hablador/habladora** becomes **habladore.**

The plural of adjectives

To form the plural of adjectives in Spanish, you follow two basic rules. First, you add **-s** to singular adjectives ending in a vowel, such as the following:

Singular	Plural	Meaning
alto	altos	*tall*
rubia	rubias	*blond*
interesante	interesantes	*interesting*

Second, you add **-es** to singular adjectives ending in a consonant:

Singular	Plural	Meaning
fácil	fáciles	*easy*
trabajador	trabajdores	*hardworking*

Just like with some nouns and pronouns, when speaking about mixed company (males and females, with no mind to number), make sure to use the masculine form of the adjective:

Mis hermanas y mi hermano son rubios. (*My sisters and my brother are blond.*)

More exceptions to the rules

Some singular Spanish adjectives don't follow the basic rules for making plurals. They follow the same or similar rules for plural formation as Spanish nouns. (See Chapter 3.)

>> Singular adjectives ending in **-z**, change **-z** to **-c** in the plural:

- **feliz → felices** (*happy*)
- **atroz → atroces** (*atrocious*)
- **sagaz → sagaces** (*astute*)

>> Some adjectives add or drop an accent mark to maintain original stress:

- **joven → jóvenes** (*young*)
- **cortés → corteses** (*courteous*)
- **inglés → ingleses** (*English*)
- **alemán → alemanes** (*German*)

You're writing an email to a friend in which you describe certain other friends and family members. Select an adjective from the list provided that more clearly describes the person. Make sure you adjust the adjective to agree in number and gender with the noun. Here's an example:

Q. Mis primos no son pesimistas. Son _____.

A. **Mis primos no son pesimistas. Son optimistas.** (*My cousins aren't pessimistic. They are optimistic.*) Although the subject is masculine plural, these adjectives always end in -a.

alemán	inglés
cómico	joven
débil	perezoso
descuidado	popular
egoísta	sagaz
fiel	sincero
francés	suspicaz
generoso	valiente

(13) Mis padres son astutos y prudentes. Son _____.

(14) Mi hermana tiene sospecha o desconfianza en todo. Es _____.

(15) Mi amiga, Linda, no es trabajadora. Es _____.

(16) Eduardo no comparte nada con nadie. Es _____.

(17) Antonio y Santiago no tienen miedo de nada. Son _____.

(18) Juanita hace reír a otros. Es _____.

(19) Enrique y Carmen siempre dicen la verdad. Son _____.

(20) Margarita no traiciona (*betray*) a nadie. Es _____.

(21) Mis abuelos nos compran muchos regalos. Son _____.

(22) Mi tío nunca tiene cuidado. Es _____.

(23) Mis hermanas tienen muchos amigos. Son _____.

(24) Mi tía es de Francia. Es _____.

(25) Mercedes no tiene suficiente fuerza física. Es _____.

(26) Mis tías no son viejas. Son _____.

(27) Mis amigos son de Inglaterra. Son _____.

(28) Mi padre es de Alemania. Es _____.

Positioning of adjectives

In Spanish, adjectives may precede or follow the noun they modify. In addition, more than one adjective may modify a noun. Each adjective must be positioned before or after the noun. Most adjectives follow the noun. The placement depends on the type of adjective being used, the connotation the speaker wants to convey, and the emphasis being used.

Sometimes, when more than one adjective describes a noun, the rules for placement vary according to the type of adjectives being used. For example, possessive adjectives (see Chapter 3), demonstrative adjectives (see Chapter 3), and adjectives of quantity (Chapter 1) precede the noun they modify, whereas descriptive adjectives (in this chapter) generally follow the noun they modify. The following sections dig deeper into these topics.

Adjectives that follow the noun

In Spanish, most descriptive adjectives follow the noun they modify. (Note that here, the possessive adjective **su** and the number **una** precede the noun.):

>**su novia francesa** (*his French girlfriend*)

>**una compañía próspera** (*a successful company*)

REMEMBER

When two adjectives follow the noun, they're joined by **y** (*and*):

>**un muchacho alto y rubio** (*a tall, blond boy*)

Adjectives that precede the noun

Non-descriptive adjectives — numbers, possessive adjectives, demonstrative adjectives, and adjectives of quantity — usually precede the noun they modify. (Here, the adjectives **feos**, **querido**, **delgado**, and **interesantes** are descriptive adjectives that follow the noun.):

>**dos gatos feos** (*two ugly cats*)

>**mi padre querido** (*my dear father*)

>**ese hombre delgado** (*that thin man*)

>**algunas cosas interesantes** (*some interesting things*)

TIP

Querido is also commonly used before the noun, particularly at the beginning of letters or messages: **Queridos amigos** (*Dear friends*).

REMEMBER

Descriptive adjectives that emphasize qualities or inherent characteristics may appear before the noun:

>**Tenemos buenos recuerdos de su fiesta.** (*We have good memories of her party.*)

In this example, the speaker is emphasizing the quality of the memories.

>**La blanca nieve es hermosa.** *White snow is beautiful.*

In this example, the inherent white color of snow may appear before the noun.

PRACTICE

Imagine that you're on a trip to a tropical island. Rearrange the words into logical order to give an accurate description of what you encounter.

Q. comida/deliciosa/mucha

A. **Hay mucha comida deliciosa.** Use the word **hay** to express *there is.* **Mucha** is an adjective that imposes limits and, therefore, precedes the noun, **comida**. **Deliciosa** is an adjective that tells the quality of the meal and, therefore, follows the noun.

29 blancas/dos/playas _____

30 americana/gente/poca _____

31 agua/azul/tanta _____

32 numerosas/magníficas/plantas _____

33 exóticos/animales/unos _____

34 grandes/árboles/algunos _____

Shortened forms of adjectives

Some Spanish adjectives get shortened in certain situations. The following list details when this occurs:

>> The following adjectives drop their final **-o** before a masculine, singular noun (note that **alguno** and **ninguno** add an accent to the **-u** when the **-o** is dropped):

- **uno** (*one*) → **un coche** (*one car*)

- **bueno** (*good*) → **un buen viaje** (*a good trip*)

- **malo** (*bad*) → **un mal muchacho** (*a bad boy*)

- **primero** (*first*) → **el primer acto** (*the first act*)

- **tercero** (*third*) → **el tercer presidente** (*the third president*)

- **alguno** (*some*) → **algún día** (*some day*)

- **ninguno** (*no*) → **ningún hombre** (*no man*)

REMEMBER

When a preposition separates the adjective from its noun, you use the original form of the adjective (don't drop the **-o**):

- **uno de tus primos** (*one of your cousins*)

>> **Grande** becomes **gran** (*great, important, famous*) before a singular masculine or feminine noun:

- **un gran profesor** (*a great teacher [male]*)

- **una gran profesora** (*a great teacher [female]*)

But it remains **grande** after the noun:

- **un escritorio grande** (*a large desk*)

- **una mesa grande** (*a large table*)

>> **Ciento** (*one hundred*) becomes **cien** before nouns and before the numbers **mil** and **millones:**

- **cien hombres y cien mujeres** (*one hundred men and one hundred women*)

- **cien mil habitantes** (*one hundred thousand inhabitants*)

- **cien millones de euros** (*one hundred million euros*)

Complete each sentence about a famous man with the correct form of the adjective.

Q. No es un _____ hombre.

A. **mal.** Use the shortened form of **malo** before a masculine singular noun.

35 Es un _____ amigo.

a. buen b. bueno c. buena d. buenos

36 Es el _____ científico que gana un premio.

a. tercera b. terceras c. tercer d. tercero

37 Es el _____ de su familia en graduarse de la universidad.

a. primer b. primero c. primera d. primeras

38 _____ biólogo es tan famoso como él.

a. Ninguna b. Ningunas c. Ningunos d. Ningún

39 _____ científicos tienen celos de él.

a. Algún b. Algunos c. Algunas d. Alguno

40 Gana _____ mil dólares al año.

a. cientos b. ciento c. cien d. doscientas

Adjectives with different meanings

The meaning of some adjectives changes depending on whether they're positioned before or after the noun they modify. Adjectives before the noun tend to have a more literal meaning, while those following the noun are more figurative.

>> **una tradición antigua** (*an old [ancient] tradition*)

 una antigua tradición (*an old [former] tradition*)

>> **una declaración cierta** (*an exact declaration*)

 una cierta declaración (*a certain [indefinite] declaration*)

>> **una mujer grande** (*a tall [large, big in size] woman*)

 una gran mujer (*a great woman [in moral character]*)

>> **la idea misma** (*the idea itself*)

 la misma idea (*the same idea*)

>> **un coche nuevo** (*a new car [brand new]*)

 un nuevo coche (*a new car [new to the owner, different]*)

» **el hombre pobre** (*the poor man [without money]*)

el pobre hombre (*the unfortunate man*)

» **un remedio simple** (*a easy remedy*)

un simple remedio (*a simple remedy*)

» **el muchacho único** (*the unique boy*)

el único muchacho (*the only boy*)

» **una amiga vieja** (*an old friend [elderly]*)

una vieja amiga (*an old friend [dear, long-time]*)

PRACTICE

In the following practice questions, place the adjective in its proper place to express the meaning indicated.

Q. (*poor*) **Es una mujer.**

A. **Es una mujer pobre. Pobre** connotes *poor (having no money)* when it follows the noun it modifies.

41 (*ancient*) Vamos a ver las ruinas. _____

42 (*simple*) Es una solución. _____

43 (*brand new*) Compran una casa. _____

44 (*same*) Tengo el problema. _____

45 (*great*) Ese hombre es un presidente. _____

It takes a bit of patience to get the hang of how to use, form, and place adjectives in Spanish. Now that you've had some practice with the rules, see whether you can apply them in the next exercise.

PRACTICE

You're a tourist who has seen many things while traveling. Create a journal entry in which you organize your notes by making all the adjectives agree and by putting them all in the proper position. I provide an adjective before the slash and another adjective after it. You must determine the correct form of the adjective (masculine or feminine; singular or plural) and place each adjective in its correct place. Here are some examples:

Q. **playa: un/espléndido**

A. **Nosotros vimos una playa espléndida.** The feminine singular demonstrative adjective **una** precedes the feminine singular noun **playa**. The descriptive adjective **espléndida** follows the noun.

Q. bosque: importante/ninguno

A. **Nosotros no vimos ningún bosque importante.** With **ninguno**, the negative, **no**, must be used before the verb. (See Chapter 8.) The masculine singular adjective **ningún** precedes the masculine singular noun **bosque**. The singular descriptive adjective importante follows the noun.

(46) flores: rojo/cien _____

(47) lagos: ninguno/largos _____

(48) nubes: blanco/mucho _____

(49) selvas: un/mágnifico _____

(50) montañas: alto/poco _____

(51) ríos: grande/un _____

(52) cascadas: estupendo/alguno _____

(53) animales: mucho/feroz _____

Using Ser and Estar in Descriptions

Spanish has two different verbs, **ser** and **estar,** that correspond to the English verb *to be.* As you can well imagine, this often causes confusion for non-native speakers, especially because both verbs have irregular forms. How do you choose the correct verb? Simply put, it depends on the context.

Using ser

The present tense forms of **ser** are highly irregular, and the only way to learn them is to memorize them. Fortunately, **ser** is used so often that this task will be rather easily accomplished.

Subject Pronoun	Verb Form	Meaning
yo	**soy**	*I am*
tú	**eres**	*you are*
él, ella, Ud.	**es**	*he, she, you are*
nosostros	**somos**	*we are*
vosotros	**sois**	*you are*
ellos, ellas, Uds.	**son**	*you are*

In descriptions, **ser** is used to express an inherent characteristic or quality (one that probably won't change anytime soon) as well as professions and nationality:

El chocolate es delicioso. (*Chocolate is delicious.*)

Clarita y Luisa son rubias. (*Clarita and Luisa are blond.*)

Nosotros somos estudiantes. (*We are students.*)

Yo soy americana. (*I am American.*)

REMEMBER

Ser is also used to express dates and times (see Chapter 1) and possession (see Chapter 3).

Using estar

The present tense forms of **estar** aren't very irregular and, except for the **yo** form, will be quite easy to internalize quickly.

Subject Pronoun	Verb Form	Meaning
yo	estoy	*I am*
tú	estás	*you are*
él, ella, Ud.	está	*he, she, you are*
nosostros	estamos	*we are*
vosotros	estáis	*you are*
ellos, ellas, Uds.	están	*you are*

Estar is used to express a physical or emotional condition or a temporary state:

Gabriel está alegre. (*Gabriel is happy.*)

Las puertas están cerradas. (*The doors are closed.*)

El café está caliente. (*The coffee is hot.*)

Common adjectives used with **estar** include:

aburrido (a)	*bored*
cansado (a)	*tired*
contento (a)	*happy, content*
emocionado (a)	*excited*
enfadado (a)	*angry*
enfermo (a)	*sick*
enojado (a)	*upset, angry*
furioso (a)	*furious*
limpio (a)	*clean*
nervioso (a)	*nervous*
ocupado (a)	*busy*
orgulloso (a)	*proud*

preocupado (a)	*worried*
preparado (a)	*prepared*
satisfecho (a)	*satisfied*
seguro (a)	*sure*
sentado (a)	*seated*
sucio (a)	*dirty*
triste	*sad*

TIP

Estar is also used to express location.

La pluma está en la mesa. (*The pen is on the table.*)

Answers to "Coloring Your Sentences with Adjectives" Practice Questions

The following are the answers to the practice questions presented in this chapter.

1. **perezosa.** Carolina receives good marks in school and works a lot. Use the feminine singular form of the adjective to express that she isn't lazy.

2. **tímido.** Paco doesn't speak a lot. Use the masculine singular form of the adjective to express that he's shy.

3. **bajo.** Ricardo isn't tall. Use the masculine singular form of the adjective to express that he's short.

4. **rica.** Isabel earns a lot of money. Use the feminine singular form of the adjective to express that she's rich.

5. **bonita.** Alicia isn't ugly. Use the feminine singular form of the adjective to express that she's pretty.

6. **rubio.** Juan doesn't have dark hair. Use the masculine singular form of the adjective to express that he is blond.

7. **hablador.** Señor Robles speaks constantly. Use the masculine singular form of the adjective to express that he's talkative.

8. **popular.** Jorge has a lot of friends. Use the masculine singular form of the adjective to express that he's popular.

9. **inglesa.** Marta is from London. Use the feminine singular form of the adjective, which doesn't require an accent, to express that she's English.

10. **sagaz.** Señora Molin is a judge. Use the feminine singular form of the adjective to express that she's astute. In this case, the feminine form is the same as the masculine form.

11. **cortés.** Patricia always says "please" and "thank you." Use the feminine singular form of the adjective to express that she's courteous. In this case, the feminine form is the same as the masculine form.

12. **puntual.** Alberto always arrives on time. Use the masculine singular form of the adjective to express that he's punctual.

13. **sagaces.** The parents are astute and wise. Use the plural form of **sagaz** to express that they're astute. With singular adjectives ending in **-z,** change **-z** to **-c** in the plural.

14. **suspicaz.** The sister has suspicions or lacks confidence in everything. Use the singular adjective **suspicaz** to express *suspicious*. The masculine and feminine forms of this adjective are the same.

15. **perezosa.** Linda isn't hardworking. Use the feminine singular form of the adjective to express that she's lazy.

16. **egoísta.** Eduardo doesn't share anything with anybody. Use the singular form of the adjective to express that he's selfish. In this case, the masculine singular adjective ends in **-a.**

17. **valientes.** Antonio and Santiago aren't afraid of anything. Use the masculine plural adjective to express that they're brave. In this case, the masculine singular adjective ends in **-e.**

(18) **cómica.** Janita makes everyone laugh. Use the feminine singular adjective to express that she's funny.

(19) **sinceros.** Enrique and Carmen always tell the truth. They're sincere. When speaking about mixed company, use the masculine plural form of the adjective.

(20) **fiel.** Margarita doesn't betray anyone. Use the singular form of the adjective to express that she's faithful. **Fiel** undergoes no change for gender.

(21) **generosos.** The grandparents are magnanimous. They're generous. When speaking about mixed company, use the masculine plural form of the adjective.

(22) **descuidado.** The uncle is never careful. Use the masculine singular form of the adjective to express that he's careless.

(23) **populares.** The sisters have many friends. Use the plural adjective to express that they're popular. Add **-es** to singular adjectives ending in a consonant to form the plural.

(24) **francesa.** The aunt is from France. Use the feminine singular adjective to express that she's French. The feminine form has no accent.

(25) **débil.** Mercedes doesn't have enough physical strength. Use the singular form of the adjective to express that she's weak. **Débil** undergoes no change for gender.

(26) **jóvenes.** The aunts aren't old. Use the feminine plural form of the adjective to express that they're young. Add an accent mark to **joven** to maintain the original stress.

(27) **ingleses.** The friends are from England. Use the masculine plural form of the adjective to express that they're English. Drop the accent mark to maintain the original stress.

(28) **alemán.** The father is from Germany. Use the masculine form of the adjective to express that he's German. The singular form has an accent mark.

(29) **Hay dos playas blancas. Dos** means *two* and, because it imposes a limit, precedes the noun. **Playas** (*beaches*) is feminine plural and follows the adjective **dos. Blancas** is a feminine plural descriptive adjective and follows the noun it modifies.

(30) **Hay poca gente americana. Poca** (*few*) imposes a limit and precedes the noun. **Gente** (*people*) is a feminine singular noun and follows the singular adjective **poca. Americana** is a feminine singular descriptive adjective and follows the noun it modifies.

(31) **Hay tanta agua azul. Tanta** (*so much*) imposes a limit and precedes the noun. **Agua** (*water*) is a feminine singular noun and follows the singular adjective **tanta. Azul** (*blue*) is a descriptive adjective and follows the noun it modifies.

(32) **Hay numerosas plantas magníficas. Numerosas** (*numerous*) imposes a limit and precedes the noun. **Plantas** (*plants*) is a feminine plural noun that follows the adjectives **numerosas. Magníficas** (*magnificent*) is a feminine plural descriptive adjective that follows the noun.

(33) **Hay unos animales exóticos. Unos** (*some*) imposes a limit and precedes the noun. **Animales** (*animals*) is a masculine plural noun and follows the adjective **unos. Exóticos** is a masculine plural descriptive adjective that follows the noun.

(34) **Hay algunos árboles grandes. Algunos** (*a few*) imposes a limit and precedes the noun. **Árboles** (*trees*) is a masculine plural noun that follows the masculine plural adjective **algunos. Grandes** (*big*) is a descriptive adjective that follows the noun.

(35) **A.** Use the shortened form of **bueno** before a masculine singular noun.

(36) **C.** Use the shortened form of **tercero** before a masculine singular noun.

(37) **B.** The original adjective **primero** is used if a preposition separates the adjective from its noun.

(38) **D.** Use the shortened form of **ninguno** before a masculine singular noun.

(39) **B.** Use the plural form of **alguno** before a masculine plural noun.

(40) **C.** Use the shortened form of **ciento** before the number **mil.** Note that the answer can't be **doscientas** because **dólares** is masculine.

(41) **Vamos a ver las ruinas antiguas. Antiguas** connotes *ancient* or *old* when it follows the noun it modifies.

(42) **Es una solución simple. Simple** connotes *simple* when it precedes the noun it modifies.

(43) **Compran una casa nueva. Nueva** connotes *brand new* when it follows the noun it modifies.

(44) **Tengo el mismo problema. Mismo** connotes *same* when it precedes the noun it modifies.

(45) **Ese hombre es un gran presidente. Grande** becomes **gran** and connotes *great* when it precedes the noun it modifies.

(46) **Nosotros vimos cien flores rojas. Cien**, the shortened form of **ciento** (*100*), which imposes a limit, is used before nouns. The plural feminine noun **flores** (*flowers*) follows the number.

(47) **Nosotros no vimos ningún lago largo.** Because **ninguno** is a negative, **no** must be placed before the verb. **Lago** (*lake*) is a masculine singular noun. The masculine singular form, **ninguno** (*not any*), which sets a limit, drops the final **-o** and adds an accent to the **-u** before a masculine noun and precedes it. **Largo** (*long*) is a masculine singular descriptive adjective that follows the noun.

(48) **Nosotros vimos muchas nubes blancas. Nubes** (*clouds*) is a feminine plural noun. The feminine plural adjective **muchas** (*many*) imposes a limit and precedes the noun. **Blancas** (*white*) is a feminine plural descriptive adjective that follows the noun.

(49) **Nosotros vimos una selva magnífica. Selva** (*jungle*) is a feminine singular noun. The feminine singular indefinite article **una** (*one, a*) imposes a limit and precedes the noun. **Magnífica** (*magnificent*) is a feminine singular descriptive adjective that follows the noun.

(50) **Nosotros vimos pocas montañas altas. Montañas** (*mountains*) is a feminine plural noun. The feminine plural adjective **pocas** (*few*) imposes a limit and precedes the noun. **Altas** (*high*) is a feminine plural descriptive adjective that follows the noun.

(51) **Nosotros vimos un río grande. Río** (*river*) is a masculine singular noun. The masculine singular indefinite article **un** (*one, a*) imposes a limit and precedes the noun. **Grande** (*big*) is a masculine singular adjective that follows the noun.

(52) **Nosotros vimos algunas cascadas estupendas. Cascadas** (*waterfalls*) is a feminine plural noun. **Algunas** (*some*) is a feminine plural adjective that imposes a limit. **Estupendas** (*stupendous*) is a feminine plural descriptive adjective that follows the noun.

(53) **Nosotros vimos muchos animales feroces. Animales** (*animals*) is a masculine plural noun. **Muchos** (*many*) is a masculine plural adjective that imposes a limit. The descriptive adjective **feroz** (*ferocious*) is the masculine singular form. To make this adjective plural, change **-z** to **-c** and add **-es**.

IN THIS CHAPTER

» **Determining when to use subject pronouns**

» **Conjugating regular verbs in the present**

» **Navigating spelling change and stem-changing verbs**

» **Understanding irregular verbs**

» **Making progress with the present progressive**

Chapter **5**

Expressing Yourself in the Present

I n Spanish, when you write or speak, you have to be careful to use verbs properly so that you can get your meaning across. Whereas English comes to many speakers naturally because they've been immersed in the language since birth, people have to internalize the rules, expressions, idioms, and idiosyncrasies of a foreign language. This requires a bit of effort and some practice until you can achieve a good comfort level with new vocabulary and a different way of expressing yourself.

It helps to understand the present tense because that's where the action and interest is — in the here and now. Although English has the reputation of being a very difficult language to learn, its present-tense verbs are rather easy to use because almost all of them follow the same set of rules. In Spanish, the overwhelming majority of present-tense verbs (known as regular verbs) are simple to master because they're predictable. However, you'll find that some verbs walk to the beat of a different drummer; for these verbs, you have to learn or memorize their patterns or irregularities. Finally, you'll find out how to say what is going on right now by using the present progressive.

In this chapter, I start you off with when to use the subject pronouns discussed in Chapter 1, because they come first in the sentence. After you successfully understand the use of Spanish subject pronouns, you're going to be able to talk about events and situations that are happening right now.

Using and Omitting Spanish Subject Pronouns

In English, you use subject pronouns all the time to explain who's doing what. In Spanish, however, you use subject pronouns a lot less frequently because the verb ending generally indicates the subject. No matter the infinitive ending of the verb (**-ar, -er, -ir**), if the verb form ends in **-o**, the subject must be **yo** because no other verb has an **-o** ending. **Hablo español,** for instance, can only mean *I speak Spanish.*

If, on the other hand, you see **Habla español,** it's unclear whether the subject is **él** (*he*), **ella** (*she*), or **Ud.** (*you*) if the sentence is taken out of context. When given the context, you usually omit the subject pronoun **él** or **ella: Le presento a mi amiga, Marta. Habla español.** (*Let me introduce you to my friend, Marta. She speaks Spanish.*)

To avoid confusion, you regularly use the subject pronoun **Ud.** to differentiate between *he, she,* and *you:*

¿Habla español? (*Do you [he, she] speak Spanish?*)

Mi novio habla español. Habla bien. (*My boyfriend speaks Spanish. He speaks well.*)

¿Habla Ud. español? (*Do you speak Spanish?*)

You regularly use the subject pronoun **Uds.** to differentiate between *they* and *you* in the plural:

Cantan bien. (*They [You] sing well.*)

Mis primos están en el coro. Cantan bien. (*My cousins are in the chorus. They sing well.*)

Uds. cantan bien también. (*You sing well, too.*)

Sometimes there may be a compound subject — a noun (or a proper name) and a pronoun, more than one proper name and a pronoun, or two pronouns as the subject. Which pronoun do you use then? Use the following chart for easy reference:

Compound Subject	Subject Pronoun Replacement
Ricardo y yo	Nosotros
María y yo (feminine)	Nosotras
Mi familia y yo (one male member)	Nosotros
Ricardo y tú	Uds.
María y tú	Uds.
Tu amigo y tú	Uds.
Ricardo y Julio (él)	Ellos
Ricardo y María (ella)	Ellos
María y Sarita	Ellas
Ricardo, María y Sarita	Ellos

In Spain, *vosotros (vosotras)* is used in place of *Uds.* in informal (familiar) situations.

REMEMBER

PRACTICE

Have you mastered the concept of compound subjects? Try your hand at the following exercise. You're speaking about yourself and people you know. Write the pronoun you'd use to refer to them.

Q. Javier, Martín, y Ana

A. **Ellos.** Use the masculine plural *they,* when speaking to a mixed group.

1. Mi hermana y yo (fem.) _____

2. Inés y tú _____

3. Sofía y Alicia _____

4. Juan y yo (masc.) _____

5. Tu padre y tú _____

6. Gabriel y Pedro _____

Expressing the Present

It must seem rather silly to read a paragraph about using the present tense. Obviously, you use the present tense to indicate what a subject is doing or does customarily:

> **Nosotros miramos la televisión cada día.** (*We watch television every day.*)

> **Ana trabaja en la ciudad.** (*Ana works in the city.*)

But I'll bet you didn't know that, in Spanish, you can also use the present to ask for instructions or to discuss an action that will take place in the future:

> **¿Preparo la cena ahora?** (*Shall I prepare dinner now?*)

> **Te veo más tarde.** (*I'll see you later.*)

Comprehending conjugations

If you want to use the present tense in Spanish, you have to figure out how to conjugate verbs. You probably haven't heard the word *conjugation* in any of your English classes, even when you had those pesky grammar lessons, because people automatically conjugate verbs in their native language without even thinking about it. So what exactly do I mean by conjugation? Plain and simple, *conjugation* refers to changing the infinitive of a verb (the *to* form — *to smile*, for example) to a form that agrees with the subject. "I *smile* and he *smiles*, too." "You *stretch* and he *stretches*, too." "We *worry* and she *worries*, too."

In Spanish, all verbs end in **-ar, -er,** or **-ir.** Most verbs are *regular*, which means that all verbs with the same infinitive ending follow the same rules of conjugation. If you memorize the endings for one regular -ar, -er, or -ir infinitive, you'll be able to conjugate all the other regular verbs within that family.

Regular present-tense -ar verbs

The **-ar** family is the largest group, by far. Here's how it works: Take the infinitive and drop its ending (**-ar**), and then add the endings for the subject pronouns as indicated in Table 5-1.

Table 5-1   Regular -ar Verb Conjugation in the Present

Subject	-ar Verbs
	HABLAR (*to earn, to win*)
yo	habl*o*
tú	habl*as*
él, ella, Ud.	habl*a*
nosotros	habl*amos*
vosotros	habl*áis*
ellos, ellas, Uds.	habl*an*

Here are some examples of **-ar** regular verbs in the present tense:

> **Hablo francés.** (*I speak French.*)
>
> **Ud. trabaja bien.** (*You work well.*)
>
> **Preparan la cena.** (*They prepare the dinner.*)

What follows is a list of many regular **-ar** verbs that follow this easy conjugation in the present. Common regular **-ar** verbs include:

-ar verb	Meaning
admirar	to admire
arreglar	to arrange, fix
ayudar	to help
bailar	to dance
bajar	to go down, descend
buscar	to look for
cambiar	to change
caminar	to walk
cantar	to sing
celebrar	to celebrate
cocinar	to cook
comprar	to buy
contestar	to answer
cortar	to cut

-ar verb	Meaning
cuidar	to take care of
descansar	to rest
desear	to desire
enseñar	to teach, to show
entrar	to enter
escuchar	to listen (to)
esperar	to wait, hope
estudiar	to study
explicar	to explain
ganar	to win, earn
hablar	to speak, to talk
invitar	to invite
lavar	to wash
limpiar	to clean
llamar	to call
llegar	to arrive
llevar	to wear, take, carry
mirar	to look at
nadar	to swim
necesitar	to need
olvidar	to forget
ordenar	to put in order
organizar	to organize
pagar	to pay (for)
pasar	to pass, spend time
planchar	to iron
practicar	to practice
preguntar	to ask
preparer	to prepare
quitar	to remove
regresar	to return
sacar	to take out
telefonear	to telephone
terminar	to finish
tomar	to take, drink
trabajar	to work
usar	to use, wear
viajar	to travel
visitar	to visit

PRACTICE

Now that you have familiarized yourself with some common **-ar** verbs, see whether you can identify the subject pronouns that are missing.

Imagine that a friend is speaking about you, himself, and other people you know. Express what each does after school. Write the pronoun you would use by referring to the verb ending.

Q. Eduardo y Clara, _____ trabajan.

A. ellos. Use the pronoun **ellos** to express *they* when speaking about a mixed group.

7. Enrique y yo, _____ tomamos un refresco.

8. _____ telefoneo a mi amiga cada noche.

9. Elena y Juanita, _____ practican la gramática.

10. _____ regresas tarde.

11. ¿César? _____ mira la televisión.

12. Francisco, Rosalina, y tú, _____ estudian.

PRACTICE

Now try your hand at conjugating **-ar** verbs so that you can refer to actions in the present.

Explain which chores each family member is responsible for.

Q. Antonio/sacar la basura

A. Antonio saca la basura. Drop the **-ar** ending from **sacar** and add **-a** for **Antonio** (*he*).

13. Mi madre/quitar el polvo _____

14. Yo/pasar la aspiradora _____

15. Clara y yo/lavar el coche _____

16. Papá/cortar el césped _____

17. Carlota y Jaime/cuidar a los niños _____

18. Tú/planchar la ropa _____

19. Ud./ordenar la sala _____

20. Luis y tú/limpiar la casa _____

21. Vosotros/cargar el lavaplatos _____

22. Blanca y Beatriz/cocinar _____

Regular present-tense -er verbs

The -**er** verb family is smaller in number but equally important. Here's how this conjugation works: Take the infinitive and drop its ending (-**er**), and then add the endings for the subject pronouns as indicated in Table 5-2.

Table 5-2   **Regular -er Verb Conjugation in the Present**

Subject	-er Verbs
	BEBER (*to drink*)
yo	**beb***o*
tú	**beb***es*
él, ella, Ud.	**beb***e*
nosotros	**beb***emos*
vosotros	**beb***éis*
ellos, ellas, Uds.	**beb***en*

Here are some examples of -**er** regular verbs in the present tense:

> **Nosotros aprendemos el español.** (*We are learning Spanish.*)
>
> **Bebo té con limón.** (*I drink tea with lemon.*)
>
> **Él corre rápidamente.** (*He runs fast.*)

The following lists common -**er** verbs.

-er Verb	Meaning
aprender	to learn
beber	to drink
comer	to eat
comprender	to understand
correr	to run
creer	to believe
deber	to have to, to owe
leer	to read
prometer	to promise
responder	to answer
vender	to sell

WARNING

The verb **deber,** when it means *to have to*, is followed by another verb in its infinitive:

> **Yo debo estudiar.** (*I have to study.*)

Here are some practice questions for **-er** verbs.

PRACTICE Express what the following people do after a day at work by conjugating the verb in parentheses.

Q. (correr) Juana _____ en el parque.

A. **corre.** Drop the **-er** ending from **correr** and add **-e** for **Juana** (*she*).

23 (prometer) Yo _____ ayudar a mis amigos.

24 (deber) Vosotros _____ descansar.

25 (comer) Gloria y yo (masc.) _____ un sandwich.

26 (beber) Tú _____ un batido (*milkshake*).

27 (responder) Enrique y Manuel _____ a sus mensajes.

28 (leer) Daniel _____ su correo electrónico.

Regular present-tense -ir verbs

Here's how the conjugation for **-ir** verbs works: Take the infinitive and drop its ending (**-ir**), and then add the endings for the subject pronouns as indicated in Table 5-3.

Table 5-3 **Regular-ir Verb Conjugation in the Present**

Subject	-ir Verbs
	DECIDIR (*to decide*)
yo	decid**o**
tú	decid**es**
él, ella, Ud.	decid**e**
nosotros	decid**imos**
vosotros	decid**ís**
ellos, ellas, Uds.	decid**en**

Here are some examples of **-ir** regular verbs in the present tense:

Ellos deciden quedarse en casa. (*They decide to stay home.*)

Abro mi periódico. (*I open my newspaper.*)

Descubrimos la verdad. (*We discover the truth.*)

Common **-ir** verbs include the following:

-ir Verb	Meaning
abrir	*to open*
asistir a	*to attend*
cubrir	*to cover*
decidir	*to decide*
describir	*to describe*
descubrir	*to discover*
dividir	*to divide*
escribir	*to write*
insistir (en)	*to insist (on)*
omitir	*to omit*
partir	*to divide, to share*
permitir	*to permit*
recibir	*to receive*
subir	*to go up, to climb*
sufrir	*to suffer*
vivir	*to live*

Here are some sentences to help you practice conjugating regular **-ir** verbs.

PRACTICE Happy Birthday! It's your **quinceañera**! Time to have a party!

Q. **Yo/decidir dar una fiesta**

A. **Yo decido dar una fiesta.** Drop the **-ir** ending from **decidir** and add **-o** for **yo** (*I*).

29 Mi padre/permitir la fiesta _____

30 Tú/escribir las invitaciones _____

31 Vosotros/dividir el trabajo necesario _____

32 Nosotros/insistir en preparar comida típica _____

33 Todos mis amigos/asistir a la fiesta _____

34 Yo/recibir muchos regalos _____

Try your hand at conjugating verbs from all the families in the following exercise.

PRACTICE

Your Spanish class is going on a trip to see a Spanish movie. Write notes in your journal to express what each person does on the trip by giving the correct present form of the verb provided in parentheses.

Q. (practicar) los muchachos _____ el español.

A. Los muchachos practican el español.

35 (tomar) Nosotros _____ el autobús para ir al cine.

36 (partir) Todos los estudiantes _____ de la escuela a las tres.

37 (esperar) Uds. _____ el autobús delante de la escuela.

38 (correr) Vosotros _____ para coger el autobús.

39 (llegar) El autobús _____ al cine a las tres y media.

40 (asistir) La clase _____ al primer pase de la película.

41 (comprar) Vosotros _____ billetes para la clase.

42 (deber) Nosotros _____ practicar el español.

43 (hablar) Tú _____ español conmigo.

44 (mirar) Entonces yo _____ la película.

45 (leer) Todo el mundo _____ los subtítulos.

46 (describir) Yo _____ bien la película en español.

47 (beber) Uds. _____ demasiado refrescos.

48 (compartir) Nosotros _____ una bolsa de dulces.

49 (comer) Yo _____ también palomitas de maíz.

50 (aprender) Tú _____ mucho.

51 (decidir) Vosotros _____ que es una buena película.

52 (aplaudir) Tú _____ la película.

Verbs with spelling changes

Some Spanish verbs undergo spelling changes to preserve the original sound of the verbs after you add a new ending. This is nothing to be overly concerned about, because the change occurs only in the first-person singular (**yo**) form of the verb. In the present tense, verbs with the endings listed in Table 5-4 undergo spelling changes.

Table 5-4   Spelling Changes in the Present Tense

Infinitive Ending	Spelling Change	Verb Examples	Present Conjugation
vowel + **-cer/-cir**	c → zc	**ofrecer** (*to offer*); **traducir** (*to translate*)	**yo ofrezco; yo traduzco**
consonant + **-cer/-cir**	c → z	**convencer** (*to convince*); **esparcir** (*to spread out*)	**yo convenzo; yo esparzo**
-ger/-gir	g → j	**escoger** (*to choose*); **exigir** (*to demand*)	**yo escojo; yo exijo**
-guir	gu → g	**distinguir** (*to distinguish*)	**yo distingo**

REMEMBER

The majority of the verbs that undergo spelling changes in the present tense end in vowel + **-cer** or vowel + **-cir**. Only a few high-frequency verbs fall under the other categories (**-ger, -gir, -guir**); in all likelihood, you'll see them rarely, if at all.

Here are the verbs with spelling changes in the present tense that you can expect to encounter most often:

Spanish Verb	Meaning
aparecer	*to appear*
conocer	*to know (to be acquainted with)*
merecer	*to deserve, merit*
nacer	*to be born*
obedecer	*to obey*
parecer	*to seem*
producir	*to produce*
reconocer	*to recognize*
reducir	*to reduce*
reproducir	*to reproduce*

Conjugating these verbs in the **yo** form can be a little tricky, so it's time to get some practice.

PRACTICE

You're bragging about what you can do and your brother can't. Fill in the correct form of the verbs in parentheses.

Q. (conducir) Yo _____ bien y él _____mal.

A. **conduzco, conduce.** To conjugate -**cir** verbs, drop the -**ir** ending. For **yo**, change the -**c** to -**cz** and then add the -**o** ending. For **él**, drop the -**ir** ending and add -**e**.

53 (merecer) Yo _____ el trofeo y él no lo _____.

54 (escoger) Yo _____ la respuesta correcta y él no la _____.

55 (reducir) Yo _____ mi consumo calórico y él no _____ el suyo (*his*).

56 (dirigir) Yo _____ las obras de teatro y él no las _____.

57 (distinguir) Yo _____ los sabores (flavors) y él no los _____.

58 (conocer) Yo _____ a todo el mundo y él no _____ a nadie (*anyone*).

Verbs with stem changes

Some Spanish verbs undergo stem changes — internal changes to the vowel in the stem of the infinitive — to preserve the original sound of the verbs after you add a new ending. In the present tense, all stem changes for these verbs occur in the **yo, tú, él (ella, Ud.)** and **ellos (ellas, Uds.)** forms. You conjugate the **nosotros** and **vosotros** forms in the normal fashion (their stems resemble the infinitive).

-AR STEM CHANGES

Many Spanish verbs with an **-ar** ending undergo stem changes in all forms except **nosotros** and **vosotros**. The following list details these changes:

» **e → ie:** For example **empezar** (*to begin*) changes to **yo empiezo** (**nosotros empezamos**). Here are the most frequently used Spanish verbs that fit into this category:

- **cerrar** (*to close*)
- **comenzar** (*to begin*)
- **despertar** (*to wake up*)
- **empezar** (*to begin*)
- **negar** (*to deny*)
- **nevar** (*to snow*)
- **pensar** (*to think*)
- **recomendar** (*to recommend*)

TIP

When the infinitive has more than one "e" in its stem (**despertar, empezar, recomendar**), the stem change occurs to the "e" immediately preceding the infinitive ending.

> **Yo recomiendo este libro.** (*I recommend this book.*)

Here are some examples for this change:

» **o/u → ue:** **mostrar** (*to show*) changes to **yo muestro** (**nosotros mostramos**), and **jugar** (*to play*) changes to **yo juego** (**nosotros jugamos**). Here are the most frequently used Spanish verbs that fit into this category:

- **acordar** (*to agree*)
- **acostar** (*to put to bed*)
- **almorzar** (*to eat lunch*)
- **colgar** (*to hang up*)
- **contar** (*to tell*)
- **costar** (*to cost*)

WARNING

- **encontrar(se)** (*to meet*)
- **probar** (*to try [on]*)
- **recordar** (*to remember*)

>> **Jugar** is the only common **-ar** verb whose stem vowel changes from **u** to **ue**:

- **Yo juego al fútbol.** (*I play soccer.*)
- **Julio y yo jugamos al golf.** (*Julio and I play golf.*)

Stem-changing verbs can be a bit confusing at first. With a little practice, you'll be able to navigate them more easily.

PRACTICE

You've made a new friend who is by nature very curious. Complete what she wants to know with the correct form of the verb in parentheses.

Q. (costar) Quiere saber cuánto _____ mi abrigo.

A. **cuesta.** The **-o** of **costar** changes to **-ue** in all forms except **nosotros** and **vosotros**.

59 (empezar) Quiere saber a qué hora _____ mis clases.

60 (jugar) Quiere saber con quién yo _____ al tenis.

61 (recomendar) Quiere saber qué restaurante mi hermano y yo _____.

62 (almorzar) Quiere saber a qué hora yo _____.

63 (encontrar) Quiere saber si mis hermanos se _____ con sus amigos cada día.

64 (pensar) Quiere saber lo que tú y yo _____ de nuestros profesores.

-ER STEM CHANGES

Many Spanish verbs with an **-er** ending undergo stem changes in all forms except **nosotros** and **vosotros.** The following list details these changes:

>> **e → ie: Querer** (*to wish, want*) changes to **yo quiero** (**nosotros queremos**). Here are the most frequently used Spanish verbs that fit into this category:

- **defender** (*to defend*)
- **encender** (*to light*)
- **entender** (*to understand*)
- **perder** (*to lose*)

>> **o → ue: Volver** (*to return*) changes to **yo vuelvo** (**nosotros volvemos**). Here are the most frequently used Spanish verbs that fit into this category:

- **devolver** (*to return*)
- **doler** (*to hurt*)

- **envolver** (*to wrap up*)
- **llover** (*to rain*)
- **mover** (*to move*)
- **poder** (*to be able to, can*)
- **Yo puedo bailar bien.** (*I can dance well.*)
- **resolver** (*to resolve*)

TIP

The verb poder is always followed by the infinitive of a verb.

REMEMBER

Some verbs with stem changes in the present tense are used impersonally in the third-person singular only:

Llueve. (*It's raining.*) (**llover; o → ue**)

Nieva. (*It's snowing.*) (**nevar; e → ie**)

Hiela. (*It's freezing.*) (**helar; e → ie**)

Truena. (*It's thundering.*) (**tronar; o → ue**)

Some practice with these additional stem-changing verbs will surely give you more confidence.

PRACTICE

You have information that you want to share about yourself and your acquaintances. Combine the elements using the correct form of the stem-changing verb.

Q. Esteban/siempre perder la paciencia.

A. **Esteban siempre pierde la paciencia.** The -e of **perder** changes to -ie in all forms except **nosotros** and **vosotros.**

(65) Felipe/poder hablar con confianza _____

(66) Carlota y yo/siempre volver tarde a casa _____

(67) Tú/querer ayudar a todo el mundo _____

(68) Yo/entender todo _____

(69) Diego y Alfonso/defender sus ideas _____

(70) Uds./resolver todos sus problemas _____

-IR STEM CHANGES

Many Spanish verbs with an -**ir** ending undergo stem changes in all forms except **nosotros** and **vosotros.** The following list outlines these changes:

>> **e → ie: Preferir** (*to prefer*) changes to **yo prefiero** (**nosotros preferimos**). Here are the most frequently used Spanish verbs that fit into this category:

- **advertir** (*to warn*)

- **consentir** (*to allow*)
- **divertir** (*to amuse*)
- **mentir** (*to lie*)
- **sentir** (*to feel, regret*)
- **sugerir** (*to suggest*)

» o → ue: **Dormir** (*to sleep*) changes to **yo duermo** (**nosotros dormimos**). Another verb conjugated like **dormir** is **morir** (*to die*).

» e → i: **Servir** (*to serve*) changes to **yo sirvo** (**nosotros servimos**). Here are the most frequently used Spanish verbs that fit into this category:

- **medir** (*to measure*)
- **pedir** (*to ask for*)
- **repetir** (*to repeat*)
- **vestir** (*to clothe*)

Practice some -**ir** stem-changing verbs to ensure you've got them down pat.

PRACTICE

Express how these people react in the situations that follow. Use the correct form of the verb in parentheses.

Q. Yo no entiendo las instrucciones del profesor. (le pedir ayuda a mi compañero de clase)

A. Yo le pido ayuda a mi compañero de clase.

71 Yo quiero comprar una cama nueva. (medir el espacio en mi habitación)

_____

72 Mi madre no quiere llegar tarde a la fiesta. (vestir a mi hermano rápidamente)

_____

73 Miguel y Gregorio hablan con su abuela pero ella no los escucha. (repetir sus palabras)

_____

74 Tú ves un accidente en la calle. (advertir a la policía)

_____

75 Mi padre prepara una cena especial. (servir la comida a la familia)

_____

76 Yo leo un libro cómico. (divertir mucho a mis hermanos)

_____

All the verbs in these sections show a spelling change in which the accent mark is added to break the diphthong and put the stress on the 'i'.

TIP

-IAR STEM CHANGE (FOR SOME VERBS)

Some Spanish verbs with an **-iar** ending undergo a stem change in all forms except **nosotros** and **vosotros**. This stem change is **i → í**. For example, **guiar** (*to guide*) changes to **yo guío** (**nosotros guiamos**). Here are the most frequently used Spanish verbs that fit into this category:

>> **enviar** (*to send*)

>> **esquiar** (*to ski*)

>> **fotografiar** (*to photograph*)

-UAR STEM CHANGE (FOR SOME VERBS)

Some Spanish verbs with a **-uar** ending undergo a stem change in all forms except **nosotros** and **vosotros**. This stem change is **u → ú**. For example, **continuar** (*to continue*) changes to **yo continúo** (**nosotros continuamos**). Here are the most frequently used Spanish verbs that fit into this category:

>> **habituar** (*to accustom someone to*)

>> **valuar** (*to value*)

-UIR (NOT -GUIR) STEM CHANGE

Some Spanish verbs with a **-uir** ending (but not a **-guir** ending) undergo a stem change in all forms except **nosotros** and **vosotros**. This stem change requires adding a **-y** after the **-u**. For example, **concluir** (*to conclude*) changes to **yo concluyo** (**nosotros concluimos**). Here are the most frequently used Spanish verbs that fit into this category:

>> **construir** (*to build*)

>> **contribuir** (*to contribute*)

>> **destruir** (*to destroy*)

>> **distribuir** (*to distribute*)

>> **incluir** (*to include*)

VERBS WITH SPELLING AND STEM CHANGES

A few Spanish verbs have both a spelling change and a stem change in the present tense. You must conjugate these verbs to accommodate both changes, as shown in Table 5-5.

Table 5-5   Verbs with Spelling and Stem Changes in the Present

Verb	English	Conjugation
corregir	*to correct*	corrijo, corriges, corrige, corregimos, corregís, corrigen
elegir	*to elect*	elijo, eliges, elige, elegimos, elegís, eligen
seguir	*to follow*	sigo, sigues, sigue, seguimos, seguís, siguen

Now's your opportunity to prove that you've completely mastered all the spelling changes listed in this section. Yes, it was an ominous task.

PRACTICE

For this exercise, write journal entries in which you express how you and your friends react to different situations. I provide the situation, as well as a verbal phrase giving the consequence of that situation in parentheses. You must conjugate the verb given in parentheses in the present tense.

Q. **Margarita quiere salir bien en su clase de español. (repetir frecuentemente las palabras del vocabulario)**

A. **Ella repite frecuentemente las palabras del vocabulario.** The second -**e** of **repetir** becomes –**i** in all forms except **nosotros** and **vosotros**.

77 El jefe piensa que Clarita y Rafael trabajan concienzudamente. (recomendar un aumento de salario para ellos)

_____

78 Mauricio no sale bien en su clase de ciencia. (mentir a su madre)

_____

79 Carlota no sabe cómo ir a la biblioteca. (pedir la ruta a un desconocido)

_____

80 Yo tengo mucho frío. (cerrar las ventanas)

_____

81 Nosotros deseamos perder peso. (empezar un régimen hoy día)

_____

82 Tu acabas de recibir un nuevo bate. (jugar al béisbol)

_____

83 Uds. tienen dos semanas de vacaciones. (querer ir a España)

_____

84 Enrique y Alfredo tienen un buen sentido del humor. (contar bromas todo el tiempo)

_____

85 Tú eres un mecánico excelente. (poder ayudarme a reparar mi coche)

_____

86 Yo no estudio mucho. (escoger a menudo respuestas incorrectas)

_____

87 Yo quiero celebrar el cumpleaños de mi mejor amiga. (le ofrecer un regalo)

_____

88 Clarita está enferma. (dormir mucho)

_____

89 Ellos prefieren el invierno. (esquiar en las montañas)

_____

90 Nilda tiene mucho que hacer. (continuar trabajando)

_____

91 Tomás es ingeniero. (construir edificios)

_____

92 Algunos alumnos cometen muchos errores. (advertir a la profesora)

_____

Irregular verbs

In Spanish, some present-tense verbs have irregular forms that you must memorize. The three categories of irregular verbs in the present tense, which I cover in detail in the following sections, are those that are irregular only in the **yo** form; those that are irregular in all forms except **nosotros** and **vosotros;** and those that are completely irregular.

IRREGULAR YO FORMS

In the present tense, some verbs are irregular only in the first-person singular (**yo**) form. You conjugate the other verb forms in the regular fashion — by dropping the infinitive ending (**-ar,** **-er,** or **-ir**) and adding the ending that corresponds to the subject. The following table presents high-frequency irregular **yo** form of these verbs.

Spanish Verb	Meaning	Form of Present Tense
caer	*to fall*	caigo
dar	*to give*	doy
hacer	*to make, to do*	hago
poner	*to put*	pongo
saber	*to know*	sé
salir	*to go out*	salgo
traer	*to bring*	traigo
ver	*to see*	veo

The following examples show these irregular forms in action:

Yo le **doy** un reloj y él le **da** aretes. (*I give her a watch and he gives her earrings.*)

Yo **pongo** el libro en mi mochila y él pone el portátil en su escritorio. (*I put the book in my backpack and he puts the laptop on his desk.*)

Yo **salgo** a la una y él **sale** a las tres. (*I go out at one o'clock and he goes out at three.*)

IRREGULAR YO, TÚ, ÉL (ELLA, UD.), AND ELLOS (ELLAS, UDS.) FORMS

In the present tense, the high-frequency verbs listed in Table 5-6 are irregular in all forms except **nosotros** and **vosotros.**

Table 5-6 Irregular Verbs in All Forms Except Nosotros and Vosotros

Verb	Meaning	Yo	Yú	El	Nosotros	Vosotros	Ellos
decir	*to say, to tell*	digo	dices	dice	decimos	decís	dicen
estar	*to be*	estoy	estás	está	estamos	estáis	están
tener	*to have*	tengo	tienes	tiene	tenemos	tenéis	tienen
venir	*to come*	vengo	vienes	viene	venimos	venís	vienen

Tener followed by **que** means *to have to* and shows obligation:

TIP

Yo tengo que trabajar ahora. (*I have to work now.*)

Nosotros tenemos que partir. (*We have to leave.*)

COMPLETELY (WELL, ALMOST) IRREGULAR VERBS

The verbs in Table 5-7 are irregular in all or most of their forms in the present tense and require a bit more of your attention for memorization.

Table 5-7   Irregular Verbs in All or Most of Their Forms

Verb	Meaning	Yo	Tú	Él	Nosotros	Vosotros	Ellos
ir	to go	voy	vas	va	vamos	vais	van
oír	to hear	oigo	oyes	oye	oímos	oís	oyen
reír	to laugh	río	ríes	ríe	reímos	reís	rien
ser	to be	soy	eres	es	somos	sois	son

PRACTICE

You're standing in line waiting to get into a concert. You overhear different people having conversations in Spanish. Complete their sentences with the correct form of the verb shown in italics in the question.

Q. ¿*Es* Ud. español?

A. Sí, yo **soy** español.

Mis padres **son** de España.

93 ¿Qué *haces* mañana?

Yo no _____ nada.

Adela y yo tampoco _____ nada.

94 ¿A qué hora *salen* para ir a la fiesta?

Nosotros _____ a las siete y media.

Yo _____ a las ocho.

95 ¿Con quién *das* un paseo?

Yo _____ un paseo con Carlos.

Esteban y Roberto _____ con Marta.

96 ¿Cuántos años *tienen* Uds.?

Yo _____ veinte años.

Mi hermana _____ treinta años.

97 ¿Adónde *van*?

Nosotros _____ al supermercado.

Yo _____ a la farmacia.

98 ¿*Oyes* algo?

Sí, yo _____ un ruido.

Estos muchachos no _____ nada.

99 ¿*Dice* siempre la verdad?

Yo siempre _____ la verdad.

Juan, a veces _____ mentiras.

100 ¿Cómo estás?

Mi abuela _____ enferma.

Yo _____ bien.

101 ¿Qué *traes* al teatro?

Mis amigas _____ refrescos.

Yo _____ dulces.

102 ¿*Ves* algo?

Sí, yo _____ un rascacielos.

Estos muchachos no _____ nada.

103 ¿Qué *pone* en su bolsillo?

Yo _____ mi dinero en mi bolsillo.

Juan _____ sus boletos en su bolsillo.

104 ¿Con quién *vienen Uds.* al teatro?

Nosotros _____ con nuestra familia.

Yo _____ con mis amigos de vez en cuando.

EXPRESSIONS WITH IRREGULAR VERBS

The irregular verbs **dar** (*to give*), **hacer** (*to make, to do*), and **tener** (*to have*), as well as a few other irregular verbs are commonly used in everyday Spanish as part of expressions. If you want to sound like you really know the language well and if you want readers of your prose to follow along without any hiccups, you need to devour the expressions that follow in this section and commit them to memory.

Verbs ending in **-se** are reflexive verbs; I discuss these in Chapter 11.

REMEMBER High-frequency expressions that use **dar** include the following:

Expression	Meaning
dar un abrazo (a)	*to hug, to embrace*
dar las gracias (a)	*to thank*

Expression	Meaning
dar recuerdos (a)	to give regards to
dar un paseo	to take a walk
dar una vuelta	to take a stroll
darse cuenta de	to realize
darse prisa	to hurry

Here are some examples of **dar** expressions:

Yo le doy un abrazo a mi novio. (*I hug my boyfriend.*)

Ellos dan un paseo por el parque. (*They take a walk in the park.*)

High-frequency expressions that use **hacer** include the following:

Expression	Meaning
hacer buen (mal) tiempo	to be nice (bad) weather
hacer frío (calor)	to be cold (hot) weather
hacer una pregunta	to ask a question
hacer una visita	to pay a visit
hacer un viaje	to take a trip
hacer viento	to be windy

Here are some examples of **hacer** expressions:

Hace mal tiempo hoy. (*The weather is bad today.*)

Hacemos un viaje a Puerto Rico. (*We are taking a trip to Puerto Rico.*)

High-frequency expressions that use **tener** include the following:

Expression	Meaning
tener calor (frío)	to be warm (cold)
tener celos de	to be jealous of (someone)
tener cuidado	to be careful
tener dolor de . . .	to have a . . . ache
tener éxito	to succeed
tener ganas de	to feel like
tener hambre (sed)	to be hungry (thirsty)
tener lugar	to take place
tener miedo de	to be afraid of
tener prisa	to be in a hurry
tener razón	to be right
tener sueño	to be sleepy
tener suerte	to be lucky

Here are some examples of **tener** expressions:

> **Tengo dolor de cabeza.** (*I have a headache.*)
>
> **Ellos tienen razón.** (*They are right.*)

WARNING

What follows is a perfect example of how you can easily make a mistake in Spanish if you try to translate your English thoughts word for word. Although the verb **tener** means *to have*, Spanish speakers often use it with a noun to express a physical condition. In English, however, you use the verb "to be" followed by an adjective to express the same physical condition:

> **Tengo sed.** (*I am thirsty.* Literally: *I have thirst.*)
>
> **Ellos tienen miedo a los perros.** (*They are afraid of dogs.* Literally: *They have fear of dogs.*)

Common expressions that use other verbs that have a spelling change or stem change in the present tense or in another tense include the following:

Expression	Meaning
oír decir que	*to hear that*
pensar + infinitive	*to intend*
querer decir	*to mean*
volverse + adjective	*to become*

Here are some examples of these expressions in action:

> **Pensamos hacer un viaje.** (*We intend to take a trip.*)
>
> **¿Qué quiere decir esto?** (*What does that mean?*)

Here are some practice questions for the expressions discussed in this section.

PRACTICE

You're practicing your Spanish vocabulary for class. Finish your homework assignment by selecting the phrase that best completes each sentence that follows. Remember to conjugate the verb as well.

Q. A Paco le interesa la medicina. Él _____ ser doctor algún día.

A. **Él piensa ser doctor algún día**. Paco is interested in medicine. Use the verb **pensar** before the infinitive to express "intends." The **-e** in **pensar** changes to **-ie** in all forms except **nosotros** and **vosotros**.

dar un paseo	pensar	tener lugar
hacer frío	querer decir	
oír decir	tener celos	

(105) No comprendo esta palabra. ¿Qué _____ "palomitas de maíz?"

(106) Siempre me informo de todo. Yo _____ que Ud. hace un viaje a México.

(107) Ramón tiene un coche nuevo. Yo también quiero comprar un coche nuevo pero no tengo bastante dinero. Yo _____ de Ramón.

(108) Hay una fiesta en casa de Emilio. ¿A qué hora _____?

(109) Hay una temperatura de cinco grados bajo cero. _____.

(110) Hay sol. Por eso yo _____ por el parque.

Progressing with the Present Progressive

For people who speak English as a first language, the concept of two present tenses — the present and the present progressive — can be confusing. How do you determine when to use the present or the present progressive in Spanish? Good news: The choice really isn't that difficult.

REMEMBER

You use the present tense when you want to express an action or event that the subject generally does at a given time or that's habitual. You use the present progressive tense to express an action or event that's in progress or that's continuing at a given time — which calls for the use of gerunds (the -*ing* form of the verb). Here are some examples:

Él va a la oficina a las siete de la mañana. (*He goes [does go] to the office at seven in the morning [every day].*)

Él está trabajando. (*He is working [at the present time].*)

Estar (*to be*) is the verb you most often use to form the present progressive because the present tense of **estar** expresses that something is taking place.

To form the present progressive with this verb, you simply include a gerund after the proper form of **estar**. Here are some examples:

Estamos escuchando. (*We are listening.*)

El niño está comiendo. (*The child is eating.*)

Forming the gerunds of regular verbs

To form the gerunds of regular verbs — verbs that end in **-ar, -er,** or **-ir** — do one of the following:

>> Drop the **-ar** from **-ar** verb infinitives and add **-ando** (the equivalent of the English -*ing*).

>> Drop the **-er** or **-ir** from **-er** or **-ir** verb infinitives, respectively, and add **-iendo** (the equivalent of the English -*ing*).

The following table shows these changes for some example verbs:

Ending	Verb	Meaning	Gerund	Meaning
-ar	hablar	*to speak*	habl*ando*	*speaking*
-er	aprender	*to learn*	aprend*iendo*	*learning*
-ir	escribir	*to write*	escrib*iendo*	*writing*

If an **-er** or **-ir** verb stem ends in a vowel, you must drop the ending and add **-yendo** (the English equivalent of *-ing*) to form the gerund:

» **construir** (*to build*): **constru*yendo***

» **creer** (*to believe*): **cre*yendo***

» **leer** (*to read*): **le*yendo***

» **oír** (*to hear*): **o*yendo***

» **traer** (*to bring*): **tra*yendo***

Forming the gerunds of stem-changing and irregular verbs

You form the gerund of a stem-changing **-ir** (**-e** to **-i** or **-o** to **-u**) verb by changing the vowel in the stem from **-e** to **-i** or from **-o** to **-u,** dropping the **-ir** infinitive ending, and then adding the proper ending for a gerund.

» **From e → i:**

- **decir** (*to say, to tell*) → **d*i*ciendo** (*saying, telling*)

- **mentir** (*to lie*) → **m*i*ntiendo** (*lying*)

- **pedir** (*to ask*) → **p*i*diendo** (*asking*)

- **repetir** (*to repeat*) → **rep*i*tiendo** (*repeating*)

- **sentir** (*to feel*) → **s*i*ntiendo** (*feeling*)

- **servir** (*to serve*) → **s*i*rviendo** (*serving*)

- **venir** (*to come*) → **v*i*niendo** (*coming*)

» **From o → u:**

- **dormir** (*to sleep*) → **d*u*rmiendo** (*sleeping*)

- **morir** (*to die*) → **m*u*riendo** (*dying*)

Answers to "Expressing Yourself in the Present" Practice Questions

The following are the answers to the practice questions presented in this chapter.

1. **Nosotras.** Use the feminine plural we when speaking about yourself and another female.

2. **Uds.** Use the polite plural *you* when speaking about another person and *yourself.*

3. **Ellas.** Use the feminine plural *they* when speaking about two females.

4. **Nosotros.** Use the masculine plural *we* when speaking about yourself and another male.

5. **Uds.** Use the polite plural *you* when speaking about another person and *yourself.*

6. **Ellos.** Use the masculine plural *they* when speaking about two males.

7. **nosotros.** The **-amos** ending indicates that the subject is **nosotros.**

8. **yo.** The **-o** ending indicates that the subject is **yo.**

9. **ellas.** The **-an** ending indicates that the subject is plural. **Ellas** is required because both subjects are female.

10. **tú.** The **-as** ending indicates that the subject is **tú.**

11. **Él.** The **-a** ending indicates that the subject is singular. **Él** is required because the subject is masculine.

12. **Uds.** The **-an** ending indicates that the subject is plural. Use **Uds.** when speaking about others and yourself.

13. **Mi madre quita el polvo.** Drop the **-ar** ending from **quitar** and add **-a** for **mi madre.**

14. **Yo paso la aspiradora.** Drop the **-ar** ending from **pasar** and add **-o** for **yo.**

15. **Clara y yo lavamos el coche.** Drop the **-ar** ending from **lavar** and add **-amos** for **nosotros.**

16. **Papá corta el césped.** Drop the **-ar** ending from **cortar** and add **-a** for **Papá.**

17. **Carlota y Jaime cuidan a los niños.** Drop the **-ar** ending from **cuidar** and add **-an** for the plural subject **Carlota y Jaime.**

18. **Tú planchas la ropa.** Drop the **-ar** ending from **planchar** and add **-as** for **tú.**

19. **Ud. ordena la sala.** Drop the **-ar** ending from **ordenar** and add **-a** for **Ud.**

20. **Luis y tú limpian la casa.** Drop the **-ar** ending from **limpiar** and add **-an** for the compound subject **Luis y tú.**

21. **Vosotros cargáis el lavaplatos.** Drop the **-ar** ending from **cargar** and add **-áis** for **vosotros.**

22. **Blanca y Beatriz cocinan.** Drop the **-ar** ending from **cocinar** and add **-an** for *they* when speaking about two females.

23. **prometo.** Drop the **-er** ending from **prometer** and add **-o** for **yo.**

(24) **debéis.** Drop the **-er** ending from **deber** and add **-éis** for **vosotros**.

(25) **comemos.** Drop the **-er** ending from **comer** and add **-emos** for the compound subject **Gloria y yo.**

(26) **bebes.** Drop the **-er** ending from **beber** and add **-es** for **tú.**

(27) **responden.** Drop the **-er** ending from **responder** and add **-en** for the compound subject **Enrique y Manuel.**

(28) **lee.** Drop the **-er** ending from **leer** and add **-e** for **Daniel.**

(29) **Mi padre permite la fiesta.** Drop the **-ir** ending from **permitir** and add **-e** for **Mi padre.**

(30) **Tú escribes las invitaciones.** Drop the **-ir** ending from **escribir** and add **-es** for **tú.**

(31) **Vosotros dividís el trabajo necesario.** Drop the **-ir** ending from **dividir** and add **-ís** for **vosotros.**

(32) **Nosotros insistimos en preparar comida típica.** Drop the **-ir** ending from **insistir** and add **-imos** for **nosotros.**

(33) **Todos mis amigos asisten a la fiesta.** Drop the **-ir** ending from **asistir** and add **-en** for **mis amigos.**

(34) **Yo recibo muchos regalos.** Drop the **-ir** ending from **recibir** and add **-o** for **yo.**

(35) **tomamos.** Drop the **-ar** ending from **tomar** and add **-amos** for **nosotros.**

(36) **parten.** Drop the **-ir** ending from **partir** and add **-en** for **todos los estudiantes.**

(37) **esperan.** Drop the **-ar** ending from **esperar** and add **-an** for **Uds.**

(38) **corréis.** Drop the **-er** ending from **correr** and add **-éis** for **vosotros.**

(39) **llega.** Drop the **-ar** ending from **llegar** and add **-a** for **el autobús.**

(40) **asiste.** Drop the **-ir** ending from **asistir** and add **-e** for **la clase.**

(41) **compráis.** Drop the **-ar** ending from **comprar** and add **-áis** for **vosotros.**

(42) **debemos.** Drop the **-er** ending from **deber** and add **-emos** for **nosotros.**

(43) **hablas.** Drop the **-ar** ending from **hablar** and add **-as** for **tú.**

(44) **miro.** Drop the **-ar** ending from **mirar** and add **-o** for **yo.**

(45) **lee.** Drop the **-er** ending from **leer** and add **-e** for **todo el mundo.**

(46) **describo.** Drop the **-ir** ending from **describir** and add **-o** for **yo.**

(47) **beben.** Drop the **-er** ending from **beber** and add **-en** for **Uds.**

(48) **compartimos.** Drop the **-ir** ending from **compartir** and add **-imos** for **nosotros.**

(49) **como.** Drop the **-er** ending from **comer** and add **-o** for **yo.**

(50) **aprendes.** Drop the **-er** ending from **aprender** and add **-es** for **tú.**

51 **decidís.** Drop the **-ir** ending from **decidir** and add **-ís** for **vosotros.**

52 **aplaudes.** Drop the **-ir** ending from **aplaudir** and add **-es** for **tú.**

53 **merezco, merece.** To conjugate **-cer** verbs, drop the **-er** ending. For **yo,** change the **-c** to **-cz** and then add the **-o** ending. For **él,** drop the **-er** ending and add **-e** as the ending.

54 **escojo, escoge.** To conjugate **-ger** verbs, drop the **-er** ending. For **yo,** change the **g** to **j** and then add the **-o** ending. For **él,** drop the **-er** ending and add **-e** as the ending.

55 **reduzco, reduce.** To conjugate **-cer** verbs, drop the **-er** ending. For **yo,** change the **-c** to **-cz** and then add the **-o** ending. For **él** drop the **-er** ending and add **-e** as the ending.

56 **dirijo, dirige.** To conjugate **-gir** verbs, drop the **-er** ending. For **yo,** change the **g** to **j** and then add the **-o** ending. For **él,** drop the **-er** ending and add **-e** as the ending.

57 **distingo, distingue.** To conjugate **-guir** verbs, For **yo,** drop **-uir** and add the **-o** ending. For **él,** drop the **-ir** ending and add **-e** as the ending.

58 **conozco, conoce.** To conjugate **-cer** verbs, drop the **-er** ending. For **yo,** change the **-c** to **-cz** and then add the **-o** ending. For **él,** drop the **-er** ending and add **-e** as the ending.

59 **empiezan.** The second **-e** of **empezar** changes to **-ie** in all forms except **nosotros** and **vosotros.** The verb agrees with the subject that follows, **mis clases.**

60 **juego.** The **-u** of **jugar** changes to **-ue** in all forms except **nosotros** and **vosotros.**

61 **recomendamos.** The **-e** of **recomendar** changes to **-ie** in all forms except **nosotros** and **vosotros.**

62 **almuerzo.** The **-o** of **almorzar** changes to **-ue** in all forms except **nosotros** and **vosotros.**

63 **encuentran.** The **-o** of **encontrar** changes to **-ue** in all forms except **nosotros** and **vosotros.**

64 **pensamos.** The **-e** of **pensar** changes to **-ie** in all forms except **nosotros** and **vosotros.** The compound subject **tú y yo** expresses **nosotros** (*we*).

65 **Felipe puede hablar con confianza.** The **-o** of **poder** changes to **-ue** in all forms except **nosotros** and **vosotros.**

66 **Carlos y yo siempre volvemos tarde a casa.** The **-o** of **volver** changes to **-ue** in all forms except **nosotros** and **vosotros.** The compound subject **Carlos y yo** expresses **nosotros** (*we*).

67 **Tú quieres ayudar a todo el mundo.** The **-e** of **querer** changes to **-ie** in all forms except **nosotros** and **vosotros.**

68 **Yo entiendo todo.** The **-e** of **entender** changes to **-ie** in all forms except **nosotros** and **vosotros.**

69 **Diego y Alfonso defienden sus ideas.** The second **-e** of **defender** changes to **-ie** in all forms except **nosotros** and **vosotros.**

70 **Uds. resuelven todos sus problemas.** The **-o** of **resolver** changes to **-ue** in all forms except **nosotros** and **vosotros.**

71 **Yo mido el espacio en mi habitación.** The **-e** of **medir** changes to **-i** in all forms except **nosotros** and **vosotros.**

72 **Mi madre viste a mi hermano rápidamente.** The **-e** of **vestir** changes to **-i** in all forms except **nosotros** and **vosotros.**

(73) **Miguel y Gregorio repiten sus palabras.** The second **-e** of **repetir** changes to **-i** in all forms except **nosotros** and **vosotros**.

(74) **Tú adviertes a la policia.** The **-e** of **advertir** changes to **-ie** in all forms except **nosotros** and **vosotros**.

(75) **Mi padre sirve la comida a la familia.** The **-e** of **servir** changes to **-i** in all forms except **nosotros** and **vosotros**.

(76) **Yo divierto mucho a mis hermanos.** The **-e** of **divertir** changes to **-ie** in all forms except **nosotros** and **vosotros**.

(77) **Él recomienda un aumento de salario para ellos.** The **-e** of **recomendar** changes to **-ie** in all forms except **nosotros** and **vosotros**.

(78) **Él miente a su madre.** The **-e** of **mentir** changes to **-ie** in all forms except **nosotros** and **vosotros**.

(79) **Ella pide la ruta a un desconocido.** The **-e** of **pedir** changes to **-i** in all forms except **nosotros** and **vosotros**.

(80) **Yo cierro las ventanas.** The **-e** of **cerrar** changes to **-ie** in all forms except **nosotros** and **vosotros**.

(81) **Nostros empezamos un régimen hoy día.** The second **-e** of **empezar** changes to **-ie** in all forms except **nosotros** and **vosotros**.

(82) **Tú juegas al béisbol.** The **-o** of **jugar** changes to **-ue** in all forms except **nosotros** and **vosotros**.

(83) **Uds. quieren ir a España.** The **-e** of **querer** changes to **-ie** in all forms except **nosotros** and **vosotros**.

(84) **Ellos cuentan bromas todo el tiempo.** The **-o** of **contar** changes to **-ue** in all forms except **nosotros** and **vosotros**.

(85) **Tú puedes ayudarme a reparar mi coche.** The **-o** of **poder** changes to **-ue** in all forms except **nosotros** and **vosotros**.

(86) **Yo escojo a menudo respuestas incorrectas.** For **yo,** change the **-g** to **-j** and then add the **-o** ending.

(87) **Yo le ofrezco un regalo.** For **yo,** change the **-c** to **-cz** and then add the **-o** ending.

(88) **Ella duerme mucho.** The **-o** of **dormir** changes to **-ue** in all forms except **nosotros** and **vosotros**.

(89) **Ellos esquían en las montañas.** For **esquiar,** change **-i** to **-í** in all forms except **nosotros** and **vosotros**.

(90) **Ella continúa trabajando.** For **continuar,** change **-u** to **-ú** in all forms except **nosotros** and **vosotros**.

(91) **Él construye edificios.** The **-i** of **construir** changes to **-y** in all forms except **nosotros** and **vosotros**.

(92) **Ellos advierten a la profesora.** The **-e** of **advertir** changes to **-ie** in all forms except **nosotros** and **vosotros**.

(93) **hago, hacemos.** The **-yo** form of **hacer** is irregular. For **nosotros,** drop the **-er** from **hacer** and add **-emos.**

(94) **salimos, salgo.** For **nosotros,** drop the **-i** from **salir** and add **-imos.** The **-yo** form of **salir** is irregular.

(95) **doy, dan.** The **-yo** form of **dar** is irregular. For **Esteban y Roberto,** drop the **-ar** from **dar** and add **-an.**

(96) **tengo, tiene.** The **-yo** form of **tener** is irregular. For **Mi hermana,** the **-e** of **tener** changes to **-ie.** Drop the **-er** from **tener** and add **-e.**

(97) **vamos, voy.** The verb **ir** is irregular and must be memorized.

(98) **oigo, oyen.** The **-yo** form of **oír** is irregular. In other forms, change the **-i** of **oír** to **-y** in all forms except **nosotros** and **vosotros.**

(99) **digo, dice.** The **-yo** form of **decir** is irregular. In other forms, change the **-e** of **decir** to **-i** in all forms except **nosotros** and **vosotros.**

(100) **está, estoy.** Add an accent to the **-a** of **estar** in all forms except **yo** and **nosotros.** The **-yo** form of **estar** is irregular.

(101) **traen, traigo.** The verb **traer** is regular in all forms except **yo.** For the plural, **mis amigas,** drop **-er** and add **-en.**

(102) **veo, ven.** The **yo** form of **ver** is irregular. For the plural, **estos muchachos,** drop **-er** and add **-en.**

(103) **pongo, pone.** The **yo** form of **poner** is irregular. For the singular, **Juan,** drop **-er** and add **-e.**

(104) **venimos, vengo.** The **yo** form of **venir** is irregular. The **-e** of **venir** changes to **-ie** in all forms except **nosotros** and **vosotros.**

(105) **quiere decir.** *What does* **palomitas de maíz** *mean?*

(106) **pienso.** *I intend to take a trip to Mexico.*

(107) **tengo celos.** *I am jealous of Ramón because I can't buy a new car.*

(108) **tiene lugar.** *At what time does it take place?*

(109) **Hace frío.** *It's cold if it's 5 degrees below zero.*

(110) **doy un paseo.** *When it's sunny, I go for a walk in the park.* The **yo** form of **dar** is irregular.

Chapter 6

Expressing Yourself with Subjunctive Feeling

So, you're unfamiliar with the subjunctive — probably as unfamiliar as I was when I first started learning a foreign language. I'm not at all surprised. Although my teachers always seemed to concentrate on grammar, I don't remember hearing about the subjunctive until my Second year of foreign language study in high school. What exactly is the subjunctive? Well, it *isn't* a tense, which tells at what time an action took place, such as present, past, or future. The subjunctive is a mood, meaning it indicates how the speaker feels about or perceives a situation.

The subjunctive expresses unreal, hypothetical, theoretical, imaginary, uncorroborated, or unconfirmed conditions or situations. These expressions are the result of the speaker's doubts, emotions, wishes, wants, needs, desires, feelings, speculations, or suppositions. Further, the subjunctive is used after verbs and expressions of advice, command, desire, hope, importance, opinion, permission, preference, prohibition, request, suggestion, and urgency. How is the present tense different from the present subjunctive? The present tense functions in the indicative mood — a mood that states a fact. Don't be intimidated; the subjunctive really isn't as difficult as it appears. With some practice, you'll quickly become comfortable using it.

In this chapter, you discover how to form the present subjunctive of regular verbs, verbs with spelling changes, verbs with stem changes, and completely irregular verbs. After you master the technique of properly conjugating these verbs, you find many of the important uses of the subjunctive. I also give you plenty of practice on determining when to use the present tense and when to use the subjunctive mood.

Forming the Present Subjunctive

If you can form the present tense, you can form the present subjunctive — with any of the types of verbs in this chapter. This is because many of the subjunctive stems use the **yo** form (first-person singular) of the present tense. (Check out more on that in Chapter 5.) You discover how to form the subjunctive with many types of verbs in the following sections.

Regular verbs

You form the present subjunctive of regular verbs by dropping the **-o** from the **yo** form of the present tense and adding the subjunctive endings shown in bold in Table 6-1. These endings are relatively easy to remember, because **-ar** verbs use the present-tense endings of **-er** verbs, and **-er** and **-ir** verbs use the present-tense endings of **-ar** verbs. This is why people say that you form the present subjunctive by using the opposite verb endings on the stem.

Table 6-1 The Present Subjunctive Endings of Regular Verbs

Yo Form of Present	-ar Verbs	-er Verbs	-ir Verbs
	hablo (*I speak*)	comprendo (*I understand*)	escribo (*I write*)
yo	hable	comprenda	escriba
tú	hables	comprendas	escribas
él, ella, Ud.	hable	comprenda	escriba
nosotros	hablemos	comprendamos	escribamos
vosotros	habléis	comprendáis	escribáis
ellos, ellas, Uds.	hablen	comprendan	escriban

Here are some examples of these verbs in the subjunctive:

Es importante que yo hable con sus padres. (*It is important that I speak to your parents.*)

Es esencial que Ud. comprenda las reglas. (*It is essential that you understand the rules.*)

Es necesario que nosotros escribamos las notas. (*It is necessary that we write the notes.*)

To get you accustomed to this reversal, here's an exercise with **-ar** verbs.

PRACTICE

Express what the following people have to do to be good citizens by using the correct form of the verb in the present subjunctive.

Q. (prestar) **Es importante que Enrique** _____ **atención a los acontecimientos** (*events*) **mundiales.**

A. **preste.** To form the present subjunctive of regular **-ar** verbs, drop **-o** from the yo form and add -e for Enrique.

1. (respetar) Es necesario que tú _____ las leyes.

2. (votar) Es preferible que nosotros _____ en las elecciones.

3. (aceptar) Es esencial que los ciudadanos _____ la responsabilidad de sus actos.

4. (escuchar) Es importante que vosotros _____ todas las ideas.

5. (trabajar) Es bueno que yo _____ por el bien de la sociedad.

6. (ayudar) Es imperativo que todo el mundo _____ a la gente desafortunada.

The following example and practice questions focus on **-er** verbs.

PRACTICE

Express what the following people have to do to maintain a healthy lifestyle by combining the two elements.

Q. **Es mejor que ella/aprender las reglas del gimnasio**

A. **Es mejor que ella aprenda las reglas del gimnasio.** To form the present subjunctive of regular **-er** verbs, drop **-o** from the **yo** form and add **-a** for **ella.**

7. Es útil que tú/correr cada día _____

8. Es importante que yo/beber mucha agua _____

9. Es necesario que vosotros/comer muchas verduras _____

10. Es imperativo que Ud./comprender cómo mantenerse sano _____

11. Es indispensable que ellos/leer artículos sobre la nutrición _____

12. Es bueno que Margarita/prometer hacer ejercicios _____

PRACTICE

Perfect! Now try your hand at **-ir** verbs. Complete each sentence with the correct form of the verb in the present subjunctive to describe how the following team players feel.

Q. (recibir) Es necesario que Julia _____ un uniforme nuevo.

A. **reciba.** To form the present subjunctive of regular **-ir** verbs, drop **-o** from the **yo** form and add **-a** for **Julia**.

(13) (decidir) Es importante que nosotras _____ ser buenas deportistas.

(14) (describir) Es necesario que la entrenadora _____ bien las reglas del deporte.

(15) (dividir) Es esencial que Ud. _____ las jugadoras en equipos.

(16) (insistir) Es increíble que tú _____ en ser árbitra.

(17) (asistir) Es preferible que vosotros _____ a las sesiones de entrenamiento.

(18) (permitir) Es bueno que las capitanas _____ a todas a jugar.

The following questions are a mixed bag of verbs. Good luck!

PRACTICE

V You and your business colleagues are going to a meeting. Complete the memo that your boss sent with instructions for everyone in the company, including himself and his family members, by inserting the proper form of the verbs provided in parentheses.

Q. (Uds.) escuchar _____ atentamente.

A. **Es importante que Uds. escuchen atentamente.**

Es importante que . . .

(19) (observar) Tú _____ como actúan los demás.

(20) (escribir) Nosotros _____ notas.

(21) (leer) Vosotros _____ los contratos antes de firmarlos.

(22) (presentar) Uds. _____ sus ideas y sus opiniones con calma.

(23) (negociar) Yo _____ de buena fe.

(24) (imprimir) Tú _____ lo importante.

(25) (participar) Enrique _____ en todas las discusiones.

(26) (proceder) Yo _____ lentamente.

(27) (hablar) Nosotros _____ lenta y claramente.

28 (responder) Rosa _____ cuidadosamente.

29 (reflexionar) Vosotros _____ antes de hablar.

30 (describir) Felipe y Raúl _____ bien nuestra posición.

Verbs that are irregular in the yo form

Some -er and -ir verbs that are irregular in the **yo** form of the present tense use the stem of the **yo** to form the present subjunctive. You drop the final -o from the **yo** form and add the opposite endings. In other words, you add an ending that starts with -a for the verbs listed in Table 6-2.

Table 6-2   Subjunctive Stems Derived from the Present-Tense Yo Form

Verb	Meaning	Yo Form	Subjunctive Forms
decir	*to say, to tell*	**digo**	**dig**a, **dig**as, **dig**a, **dig**amos, **dig**áis, **dig**an
hacer	*to make, to do*	**hago**	**hag**a, **hag**as, **hag**a, **hag**amos, **hag**áis, **hag**an
oír	*to hear*	**oigo**	**oig**a, **oig**as, **oig**a, **oig**amos, **oig**áis, **oig**an
poner	*to put*	**pongo**	**pong**a, **pong**as, **pong**a, **pong**amos, **pong**áis, **pong**an
salir	*to go out*	**salgo**	**salg**a, **salg**as, **salg**a, **salg**amos, **salg**áis, **salg**an
tener	*to have*	**tengo**	**teng**a, **teng**as, **teng**a, **teng**amos, **teng**áis, **teng**an
traer	*to bring*	**traigo**	**traig**a, **traig**as, **traig**a, **traig**amos, **traig**áis, **traig**an
valer	*to be worth*	**valgo**	**valg**a, **valg**as, **valg**a, **valg**amos, **valg**áis, **valg**an
venir	*to come*	**vengo**	**veng**a, **veng**as, **veng**a, **veng**amos, **veng**áis, **veng**an
ver	*to see*	**veo**	**ve**a, **ve**as, **ve**a, **ve**amos, **ve**áis, **ve**an

Here are some examples of these types of verbs:

Es importante que todos vengan a tiempo. (*It's important that everyone come on time.*)

Es urgente que Uds. hagan todo este trabajo ahora. (*It is urgent that you do all this work now.*)

Try your hand at forming the present subjunctive of these verbs with irregular **yo** forms in the present tense.

PRACTICE

Use the present subjunctive to express what the teacher tells the students it is necessary for them to do.

Q. Es necesario que Uds/no salir de la clase sin permiso

A. **Es necesario que Uds. no salgan de la clase sin permiso.** To form the present subjunctive, take the irregular **yo** form of **salir** in the present tense (**salgo**). Drop the -o and add -an as the ending for **Uds**.

Es necesario que Uds. . . .

31 no decir mentiras _____

32 tener cuidado en la sala de clase _____

33 ver bien las reglas escritas en la pizarra _____

34 valer mucho como alumnos _____

35 hacer todo el trabajo escolar _____

36 venir a clase preparados _____

Verbs with spelling changes in the yo form

Some Spanish verbs have the same spelling change in the present subjunctive as they have in the present tense. Namely, verbs ending in **-cer/-cir, -ger/-gir,** and **-guir** (not **-uir**) undergo the same changes that occur in the **yo** form of the present. These changes are

>> vowel + **-cer/-cir** verbs: **c → zc**

>> consonant + **-cer /-cir** verbs: **c → z**

>> **-ger/-gir** verbs: **g → j**

>> **-guir** verbs: **gu → g**

Table 6-3 shows these changes in the subjunctive.

Table 6-3   Present Subjunctive of Verbs with Spelling Changes

Infinitive	Present Yo Form	Stem	Subjunctive + Endings
ofrecer (*to offer*)	**ofrezco**	**ofrezc-**	**-a, -as, -a, -amos, -áis, -an**
traducir (*to translate*)	**traduzco**	**traduzc-**	**-a, -as, -a, -amos, -áis, -an**
convencer (*to convince*)	**convenzo**	**convenz-**	**-a, -as, -a, -amos, -áis, -an**
esparcir (*to spread*)	**esparzo**	**esparz-**	**-a, -as, -a, -amos, -áis, -an**
escoger (*to choose*)	**escojo**	**escoj-**	**-a, -as, -a, -amos, -áis, -an**
exigir (*to demand*)	**exijo**	**exij-**	**-a, -as, -a, -amos, -áis, -an**
distinguir (*to distinguish*)	**distingo**	**disting-**	**-a, -as, -a, -amos, -áis, -an**

The following examples illustrate these spelling changes:

Es una lástima-que el director no le ofrezca un aumento de salario. (*It is regrettable that the director isn't offering him a raise.*)

Es natural que el jefe exija mucho de sus empleados. (*It is natural that the boss demands a lot from his employees.*)

REMEMBER

You see some different spelling changes for verbs in the present subjunctive than you see for verbs with spelling changes in the present tense. In the present subjunctive, verbs ending in **-car, -gar,** and **-zar** undergo changes. They have the same changes as in the preterite (or the past tense; see Chapter 13). These changes are as follows:

>> **-car** verbs: **c → qu**

>> **-gar** verbs: **g → gu**

>> **-zar** verbs: **z → c**

The following table (and examples) shows the full conjugation:

Infinitive	Stem	Subjunctive Endings
tocar (*to touch*)	**toqu-**	**-e, -es, -e, -emos, -éis, -en**
pagar (*to pay*)	**pagu-**	**-e, -es, -e, -emos, -éis, -en**
organizar (*to organize*)	**organic-**	**-e, -es, -e, -emos, éis, -en**

Es importante que no toques nada. (*It is important that you not touch anything.*)

Es imperativo que nosotros paguemos esta factura. (*It is imperative that we pay this bill.*)

Es necesario que él organice los datos. (*It is necessary for him to organize the data.*)

These verbs with spelling changes can prove to be quite tricky, so it's imperative to practice them.

PRACTICE

Express what a parent tells a babysitter it is essential to do. Start with the phrase **Es esencial que . . .**

Q. tú/llegar temprano

A. **Es esencial que tu llegues temprano.** Verbs that end in **-gar** change **-g** to **-gu** in all forms of the subjunctive. To form the present subjunctive of **-ar** verbs, drop **-o** from the **yo** form and add **-es** for **tú.**

Es esencial que . . .

37 Roberto/no utilizar tijeras (*scissors*) _____

38 los niños/no desobedecer _____

39 yo/te pagar bastante dinero _____

40 Eva/no sacar todas sus muñecas _____

41 tú/no conducir al centro _____

42 Eva/no coger todos los juguetes _____

(43) todos/distinguir entre el bien y el mal _____

(44) los niños/no esparcir sus juguetes por todo el suelo _____

(45) Roberto no fingir (*to pretend*) tener hambre _____

(46) los niños/no apagar todas las luces _____

Verbs with stem changes

Just like in the present tense, stem-changing **-ar** and **-er** verbs in the present subjunctive undergo changes in all forms except **nosotros** and **vosotros**. Table 6-4 outlines these changes.

Table 6-4   Verbs with Stem Changes in the Present Subjunctive

Infinitive Ending	Stem Change in the Present	Example Verb	Yo, Tú, Él, Ellos Subjunctive Stem	Nosotros/Vosotros Subjunctive Stem
-ar	e → ie	**cerrar** (*to close*)	**cierr-**	**cerr-**
-ar	o → ue	**mostrar** (*to show*)	**muestr-**	**mostr-**
-er	e → ie	**querer** (*to wish, to want*)	**quier-**	**quer-**
-er	o → ue	**volver** (*to return*)	**vuelv-**	**volv-**

Here are two examples sentences with these verbs:

> **Quiero que Ud. cierre la ventana.** (*I want you to close the window.*)

> **Es dudoso que ellos vuelvan temprano.** (*It is doubtful that they will return early.*)

REMEMBER

And what about **-ir** verbs? Well, **-ir** verbs with an **-e** to **-i** stem change make the change from **-e** to **-i** in all forms, including **nosotros** and **vosotros**. Stem-changing verbs ending in **-ir**, however, also have changes unique to the **nosotros** and **vosotros** forms, as shown in the Table 6-5.

Table 6-5   Certain -ir Verbs with Stem Changes

Infinitive	Stem Change	Stem	Nosotros and Vosotros Stems
preferir (*to prefer*)	e → ie	**prefier-**	**prefir-**
dormir (*to sleep*)	o → ue	**duerm-**	**durm-**
servir (*to serve*)	e → i	**sirv-**	**sirv-**

Here are some examples of **-ir** verbs in the subjunctive:

> **La profesora está contenta de que nosotros prefiramos ver una película española.** (*The teacher is happy that we prefer to see a Spanish film.*)

Su padre está asombrado de que él duerma hasta las diez. (*His father is astonished that he sleeps until ten o'clock.*)

Es dudoso que sirvan vino en la conferencia. (*It is doubtful that they will serve wine at the conference.*)

The changes don't end with simple **-ar, -er,** and **-ir** verbs, however. Note the stem changes for the following categories of verbs that end with an additional vowel:

>> Verbs that end in **-iar** have accent marks in all present subjunctive forms except **nosotros:**

● **enviar** (*to send*): **envíe, envíes, envíe, enviemos, enviéis, envíen**

>> Verbs that end in **-uar** have accent marks in all present subjunctive forms except **nosotros:**

● **continuar** (*to continue*): **continúe, continúes, continúe, continuemos, continuéis, continúen**

>> Verbs that end in **-uir** (but not **-guir**) add a **y** after the **u** in all present subjunctive forms:

● **concluir** (*to conclude*): **concluya, concluyas, concluya, concluyamos, concluyáis, concluyan**

The following examples show these rules in action:

Es importante que Ud. envíe este paquete inmediatamente. (*It is important that you send this package immediately.*)

Me enfada que Ud. no continúe estudiando español. (*I'm displeased that you don't continue to study Spanish.*)

El profesor desea que los estudiantes concluyan su trabajo. (*The teacher wants the students to complete their work.*)

Verbs with spelling and stem changes

Some very common Spanish verbs have both spelling and stem changes in the present subjunctive form, as shown in Table 6-6.

Table 6-6   Stem and Spelling Changes in the Present Subjunctive

Verb	Stem Change	Spelling Change	Present Subjunctive Forms
colgar (*to hang*)	**o** to **-ue**	**-g** to **-gu**	**cuelgue, cuelgues, cuelgue, colguemos, colguéis, cuelguen**
jugar (*to play*)	**-u** to **-ue**	**-g** to **-gu**	**juegue, juegues, juegue, juguemos, juguéis, jueguen**
comenzar (*to begin*)	**-e** to **-ie**	**-z** to **-c**	**comience, comiences, comience, comencemos, comencéis, comiencen**
empezar (*to begin*)	**-e** to **-ie**	**-z** to **-c**	**empiece, empieces, empiece, empecemos, empecéis, empiecen**
almorzar (*to eat lunch*)	**-o** to **-ue**	**-z** to **-c**	**almuerce, almuerces, almuerce, almorcemos, almorcéis, almuercen**

The following examples show both changes in action:

María está contenta de que sus perros jueguen en el jardín. (*Maria is happy that her dogs play in the backyard.*)

Estoy encantada de que el espectáculo empiece ahora. (*I am delighted that the show will begin now.*)

La madre no permite que sus hijos almuercen en la sala. (*The mother doesn't permit her children to eat in the living room.*)

Before moving on to verbs that are completely irregular in the present subjunctive, it's important to practice verbs with spelling changes.

PRACTICE

The Gómez family has certain habits. Express them using the present subjunctive of the verb indicated.

Q. (volver) Es interesante que toda la familia _____ a casa a eso de las cinco.

A. **vuelva. Volver** changes **-o** to **-ue** in all forms of the present subjunctive except **nosotros** and **vosotros**.

47 (almorzar) Es interesante que tú _____ a la una.

48 (enviar) Es interesante que, de vez en cuando, Linda _____ una invitación a su novio a comer con ellos.

49 (jugar) Es interesante que Julio _____ afuera antes de cenar.

50 (morir) Es interesante que todo el mundo _____ de hambre a las cinco.

51 (empezar) Es interesante que mamá _____ a preparar la cena a las cinco y cuarto.

52 (preferer) Es interesante que nosotros _____ platos cubanos.

53 (querer) Es interesante que papá _____ comer en la cocina.

54 (servir) Es interesante que yo _____ la comida a las siete.

55 (mostrar) Es interesante que María y Clara _____ el postre a la familia.

56 (concluir) Es interesante que la cena _____ a las ocho.

(Very) irregular verbs

Some verbs are completely irregular in the subjunctive mood, which means you can't follow any rules or patterns to form them. You can do nothing else but memorize them. Table 6-7 will help.

Table 6-7   (Very) Irregular Verbs in the Subjunctive

Spanish Verb	Meaning	Subjunctive Forms
dar	*to give*	**dé, des, dé, demos, deis, den**
estar	*to be*	**esté, estés, esté, estemos, estéis, estén**
ir	*to go*	**vaya, vayas, vaya, vayamos, vayáis, vayan**
saber	*to know*	**sepa, sepas, sepa, sepamos, sepáis, sepan**
ser	*to be*	**sea, seas, sea, seamos, seáis, sean**

Here are some examples of irregular verbs in the subjunctive:

Estamos tristes de que tu abuela esté enferma. (*We are sad that your grandmother is sick.*)

Yo dudo que él sepa reparar la computadora. (*I doubt that he knows how to repair the computer.*)

You and your classmates know exactly what your Spanish teacher expects from you. Write an email to your friend explaining your class rules. In the spaces provided, insert the correct form of the verb in parentheses.

Q. (saber) Nosotros _____ conjugar los verbos.

A. **Es importante que nosotros sepamos conjugar todos los verbos.** (*It is important that we know how to conjugate all the verbs.*)

Querido Federico,

Es importante que . . .

57 (llegar) tú no _____ tarde a la clase y que Isabel y yo no _____ tarde a la clase.

58 (perder) tú no _____ el tiempo en clase y que Isabel y yo no lo _____ tampoco.

59 (tener) tú no _____ miedo y que Isabel y yo no to _____ tampoco.

60 (continuar) tú no _____ hablando todo el tiempo y que Isabel y yo no _____ hablando tampoco.

61 (mostrar) tú no _____ la tarea a su compañero de clase y que Isabel y yo no la _____ a nuestra compañera de clase tampoco.

62 (estar) tú no _____ nervioso en clase y que Isabel y yo no _____ nerviosas tampoco.

63 (masticar) tú no _____ chicle y que Isabel y yo no lo _____ tampoco.

64. (ir) tú no _____ al baño y que Isabel y yo no _____ al baño tampoco.

65. (mentir) tú no _____ y que Isabel y yo no _____ tampoco.

66. (empezar) tú no _____ la tarea en clase y que Isabel y yo no la _____ tampoco.

67. (enviar) tú no _____ notas a los demás y que Isabel y yo no las _____ tampoco.

68. (dormir) tú no _____ en clase y que Isabel y yo no _____ en clase tampoco.

69. (hacer) tú no _____ la tarea en clase y que Isabel y yo no la _____ en clase tampoco.

70. (salir) tú no _____ de la clase sin permiso y que Isabel y yo no _____ de ella tampoco.

71. (cerrar) tú no _____ el libro y que Isabel y yo no _____ el libro tampoco.

72. (traducir) tú no _____ las frases en inglés y que Isabel y yo no las _____ tampoco.

73. (pedir) tú no _____ el permiso y que Isabel y yo no lo _____ tampoco.

74. (escoger) tú no _____ respuestas incorrectas y que Isabel y yo no las _____ tampoco.

75. (jugar) tú no _____ en clase y que Isabel y yo no _____ en ella tampoco.

76. (almorzar) tú no _____ en clase y que Isabel y yo no _____ en ella tampoco.

77. (ser) tú no _____ irresponsable y que Isabel y yo no _____ irresponsables tampoco.

78. 78 (dar) tú no _____ tu tarea a tus amigos y que Isabel y yo no la _____ a nuestros amigos tampoco.

Tu amiga,

Pilar

Spanning the Uses of the Present Subjunctive

The present subjunctive has many applications, which makes it a very useful tool. The subjunctive allows you to express your innermost hopes, desires, and dreams; your most pressing needs; your wildest doubts; and your most humble opinions. Furthermore, it allows you to give advice, to insist on receiving what you want, to offer suggestions, and to demand the necessities of life. And you can execute these expressions in a very low-key, gentle way.

How do you know when to use the present subjunctive? Allow me to make it clear. You must use the present subjunctive in Spanish (whether or not you'd use it in English) when all the following conditions exist within a sentence:

>> The sentence contains a *main* (or *independent*) *clause* — a group of words containing a subject and a verb that can stand alone as a sentence — and a *subordinate* (or *dependent*) *clause* — a group of words containing a subject and a verb that can't stand alone. Generally, each clause must contain a different subject.

>> The main clause shows, among other things, fear, wishing, wanting, emotion, doubt, need, necessity, feelings, emotions, commands or orders, supposition, speculation, or opinion.

>> **Que** (*that*) joins the main clause to the dependent clause, which contains a verb in the subjunctive.

TIP

When you use the subjunctive in English (and most people do so without even realizing it), you often omit the word *that*. In Spanish, however, you must always use **que** to join the two clauses:

>> **Es improbable que yo salga esta noche.** (*It is improbable [that] I'll go out tonight.*)

>> **(No) Es extraño que él haga eso.** (*It is [not] strange [that] he's doing that.*)

Here are two examples to get you into the swing of things before the following sections dig deeper into the inner workings of the present subjunctive.

La profesora de español quiere que los estudiantes no hablen inglés en clase. (*The Spanish teacher doesn't want the students to speak English in class.*)

El gerente insiste en que los empleados trabajen el sábado. (*The manager insists that the workers work on Saturday.*)

Using the present subjunctive after impersonal expressions

Just because you use an impersonal expression doesn't mean you're being impersonal. On the contrary, you can use this construction to convey some very personal information and ideas. An impersonal expression acts as the main clause of the sentence and is joined to the thoughts you want to relate by **que** (*that*). When this expression shows wishing, uncertainty, need, emotion, and so on, it requires the subjunctive in the dependent clause that follows.

REMEMBER

Because it isn't a tense but a mood, the present subjunctive may refer to present or future actions:

Conviene que Ud. estudie mucho. (*It is advisable that you study a lot.*)

Es dudoso que yo termine todo mi trabajo esta noche. (*It is doubtful that I will finish all my work tonight.*)

Many (although not all) impersonal expressions begin with **es** (*it is*) and are followed by adjectives showing wishing, emotion, doubt, need, and so on. They require the subjunctive even if they're negated:

No es urgente que me telefonee. (*It isn't urgent that you call me.*)

The following list shows some of the most common Spanish impersonal expressions that require the subjunctive:

English	Spanish
it is absurd that	es absurdo que
it is advisable that	conviene que
it is amazing that	es asombroso que
it is amusing that	es divertido que
it is bad that	es malo que
it is better that	es mejor que, más vale que
it is curious that	es curioso que
it is difficult that	es difícil que
it is doubtful that	es dudoso que
it is easy that	es fácil que
it is enough that	es suficiente que, basta que
it is essential that	es esencial que
it is fair that	es justo que
it is fitting that	es conveniente que
it is good that	es bueno que
it is imperative that	es imperativo que
it is important that	es importante que, importa que
it is impossible that	es imposible que
it is improbable that	es improbable que
it is incredible that	es increíble que
it is indispensable that	es indispensable que
it is interesting that	es interesante que
it is ironic that	es irónico que
it is natural that	es natural que
it is necessary that	es necesario que, es preciso que, es menester que
it is nice that	es bueno que
it is a pity that	es una lástima que
it is possible that	es posible que
it is preferable that	es preferible que
it is probable that	es probable que
it is rare that	es raro que
it is regrettable that	es lamentable que
it seems untrue that	parece mentira que
it is strange that	es extraño que

English	Spanish
it is surprising that	es sorprendiente que
it is unfair that	es injusto que
it is urgent that	es urgente que
it is useful that	es útil que

Here are some examples that show how an impersonal expression can communicate a very personal thought, feeling, or opinion:

Es sorprendiente que esa mujer sea tan irresponsable. (*It is surprising that that woman is so irresponsible.*)

Es injusto que estas personas no puedan votar. (*It is unfair that these people can't vote.*)

Be careful! When impersonal expressions show certainty, you must use the indicative (present, past, or future):

English	Spanish
it is certain, it is sure	es cierto
it is clear	está claro
it is evident	es evidente
it is exact	es exacto
it is obvious	es obvio
it is sure	es seguro
it is true	es verdad
it seems	parece

Here are some examples where certainty is shown:

Es obvio que nuestros precios son competitivos. (*It is obvious that our prices are competitive.*)

Está claro que Ud. tiene razón. (*It is clear that you are right.*)

However, impersonal expressions that show certainty when used in the affirmative express doubt or denial when they're negated and, therefore, require the subjunctive:

Es cierto el avión despega pronto. (*It is certain that the plane will take off soon.*)

No es cierto que el avión despegue pronto. (*It is uncertain that the plane will take off soon.*)

Your friend is having a party, and you want to offer suggestions on what people have to do to prepare for the party and what the party will be like. Do so by writing her a note, in which you combine the fragments provided to form your sentences.

Q. importante/Yolanda/hablar con los invitados

A. Es importante que Yolanda hable con los invitados.

Querida Linda,

(79) preciso/todos/buscar una orquesta

_____

(80) urgente/Daniel/le decir el menú al cocinero

_____

(81) seguro/todo el mundo/estar nervioso

_____

(82) indispensable/yo/enviar las invitaciones

_____

(83) importante/vosotros/escoger un buen restaurante

_____

(84) no/evidente/todos los invitados/venir

_____

(85) imperativo/tú/saber a quienes quieres invitar

_____

(86) cierto/vosotros/tener muchos amigos

_____

(87) esencial/tu esposo/pagar con antelación

_____

(88) necesario/Estela/le dar una lista de los invitados al propietario

_____

89   conviene que/yo/organizar actividades

_____

 90   claro/esta fiesta/ir a ser maravillosa

_____

Susana

Using the present subjunctive to express wishing, emotion, need, and doubt

When used in a main clause, certain verbs require the use of the subjunctive in the dependent clause. This is because these verbs show not only wishing, emotion, need, or doubt but also other related thoughts such as advice, command, demand, desire, hope, permission, preference, prohibition, request, suggestion, or wanting. The following table lists some of these verbs:

Spanish	English
aconsejar	to advise
alegrarse (de)	to be glad, to be happy
avergonzarse de	to be ashamed of
desear	to desire, to wish, to want
dudar	to doubt
enfadarse	to become angry
enojarse	to become angry
esperar	to hope
exigir	to require, to demand
insistir en	to insist
lamentar	to regret
mandar	to command, to order
necesitar	to need
negar	to deny
ojalá	if only . . .
ordenar	to order
pedir	to ask for, to request
permitir	to permit
preferir	to prefer
prohibir	to forbid
querer	to wish, to want
reclamar	to demand
recomendar	to recommend
requerir	to require
rogar	to beg, to request

Spanish	English
sentir	to be sorry, to regret
solicitar	to request
sorprenderse de	to be surprised
sugerir	to suggest
suplicar	to beg, to plead
temer	to fear
tener miedo de	to fear

Here's how you use many of these verbs:

Siento que Uds. no vengan a mi fiesta. (*I am sorry that you aren't coming to my party.*)

El patrón manda que Ud. llegue a tiempo. (*The boss demands that you arrive on time.*)

Ojalá que yo gane la lotería. (*If only I win the lottery.*)

REMEMBER

If no doubt exists in the thought you want to express, you use the indicative (past, present, or future):

Él no duda que yo merezco el premio. (*He doesn't doubt that I deserve the price.*)

Yo creo que ella es muy inteligente. (*I believe she is very intelligent.*)

If the certainty is negated or questioned, however, you use the subjunctive:

¿No piensas que ese libro sea interesante? (*Don't you think that book is interesting?*)

PRACTICE

You and your classmates are practicing for a school play. The teacher has written out some suggestions for the cast. Complete their sentences by filling in the missing words, using the correct forms of the verbs provided in parentheses.

Q. (prestar) Quiero que todos _____ atención.

A. Quiero que todos presten atención.

91 (hacer) Deseo que Blanca _____ lo que yo le digo.

92 (seguir) Aconsejo que todos _____ las instrucciones.

93 (cantar) No niego que Guillermo _____ bien.

94 (aprender) Exijo que Rosa _____ su papel de memoria.

95 (saber) Ojalá que Gregorio y Salvador _____ la letra de la canción.

96 (ir) Prefiero que Ricardo _____ a la derecha en esta escena.

97 (hablar) Creo que los muchachos siempre _____ con voz firme.

98 (poder) Dudo que el público _____ oír a Esteban.

Using the present subjunctive after adjectives that express feelings or emotions

When the main clause of a Spanish sentence contains the word **estar** (*to be*) followed by an adjective that expresses feelings or emotions, you use the subjunctive in the dependent clause. To complete the sentences, you insert words **de que** (*that*) after the adjective:

> **Estoy alegre de que Uds. me acompañen al cine.** (*I'm happy that you are accompanying me to the movies.*)

> **No estamos contentos de que tú pierdas el tiempo.** (*We are not happy that you are wasting time.*)

The following list shows many Spanish adjectives that express feelings or emotions (for more on adjectives, head to Chapter 8):

Spanish Adjective	English Meaning
alegre	*happy*
asombrado (-a)	*astonished, surprised*
asustado (-a)	*afraid*
avergonzado (-a)	*embarrassed, ashamed*
contento (-a)	*happy*
elogiado (-a)	*flattered*
encantado (-a)	*delighted*
enfadado (-a)	*displeased*
enojado (-a)	*angry*
fastidiado (-a)	*bothered*
feliz	*happy*
furioso (-a)	*furious*
infeliz	*unhappy*
irritado (-a)	*irritated*
orgulloso (-a)	*proud*
triste	*sad*

TIP

Note that the following verbs showing feelings and emotions are used with indirect object pronouns (see Chapter 9) to avoid sounding overly literal:

> **Me molesta (Me irrita) (Me fastidia) que él no pueda venir**. (*It bothers me that he can't come.*)

> **Le alegra que tú trabajes.** (*He's [She's] happy that you art working.*)

Josefina is very happy today. Complete the email she plans to send to a friend, in which she wants to explain why she's happy, by joining the phrases. Provide any missing parts and conjugate the verbs as necessary.

Q. **contenta/mi hija/recibir buenas notas**

A. **Estoy contenta de que mi hija reciba buenas notas.**

Verónica

99   alegre/mi casa/valer mucho

100   contenta/mi jefe/me ofrecer un aumento de salario

101   feliz/mi hijo/demostrar una aptitud para las ciencias

102   orgullosa/mis hijos/salir bien en la escuela

103   encantada/mi familia/venir a visitarnos

104   asombrada/tú/querer acompañarnos a Costa Rica

Josefina

Using the present subjunctive in relative clauses

You use the subjunctive in relative clauses, where the person or thing mentioned in the main clause

>> Is indefinite

>> Is nonexistent

>> Is sought after but not yet attained

>> May or may not exist

In other words, the subject of the sentence just isn't sure or is in doubt about the availability of the person or thing. Here are two examples:

Busco a un mecánico que *sepa* reparar mi coche. (*I am looking for a mechanic who knows how to repair my car.*)

Conozco a un mecánico que *sabe* reparar mi coche. (*I know a mechanic who knows how to repair my car.*)

Note that in the first sentence, the subject is unsure whether such a person can be found. In the second sentence, however, the subject has no doubt that the person exists, so the present tense, rather than the present subjunctive, is required.

PRACTICE

You're on a tour in a Spanish-speaking country. Write an email to practice your Spanish in which you explain what's happening on your trip. For each sentence, I provide two shorter sentences. You must join them with **que** and use either the present tense or the present subjunctive in the second part of your new sentence.

Q. No es evidente. El guía conoce bien la región

A. No es evidente que el guía conozca bien la región.

Diego

(105) Yo busco una tienda. Vende recuerdos.

(106) Yo estoy sorprendido. El tren no va al centro.

(107) Es natural. El guía sabe las rutas más bellas.

(108) ¿Conoces a un chófer aquí? ¿Conduce bien?

(109) Yo no dudo. La visita turística es interesante.

(110) Yo no creo. El museo está cerrado.

(111) Es una lástima. Estos hombres cuelgan un cartel que indica: "No hay billetes."

(112) Está claro. El guía es bueno.

Felipe

Answers to "Expressing Yourself with Subjunctive Feeling" Practice Questions

This section provides the answers and explanations to the practice questions presented in this chapter.

1. **respetes.** To form the present subjunctive of regular -**ar** verbs, drop -**o** from the **yo** form and add -**es** for **tú.**

2. **votemos.** To form the present subjunctive of regular -**ar** verbs, drop -**o** from the **yo** form and add -**emos** for **nosotros.**

3. **acepten.** To form the present subjunctive of regular -**ar** verbs, drop -**o** from the **yo** form and add -**en** for **los ciudadanos.**

4. **escuchéis.** To form the present subjunctive of regular -**ar** verbs, drop -**o** from the **yo** form and add -**eis** for **vosotros.**

5. **trabaje.** To form the present subjunctive of regular -**ar** verbs, drop -**o** from the **yo** form and add -**e** for **yo.**

6. **ayude.** To form the present subjunctive of regular -**ar** verbs, drop -**o** from the **yo** form and add -**e** for **todo el mundo.**

7. **Es útil que tú corras cada día.** To form the present subjunctive of regular -**er** verbs, drop -**o** from the **yo** form and add -**as** for **tú.**

8. **Es importante que yo beba mucha agua.** To form the present subjunctive of regular -**er** verbs, drop -**o** from the **yo** form and add -**a** for **yo.**

9. **Es necesario que vosotros comáis muchas verduras.** To form the present subjunctive of regular -**er** verbs, drop -**o** from the **yo** form and add -**áis** for **vosotros.**

10. **Es imperativo que Ud. comprenda cómo mantenerse sano.** To form the present subjunctive of regular -**er** verbs, drop -**o** from the **yo** form and add -**a** for **Ud.**

11. **Es indispensable que ellos lean artículos sobre la nutrición.** To form the present subjunctive of regular -**er** verbs, drop -**o** from the **yo** form and add -**an** for **ellos.**

12. **Es bueno que Margarita prometa hacer ejercicios.** To form the present subjunctive of regular -**er** verbs, drop -**o** from the **yo** form and add -**a** for **Margarita.**

13. **decidamos.** To form the present subjunctive of regular -**ir** verbs, drop -**o** from the **yo** form and add -**amos** for **Julia.**

14. **describa.** To form the present subjunctive of regular -**ir** verbs, drop -**o** from the **yo** form and add -**a** for **la entrenadora.**

15. **divida.** To form the present subjunctive of regular -**ir** verbs, drop -**o** from the **yo** form and add -**a** for **Ud.**

16. **insistas.** To form the present subjunctive of regular -**ir** verbs, drop -**o** from the **yo** form and add -**as** for **tú.**

17. **asistáis.** To form the present subjunctive of regular -**ir** verbs, drop -**o** from the **yo** form and add -**áis** for **vosotros.**

(18) **permitan.** To form the present subjunctive of regular **-ir** verbs, drop **-o** from the **yo** form and add **-an** for **las capitanas.**

(19) **observes.** To form the present subjunctive of regular **-ar** verbs, drop **-o** from the **yo** form and add **-es** for **tú.**

(20) **escribamos.** To form the present subjunctive of regular **-ir** verbs, drop **-o** from the **yo** form and add **-amos** for **nosotros.**

(21) **leáis.** To form the present subjunctive of regular **-er** verbs, drop **-o** from the **yo** form and add **-áis** for **vosotros.**

(22) **presenten.** To form the present subjunctive of regular **-ar** verbs, drop **-o** from the **yo** form and add **-en** for **Uds.**

(23) **negocie.** To form the present subjunctive of regular **-ar** verbs, drop **-o** from the **yo** form and add **-e** for **yo.**

(24) **imprimas.** To form the present subjunctive of regular **-ir** verbs, drop **-o** from the **yo** form and add **-as** for **tú.**

(25) **participe.** To form the present subjunctive of regular **-ar** verbs, drop **-o** from the **yo** form and add **-e** for **Enrique.**

(26) **proceda.** To form the present subjunctive of regular **-er** verbs, drop **-o** from the **yo** form and add **-a** for **yo.**

(27) **hablemos.** To form the present subjunctive of regular **-ar** verbs, drop **-o** from the **yo** form and add **-emos** for **nosotros.**

(28) **responda.** To form the present subjunctive of regular **-er** verbs, drop **-o** from the **yo** form and add **-a** for **Rosa.**

(29) **reflexionéis.** To form the present subjunctive of regular **-ar** verbs, drop **-o** from the **yo** form and add **-éis** for **vosotros.**

(30) **describan.** To form the present subjunctive of regular **-ir** verbs, drop **-o** from the **yo** form and add **-an** for **Felipe y Raúl.**

(31) **Es necesario que Uds. no digan mentiras.** To form the present subjunctive, take the irregular **yo** form of **decir** in the present tense (**digo**). Drop the **-o** and add **-an** as the ending for **Uds.**

(32) **Es necesario que Uds. tengan cuidado en la sala de clase.** To form the present subjunctive, take the irregular **yo** form of **tener** in the present tense (**tengo**). Drop the **-o** and add **-an** as the ending for **Uds.**

(33) **Es necesario que Uds. vean bien las reglas escritas en la pizarra.** To form the present subjunctive, take the irregular **yo** form of **ver** in the present tense (**veo**). Drop the **-o** and add **-an** as the ending for **Uds.**

(34) **Es necesario que Uds. valgan mucho como alumnos.** To form the present subjunctive, take the irregular **yo** form of **valer** in the present tense (**valgo**). Drop the **-o** and add **-an** as the ending for **Uds.**

(35) **Es necesario que Uds. hagan todo el trabajo escolar.** To form the present subjunctive, take the irregular **yo** form of **hacer** in the present tense (**hago**). Drop the **-o** and add **-an** as the ending for **Uds.**

36. **Es necesario que Uds. vengan a clase preparados.** To form the present subjunctive, take the irregular **yo** form of **venir** in the present tense (**vengo**). Drop the **-o** and add **-an** as the ending for **Uds.**

37. **Es esencial que Roberto no utilice tijeras.** Verbs that end in **-zar** change **-z** to **-c** in all forms of the subjunctive. To form the present subjunctive of **-ar** verbs, drop **-o** from the **yo** form and add **-e** for **Roberto.**

38. **Es esencial que los niños no desobedezcan.** Desobedecer changes **-c** to **-zc** in its present tense **yo** form. To form the present subjunctive, drop the **-o** from **desobedezco** and add **-an** as the ending for **los niños.**

39. **Es esencial que yo te pague bastante dinero.** Verbs that end in **-gar** change **-g** to **-gu** in all forms of the subjunctive. To form the present subjunctive of **-ar** verbs, drop **-o** from the **yo** form and add **-e** for **yo.**

40. **Es esencial que Eva no saque todas sus muñecas.** Verbs that end in **-car** change **-c** to **-qu** in all forms of the subjunctive. To form the present subjunctive of **-ar** verbs, drop **-o** from the **yo** form and add **-e** for **Eva.**

41. **Es esencial que tú no conduzcas al centro.** Conducir changes **-c** to **-zc** in its present tense **yo** form. To form the present subjunctive, drop the **-o** from **conduzco** and add **-as** as the ending for **tú.**

42. **Es esencial que Eva no coja todos los juguetes.** Verbs that end in **-ger** change **-g** to **-j** in all forms of the subjunctive. To form the present subjunctive of **-er** verbs, drop **-o** from the **yo** form and add **-a** for **Eva.**

43. **Es esencial que todos no distingan entre el bien y el mal.** Distinguir changes **-gu** to **-g** in its present tense **yo** form. To form the present subjunctive, drop the **-o** from **distingo** and add **-an** as the ending for **todos.**

44. **Es esencial que los niños no esparzan sus juguetes por todo el suelo.** Verbs that end in **-cer** change **-c** to **-z** in all forms of the subjunctive. To form the present subjunctive of **-ir** verbs, drop **-o** from the **yo** form and add **-an** for **los niños.**

45. **Es esencial que Roberto no finja tener hambre.** Verbs that end in **-gir** change **-g** to **-j** in all forms of the subjunctive. To form the present subjunctive of **-ir** verbs, drop **-o** from the **yo** form and add **-a** for **Roberto.**

46. **Es esencial que los niños no apaguen todas las luces.** Verbs that end in **-gar** change **-g** to **-gu** in all forms of the subjunctive. To form the present subjunctive of **-ar** verbs, drop **-o** from the **yo** form and add **-en** for **los niños.**

47. **almuerces.** Almorzar changes **-o** to **-ue** in all forms of the present subjunctive except **nosotros** and **vosotros.** In the present subjunctive, verbs ending in **-zar** change **-z** to **-c** in all forms. For **-ar** verbs, add **-es** for the subject **tú.**

48. **envíe.** Verbs that end in **-iar** have accent marks in all present subjunctive forms except **nosotros.** For **-ar** verbs, add **-e** for the subject **Linda.**

49. **juegue.** Jugar changes **-u** to **-ue** in all forms of the present subjunctive except **nosotros** and **vosotros.** In the present subjunctive, verbs ending in **-gar** change **-g** to **-gu** in all forms. For **-ar** verbs, add **-e** for the subject **Julio.**

50. **muera.** Morir changes **-o** to **-ue** in all forms of the present subjunctive except **nosotros** and **vosotros,** when **-o** changes to **-u.** For **-ir** verbs, add **-a** for the subject **todo el mundo.**

(51) **empiece. Empezar** changes **-e** to **-ie** in all forms of the present subjunctive except **nosotros** and **vosotros**. In the present subjunctive, verbs ending in **-zar** change **-z** to **-c** in all forms. For **-ar** verbs, add **-e** for the subject **mamá**.

(52) **prefiramos. Preferir** changes **-e** to **-ie** in all forms of the present subjunctive except **nosotros** and **vosotros** when **-e** changes to **-i**. For **-ir** verbs, add **-amos** for the subject **nosotros**.

(53) **quiera. Querer** changes **-er** to **-ie** in all forms except **nosotros** and **vosotros**. For **-er** verbs, add **-a** for the subject **papá**.

(54) **sirva. Servir** changes **-e** to **-i** in all forms of the present subjunctive. For **-ir** verbs, add **-a** for the subject **yo**.

(55) **muestren. Mostrar** changes **-o** to **-ue** in all forms of the present subjunctive except **nosotros** and **vosotros**. For **-ar** verbs, add **-en** for the subject **María y Clara**.

(56) **concluya.** Verbs that end in **-uir** (but not **-guir**) add a **-y** after the **-u** in all present subjunctive forms.

(57) **llegues, lleguemos.** In **-gar** verbs, **-g** changes to **-gu** in the subjunctive.

(58) **pierdas, perdamos.** The stem vowel changes from **-e** to **-ie** in all forms except **nosotros** and **vosotros**.

(59) **tengas, tengamos.** To form the subjunctive, take the **yo** form of the present tense and drop **-o**.

(60) **continúes, continuemos.** The stem vowel changes from **-u** to **-ú** in all forms except **nosotros** and **vosotros**.

(61) **muestres, mostremos.** The stem vowel changes from **-o** to **-ue** in all forms except **nosotros** and **vosotros**.

(62) **estés, estemos. Estar** has irregular subjunctive forms that must be memorized.

(63) **mastiques, mastiquemos.** In **-car** verbs, **-c** changes to **-qu** in the subjunctive.

(64) **vayas, vayamos. Ir** has irregular subjunctive forms that must be memorized.

(65) **mientas, mintamos.** The stem vowel changes from **e** to **ie** in all forms except **nosotros** and **vosotros**. In the nosotros and vosotros forms, the stem vowel **e** changes to **i**.

(66) **empieces, empecemos.** In **-zar** verbs, **-z** changes to **-c** in the subjunctive. The stem vowel changes from **-e** to **-ie** in all forms except **nosotros** and **vosotros**.

(67) **envíes, enviemos.** The stem vowel changes from **-i** to **-í** in all forms except **nosotros** and **vosotros**.

(68) **duermas, durmamos.** The stem vowel changes from **-o** to **-u** in all forms except **nosotros** and **vosotros**. In the nosotros and vosotros forms, the stem vowel changes o to u.

(69) **hagas, hagamos.** To form the subjunctive, take the **yo** form of the present tense and drop **-o**.

(70) **salgas, salgamos.** To form the subjunctive, take the **yo** form of the present tense and drop **-o**.

(71) **cierres, cerremos.** The stem vowel changes from **-e** to **-ie** in all forms except **nosotros** and **vosotros**.

(72) **traduzcas, traduzcamos.** In vowel + **-cir** verbs, **-z** changes to **-zc** in the subjunctive.

(73) **pidas, pidamos.** The stem vowel changes from **-e** to **-i** in all forms except **nosotros** and **vosotros.** In the nosotros and vosotros forms, the stem vowel -e changes to -i.

(74) **escojas, escojamos.** In **-ger** verbs, **-g** changes to **-j** in the subjunctive.

(75) **juegues, juguemos.** The stem vowel changes from **-u** to **-ue** in all forms except **nosotros** and **vosotros.** In **-gar** verbs, **-g** changes to **-gu** in the subjunctive.

(76) **almuerces, almorcemos.** In **-zar** verbs, **-z** changes to **-c** in the subjunctive. The stem vowel changes from **-o** to **-ue** in all forms except **nosotros** and **vosotros.**

(77) **seas, seamos. Ser** has irregular subjunctive forms that must be memorized.

(78) **des, demos. Dar** has irregular subjunctive forms that must be memorized.

(79) **Es preciso que todos busquen una orquesta.** In **-car** verbs, **-c** changes to **-qu** in the subjunctive.

(80) **Es urgente que Daniel le diga el menú al cocinero.** To form the subjunctive, take the **yo** form of the present tense and drop **-o.**

(81) **Es seguro que todo el mundo está nervioso.** You use the indicative because there is no doubt. **Estar** has irregular present tense forms that must be memorized.

(82) **Es indispensable que yo envíe las invitaciones.** The stem vowel changes from **-i** to **-í** in all forms except **nosotros** and **vosotros.**

(83) **Es importante que vosotros escojáis un buen restaurante.** In **-ger** verbs, **-g** changes to **-j** in the subjunctive.

(84) **No es evidente que todos los invitados vengan.** You need the subjunctive because the fact isn't evident, and, therefore, there is doubt. To form the subjunctive, take the **yo** form of the present tense and drop **-o.**

(85) **Es imperativo que tú sepas a quiénes quieres invitar. Saber** has irregular subjunctive forms that must be memorized.

(86) **Es cierto que vosotros tenéis muchos amigos.** You use the indicative because there is no doubt.

(87) **Es esencial que tu esposo pague con antelación.** In **-gar** verbs, **-g** changes to **-gu** in the subjunctive.

(88) **Es necesario que Estela le dé una lista de los invitados al propietario. Dar** has irregular subjunctive forms that must be memorized.

(89) **Conviene que yo organice actividades.** In **-zar** verbs, **-z** changes to **-c** in the subjunctive.

(90) **Está claro que esta fiesta va a ser maravillosa.** You use the indicative because there is no doubt.

(91) **haga.** To form the subjunctive, take the **yo** form of the present tense and drop **-o.**

(92) **sigan.** The stem vowel changes from **-e** to **-i** in all forms except **nosotros** and **vosotros.**

(93) **canta.** You use the indicative because there is no doubt.

(94) **aprenda. Aprender** is a regular verb in the subjunctive.

(95) **sepan. Saber** has irregular subjunctive forms that must be memorized.

(96) **vaya. Ir** has irregular subjunctive forms that must be memorized.

(97) **hablan.** You use the indicative because there is no doubt.

(98) **pueda.** The stem vowel changes from **-o** to **-ue** in all forms except **nosotros** and **vosotros.**

(99) **Estoy alegre de que mi casa valga mucho.** To form the subjunctive, take the **yo** form of the present tense and drop **-o.**

(100) **Estoy contenta de que mi jefe me ofrezca un aumento de salario.** In vowel + **-cer** verbs, **-z** changes to **-zc** in the subjunctive.

(101) **Estoy feliz de que mi hijo demuestre una aptitud para las ciencias.** The stem vowel changes from **-o** to **-ue** in all forms except **nosotros** and **vosotros.**

(102) **Estoy orgullosa de que mis hijos salgan bien en la escuela.** To form the subjunctive, take the **yo** form of the present tense and drop **-o.**

(103) **Estoy encantada de que mi familia venga a visitarnos.** To form the subjunctive, take the **yo** form of the present tense and drop **-o.**

(104) **Estoy asombrada de que tú quieras acompañarnos a Costa Rica.** The stem vowel changes from **-e** to **-ie** in all forms except **nosotros** and **vosotros.**

(105) **Yo busco una tienda que venda recuerdos. Vender** is a regular verb in the subjunctive.

(106) **Yo estoy sorprendido de que el tren no vaya al centro. Ir** has irregular subjunctive forms that must be memorized.

(107) **Es natural que el guía sepa las rutas más bellas. Saber** has irregular subjunctive forms that must be memorized.

(108) **¿Conoces a un chófer aquí que conduzca bien?** In vowel + **-cer** verbs, **-z** changes to **-zc** in the subjunctive. The question implies doubt.

(109) **Yo no dudo que la visita turística es interesante.** You use the indicative because there is no doubt.

(110) **Yo no creo que el museo esté cerrado. Estar** has irregular subjunctive forms that must be memorized.

(111) **Es una lástima que estos hombres cuelguen un cartel que indica: "No hay billetes."** The stem vowel changes from **-o** to **-ue** in all forms except **nosotros** and **vosotros.** In **-gar** verbs, **-g** changes to **-gu** in the subjunctive.

(112) **Está claro que el guía es bueno.** You use the indicative because there is no doubt.

Chapter **7**

Enriching Your Sentences with Adverbs and Comparisons

The adjectives presented in Chapter 4 certainly help you to be descriptive. Adverbs can also assist in accomplishing this objective. Your writing will be much more informative if you can vividly describe how the objects in your environment work or how the people who surround you act. Another useful tool is making comparisons, which will enrich your emails, notes, letters, prose, and compositions.

In this chapter, you discover how to form and place adverbs within Spanish sentences. Then you find out how to compare and contrast people, places, things, ideas, and activities. By the end of this chapter, you'll be able to express all your descriptive thoughts in Spanish.

Describing Verbs with Adverbs

The function of an adverb is to describe a verb, another adverb, or an adjective so your audience has a better understanding of how or to what degree or intensity an action is performed. Does a person run (very) quickly? Is their house very big? You use adverbs frequently when you express the manner in which things are done or to express time, frequency, and quantity. The following sections work on helping you form adverbs and position them correctly in sentences.

Forming adverbs

Many English adverbs end in **-ly,** and the equivalent Spanish ending is **-mente.** To form an adverb in Spanish, you add **-mente** to the feminine singular form of an adjective. Table 7-1 shows how it's done.

Table 7-1   Forming Various Types of Adverbs

Masc. Adj.	Fem. Adj.	Adverb	Meaning
completo	completa	completamente	*completely*
lento	lenta	lentamente	*slowly*
rápido	rápida	rápidamente	*quickly*
alegre	alegre	alegremente	*happily*
breve	breve	brevemente	*briefly*
frecuente	frecuente	frecuentemente	*frequently*
especial	especial	especialmente	*especially*
final	final	finalmente	*finally*
feroz	feroz	ferozmente	*ferociously*

REMEMBER

Unlike adjectives, which require agreement in gender and number with the nouns they describe, adverbs require no agreement because they modify verbs and not nouns or pronouns.

The following example shows an adverb in action:

> **Él entra rápidamente y ella sale rápidamente.** (*He enters quickly and she leaves quickly.*)

Adverbial phrases

Sometimes, using the feminine singular form of an adjective to form an adverb in Spanish can be quite awkward. When writing, you may find the spelling tricky. And at other times, you may not recall the feminine form of the adjective. Luckily, you have an easy way out. You can use the preposition **con** (*with*) + the noun to form an adverbial phrase, which functions in the same way as an adverb.

For instance, if you have trouble remembering or writing **cuidadosamente** (*carefully*), you can substitute **con cuidado** (*with care*) and your Spanish will be perfect. Here are some examples of how this works:

Con + Noun	Adverb	Meaning
con alegría	alegremente	*happily*
con claridad	claramente	*clearly*
con cortesía	cortésmente	*courteously*
con energía	enérgicamente	*energetically*
con habilidad	hábilmente	*skillfully*
con paciencia	pacientemente	*patiently*
con rapidez	rápidamente	*quickly*
con respeto	respetuosamente	*respectfully*

Here's an example of this construction:

Ella habla con respeto/respetuosamente. (*She speaks with respect/respectfully.*)

PRACTICE

Express how different people in your office work by replacing the phrase **con** + noun and using an adverb in the following sentences. This example shows you the way.

Q. **Jaime responde con respeto.**

A. **Jaime responde respetuosamente.** Change the adverbial phrase to an adverb. To the feminine adjective, **respetuosa**, add the adverbial ending **-mente**.

1 Estas mujeres hablan con franqueza.

_____

2 Ese hombre trabaja con cuidado.

_____

3 El jefe reacciona con rapidez.

_____

4 Yo escucho con atención.

_____

5 Clara se explica con claridad.

_____

6 Pilar contesta con cortesía.

_____

CHAPTER 7 Enriching Your Sentences with Adverbs and Comparisons   151

7 Miguel hace preguntas con frecuencia.

_____

8 Ana participa con felicidad.

_____

Now use an adverbial phrase to replace the adverb in each sentence.

PRACTICE

Express how the team members interact with each other.

Q. **El entrenador habla claramente.**

A. **El entrenador habla con claridad.**

9 Miguel ayuda a sus compañeros de equipo enérgicamente. _____

10 Los jugadores escuchan pacientemente. _____

11 Guillermo siempre responde respetuosamente. _____

12 Carlos y Nicolás corren rápidamente. _____

13 Domingo juega hábilmente. _____

14 Ramón anota (scores) frecuentemente. _____

Working with adverbs not formed from adjectives

Some adverbs and adverbial expressions aren't formed from adjectives; they're words or phrases in and of themselves. Table 7-2 lists some of the most frequently used words and phrases that fit this description.

Here's an example of one of these phrases in use:

Él acepta la responsabilidad de buena gana. (*He willingly accepts the responsibility.*)

Table 7-2   Frequently Used Adverbs and Adverbial Phrases

Adverb	Meaning	Adverb	Meaning
a menudo	*often*	**más**	*more*
a veces	*sometimes*	**más tarde**	*later*
ahora	*now*	**mejor**	*better*
ahora mismo	*right now*	**menos**	*less*
al fin	*finally*	**mientras**	*meanwhile*
allá	*there*	**muy**	*very*

Adverb	Meaning	Adverb	Meaning
aquí	*here*	peor	*worse*
ayer	*yesterday*	poco	*little*
bastante	*quite, rather, enough*	por consiguiente	*consequently*
casi	*almost*	por supuesto	*of course*
cerca	*near*	pronto	*soon*
de buena gana	*willingly*	pues	*then*
de nuevo	*again*	siempre	*always*
de repente	*suddenly*	sin embargo	*however, nevertheless*
de vez en cuando	*from time to time*	tal vez	*perhaps*
demasiado	*too*	también	*also, too*
despacio	*slowly*	tan	*as, so*
después	*afterward*	tarde	*late*
en seguida	*immediately*	temprano	*soon, early*
hoy	*today*	todavía	*still, yet*
hoy día	*nowadays*	todos los días	*everyday*
lejos	*far*	ya	*already*
mañana	*tomorrow*	ya no	*no longer*

Describe the actions of your friends by completing each sentence with an appropriate adverb or adverbial phrase from the list provided.

ahora	despacio	más tarde	por consiguiente
pronto	siempre	también	

Q. Carolina habla por teléfono en este momento. Ella habla _____.

A. ahora. She is speaking at this moment; therefore, she is speaking now.

15 Dolores estudia mucho. _____ recibe buenas notas.

16 Salvador es muy respetuoso. Él _____ dice "por favor" y "gracias."

17 Felipe es perezoso. Siempre quiere hacer su trabajo _____.

18 Yolanda escucha la música clásica y _____ la música rock.

19 Jaime no corre rápidamente. Al contrario, corre _____.

20 Paz va a llegar en cinco minutos. Va a llegar _____.

Adjectives versus adverbs

The use of certain adjectives and adverbs can require some thought and an understanding of the function of the parts of speech in English. Alas, their use in Spanish can be just as tricky. The following list presents some adjective/adverb situations that can trip you up when figuring out how to write these tools in Spanish:

» **Buen(o)(s)** and **mal(o)(s)** are adjectives (and must agree in number and gender with the nouns they modify) that mean *good* and *bad*, respectively, and **bien** and **mal** are adverbs (requiring no agreement) that mean *well* and *badly/poorly*, respectively.

  ● **Ellas tienen muchas buenas/malas ideas.** (*They have many good/bad ideas.*)

  ● **Elena juega bien/mal.** (*Elena plays well/poorly.*)

» The Spanish words **más** (*more*), **menos** (*less, fewer*), **mejor** (*better*), **peor** (*worse*), **mucho** (*much, many*), **poco** (*little, few*), and **demasiado** (*too [much], too [many]*) may be used as adjectives or adverbs.

  As adjectives, **más** and **menos** don't add any endings; **mejor** and **peor** add **-es** to agree only with noun plurals that they modify; and **mucho, poco,** and **demasiado** agree in number and gender with the nouns they modify. As adverbs, all these words don't add or change any endings. Look at the following sentences where adjectives appear in the first examples and adverbs are used in the second examples:

  ● **Samuel tiene más/menos energía.** (*Samuel has more/less energy.*)

    Samuel trabaja más/menos enérgicamente. (*Samuel works more/less energetically.*)

  ● **Teodoro tiene mejores/peores notas.** (*Theodore has better/worse notes.*)

    Teodoro se aplica mejor/peor. (*Theodore applies himself better/worse.*)

  ● **Da muchas/pocas/demasiadas excusas.** (*He gives many/few/too many excuses.*)

    Piensa mucho/poco/demasiado. (*He thinks a lot/a little/too much.*)

Describe the following workers by completing each sentence with the correct form of the adjective or adverb indicated.

PRACTICE

Q. (mucho) Alonso gana _____ porque hace _____ trabajo.

A. **Alonso gana mucho porque hace mucho trabajo. Mucho** is used as an adverb to describe the verb, **gana. Mucho** is a masculine singular adjective that describes the noun, **trabajo.**

21 (malo) Antonio reacciona _____ porque recibe _____ noticias.

22 (mejor) Carolina tiene _____ resultados porque trabaja _____.

23 (bien) El señor López es un _____ profesor porque enseña _____.

24 (más) Vicente tiene _____ dinero porque ahorra (*saves*) _____.

25 (demasiado) Felipe tiene _____ problemas porque se preocupa _____ de todo.

26 (poco) Clara tiene _____ energía porque come _____.

Positioning of adverbs

You generally place adverbs directly after the verb they modify. Sometimes, however, the position of the adverb is variable and is placed where you'd logically put an English adverb, as in the following examples:

¿Hablas español elocuentemente? (*Do you speak Spanish eloquently?*)

Afortunadamente, yo recibí el paquete. (*Fortunately, I received the package.*)

PRACTICE

Verónica and Juana are having an argument. Express how Verónica acts by putting the adverb in its appropriate place.

Q. Escucha. (atentamente)

A. **Escucha atentamente.** Adverbs are generally placed after the verbs they modify.

27 Habla. (francamente) _____

28 Grita en voz alta. (a menudo) _____

29 Culpa a su amiga. (frecuentemente) _____

30 Explica la situación. (mal) _____

31 Responde a su amiga. (impulsivamente) _____

32 Presenta su punto de vista. (bien) _____

Making Comparisons

You generally make comparisons by using adjectives or adverbs. You can make comparisons of equality or inequality, and you can use superlatives. Making comparisons in Spanish isn't always easy, but this section gives you all the tools you need to succeed.

Comparisons of equality

Comparisons of equality show that two things or people are the same. In Spanish, whether you're using an adjective or an adverb, you make the comparison the same way.

You use **tan** (*as*) + adjective or adverb + **como** (*as*), as shown here:

> **Dolores es tan concienzuda como Jorge.** (*Dolores is as conscientious as George.*)
>
> **Ella estudia tan diligentemente como él.** (*She studies as diligently as he does.*)

Remember that when you use an adjective, it must agree in number and gender with the subject.

REMEMBER You can make negative comparisons by putting **no** before the verb:

> **Tú no eres tan trabajadora como él.** (*You are not as hardworking as he is.*)
>
> **Tú no escuchas tan atentamente como Juan.** (*You don't listen as attentively as Juan.*)

TIP

Comparisons of inequality

Comparisons of inequality show that two things or people are not the same. As with comparisons of equality, whether you're using an adjective or an adverb, you make the comparison the same way. You create the comparison of inequality with **más** (*more*) or **menos** (*less*):

> **más** (**menos**) + adjective or adverb + **que** (*than*)

Here are two examples:

> **Diego es más/menos hablador que yo.** (*Diego is more/less talkative than I.*)
>
> **Diego habla más/menos que yo.** (*Diego talks more/less than I.*)

To form comparisons of inequality in Spanish, you must use the words **más** (*more*) or **menos** (*less*) before the adjective or after the verb you are describing. In other words, there is no way to express "taller" as one word in Spanish. You must say "*more tall*" or **más grande**.

WARNING

The superlative

The *superlative* shows that something (or someone) is the best or worst of its (or their) kind. You form the superlatives of adjectives as follows:

> Subject + verb + definite article (**el/la/los/las**) + **más/menos** (*more/less*) + adjective + **de** (*in*)

Here are two examples:

> **Ella es la más alta de su clase.** (*She is the tallest in her class.*)
>
> **Él es el menos atlético del equipo.** (*He is the least athletic on the team.*)

Note that a noun may be included as follows:

> Subject + **más/menos** + adjective + **de** + noun + verb + noun.

Here are some examples:

> **La estudiante más alta de la clase es Ana.** (*The tallest student in the class is Ana.*)

> **El jugador menos atlético del equipo es Juan.** (*The least athletic player on the team is Juan.*)

A shortened version is also acceptable:

> **La más alta es Ana.** (*Ana is the tallest.*)

> **El menos atlético es Juan.** (*Juan is the least athletic.*)

TIP

If the sentence contains a direct object, you form the superlative by inserting the noun after the definite article (**el/la/los/las**):

> **Ella prepara la paella más deliciosa del mundo.** (*She prepares the best paella in the world.*)

Now we come to adverbs. Superlatives of adverbs aren't distinguished from their comparative forms (see the previous sections):

WARNING

To form superlatives in Spanish, you must use the words **más** (*more*) or **menos** (*less*) before the adverb you are describing. In other words, there is no way to express "fastest" as one word in Spanish. You must say "*more fast*" or **más rápidamente** Note how adverbs are compared and that "**que**" followed by a noun indicates the superlative:

> Positive: **Él acepta críticas pacientemente.** (*He accepts criticism patiently.*)

> Comparative: **Él acepta críticas más (menos) pacientemente.** (*He accepts criticism more (less) patiently.*)

> Superlative: **Él acepta críticas más/menos pacientemente que los otros.** (*He accepts criticism more/less patiently than others.*)

REMEMBER

The adverbs **bien** (*well*) and **mal** (*poorly*) become **mejor** (*better*) and **peor** (*worse*), respectively, in their comparative and superlative (in parenthesis) forms and follow the verb or verb phrase they modify:

> **Tomás juega al fútbol mejor (que Javier).** (*Thomas plays soccer better than Javier.*)

> **Ella cocina peor (que yo).** (*She cooks worse than I do.*)

PRACTICE

For this exercise, write a journal entry in which you describe the things and people in town by forming comparisons with adjectives and adverbs. For each question, I provide the noun and the verb. Use the +, −, and = signs to determine the type of comparison and whether to use an adjective or an adverb. Make sure that all your adjectives agree with the nouns they modify. The following examples get you started.

Q. la iglesia es = magnífico/la catedral

A. **La iglesia es tan magnífica como la catedral.** Use **tan** to express *as* before the adjective and **como** to express *as* after the adjective.

Q. el metro llega + frecuente/el autobús

A. **El metro llega más frecuentemente que el autobús**. Use **más** to express *more* before the adjective and **que** to express *than* after the adjective.

(33) este rascacielos es + alto/ese edificio

_____

(34) estas calles son − estrecho/esas avenidas

_____

(35) esta boutique es = elegante/esos almacenes

_____

(36) este juez escucha − atento/ese abogado

_____

(37) estos chóferes de autobús conducen + bien/esos choferes de taxi

_____

(38) este doctor reflexiona = profundo/ese cirujano

_____

The absolute superlative

The *absolute superlative* it is used when no comparison is made. To form this basic construction, you add **-ísimo** (masc.); **-ísima** (fem.); **-ísimos** (masc. plural.); **-ísimas** (fem. plural.) to the adjective according to the gender (masculine or feminine) and number (singular or plural) of the noun being described. The meaning is the same as **muy** (*very*) + adjective:

> **La catedral es muy bella / La catedral es bellísima.** (*The cathedral is very beautiful.*)

> **Los edificios son muy altos / Los edificios son altísimos.** (*The buildings are very tall.*)

TIP

If the adjective ends in a consonant, simply add the correct superlative ending:

> **Esas muchachas son popularísimas.** (*Those girls are very popular.*)

Here are some more things you need to know to form the absolute superlative:

≫ You drop the final vowel of an adjective before adding **-ísimo** (**-a, -os, -as**):

  • **La casa es muy grande / La casa es grandísima.** (*The house is very large.*)

≫ You use **muchísimo** to express *very much*:

- **Te adoro muchísimo.** (*I adore you very much.*)

» Adjectives ending in **-co (-ca)**, **-go (-ga)**, or **-z** change **c** to **qu**, **g** to **gu**, and **z** to **c**, respectively, before adding **-ísimo:**

- **La torta es muy rica / La torta es riquísima.** (*The pie is very tasty.*)

- **El suéter es muy largo / El suéter es larguísimo.** (*The sweater is very long.*)

- **El juez es muy sagaz / El juez es sagacísimo.** (*The judge is very shrewd.*)

PRACTICE

Your friend is having a very bad day and is complaining about *everything*. Write down what they say so you can show it to them at a later date for a laugh. I provide the adjective in parentheses, and you create the absolute superlative form. Here's an example.

Q. (grande) Mis problemas son _____.

A. **Mis problemas son grandísimos. Problemas** is a masculine plural noun. Drop the **-e** from grande and add **-ísimos**.

39 (rico) Este pastel es _____.

40 (atroz) Estos crímenes son _____.

41 (largo) Este día es _____.

42 (mal) Estos hombres son _____.

43 (difícil) Esta situación es _____.

44 (aburrido) Estas películas son _____.

Answers to "Enriching Your Sentences with Adverbs and Comparisons" Practice Questions

The following are the answers to the practice questions presented in this chapter.

1. **Estas mujeres hablan francamente.** Change the adverbial phrase to an adverb. To the feminine adjective, **franca**, add the adverbial ending **-mente.**

2. **Ese hombre trabaja cuidadosamente.** Change the adverbial phrase to an adverb. To the feminine adjective, **cuidadosa,** add the adverbial ending **-mente.**

3. **El jefe reacciona rápidamente.** Change the adverbial phrase to an adverb. To the feminine adjective, **rápida,** add the adverbial ending **-mente.**

4. **Yo escucho atentamente.** Change the adverbial phrase to an adverb. To the feminine adjective, **atenta,** add the adverbial ending **-mente.**

5. **Clara se explica claramente.** Change the adverbial phrase to an adverb. To the feminine adjective, **clara,** add the adverbial ending **-mente.**

6. **Pilar contesta cortésmente.** Change the adverbial phrase to an adverb. To the feminine adjective, **cortés,** add the adverbial ending **-mente.**

7. **Miguel hace preguntas frecuentemente.** Change the adverbial phrase to an adverb. To the feminine adjective, **frecuente,** add the adverbial ending **-mente.**

8. **Ana participa felizmente.** Change the adverbial phrase to an adverb. To the feminine adjective, **feliz,** add the adverbial ending **-mente.**

9. Use **con** and the noun **energía.**

10. Use **con** and the noun **paciencia.**

11. Use **con** and the noun **respeto.**

12. Use **con** and the noun **rapidez.**

13. Use **con** and the noun **habilidad.**

14. Use **con** and the noun **frequencia.**

15. **por consiguiente.** (*Dolores studies a lot, consequently she receives good grades.*)

16. **siempre.** (*Salvador is very respectful and always says please and thank you.*)

17. **más tarde.** (*Felipe is lazy and always wants to do his work later.*)

18. **también.** (*Yolanda listens to classical music and also to rock music.*)

19. **despacio.** (*Jaime doesn't run quickly. On the contrary, he runs slowly.*)

20. **pronto.** (*Paz is going to arrive in five minutes. She is going to arrive soon.*)

(21) **mal/malas. Mal** is used as an adverb to describe the verb, **reacciona. Malas** is a feminine plural adjective that describes the noun, **noticias.**

(22) **mejores/mejor. Mejores** is a masculine plural adjective that describes the noun, **resultados. Mejor** is used as adverb to describe the verb, **trabaja.**

(23) **buen/bien. Buen** is a masculine singular adjective that describes the noun, **profesor.** Drop the **-o** from **bueno** before a masculine singular adjective. **Bien** is used as adverb to describe the verb, **enseña.**

(24) **más/más. Más** is a masculine singular adjective that describes the noun, **dinero. Más** is used as adverb to describe the verb, **ahorra.**

(25) **demasiadados/demasiado. Demasiados** is a masculine plural adjective that describes the noun, **problemas** (a masculine noun that ends in **-a**). **Demasiado** is used as adverb to describe the verb, **se preocupa.**

(26) **poca/poco. Poca** is a feminine singular adjective that describes the noun, **energía. Poco** is used as an adverb to describe the verb, **come.**

(27) **Habla francamente.** Adverbs are generally placed after the verbs they modify.

(28) **A menudo, grita en voz alta.** Sometimes the position of the adverb is variable and is placed where you'd logically put an English adverb.

(29) **Culpa frecuentemente a su amiga.** Adverbs are generally placed after the verbs they modify.

(30) **Explica mal la situación.** Adverbs are generally placed after the verbs they modify.

(31) **Responde impulsivamente a su amiga.** Adverbs are generally placed after the verbs they modify.

(32) **Presenta bien su punto de vista.** Adverbs are generally placed after the verbs they modify.

(33) **Este rascacielos es más alto que ese edificio.** Use **más** to express *more* before the adjective and **que** to express *than* after the adjective.

(34) **Estas calles son menos estrechas que esas avenidas.** Use **menos** to express *less* before the adjective and **que** to express *than* after the adjective.

(35) **Esta boutique es tan elegante como esos almacenes.** Use **tan** to express *as* before the adjective and **como** to express *as* after the adjective.

(36) **Este juez escucha menos atentamente que ese abogado.** Use **menos** to express *less* before the adverb and **que** to express *than* after the adjective.

(37) **Estos chóferes de autobús conducen mejor que esos choferes de taxi.** Use **mejor** to express *better* and **que** to express *than* before the noun.

(38) **Este doctor reflexiona tan profundamente como ese cirujano.** Use **tan** to express *as* before the adverb and **como** to express *as* after the adjective.

(39) **riquísimo. Pastel** is a masculine plural noun. Drop the **-o** from **rico**, change **-c** to **-qu**, and add **-ísimo.**

(40) **atrocísimos. Crímenes** is a masculine plural noun. Change **-z** from **atroz** to **-c** and add **-ísimos.**

(41) **larguísimo. Día** is a masculine singular noun. Drop the **-o** from **largo,** change **-g** to **-gu**, and add **-ísimo.**

(42) **malísimos. Hombres** is a masculine plural noun. **Mal** ends in a consonant. Add **-ísimos.**

(43) **dificilísima. Situación** is a feminine singular noun. **Difícil** ends in a consonant. Drop the accent and add **-ísima.**

(44) **aburridísimas. Películas** is a feminine plural noun. Drop the **-o** from **aburrido** and add **-ísimas.**

3
Giving and Obtaining Information

Chapter 8

Getting Answers with the Right Questions

Sometimes when you ask a question, all you want in return is a simple yes or no answer. No explanations needed. Other times, however, you're really interested in getting information. You want all the facts. As a student, traveler, or businessperson speaking Spanish, you'll need to know names, phone numbers, addresses, how much you have to pay — any one of a thousand possible things that beg for questions and answers.

Maybe the answers you're looking for are imperative, or perhaps you just want to give in to your curiosity. It doesn't matter. You need to know how to ask questions properly in Spanish so you receive the correct answers. And, of course, many people will have questions for you, and you'll have to provide the answers. There's no getting around that.

In this chapter, you find out how to obtain all the information you need — from easy yes or no questions to more detailed inquiries about who, what, when, where, how, or why. By the time you finish this chapter, you'll be proficient at not only asking questions but also giving appropriate answers to the questions others ask you.

Inquiring in Spanish

Curiosity has always been one of my most endearing personality traits. What can I say? I'm inquisitive about everything. And I'd venture to guess that many of you share my desire to learn as much as I can about everything I can. People like us ask a lot of questions. There's nothing wrong with that. Fortunately for you, asking questions in Spanish is a rather simple task.

You'll certainly need to use two main types of questions in Spanish: those that call for a "yes" or "no" answer and those that ask for more detailed facts. I cover these questions in the sections that follow

WARNING

The words *do* and *does* and sometimes *am*, *is*, and *are* don't translate from English into Spanish. In Spanish, these words are part of the meaning of the conjugated verb:

¿Te gusta este restaurante? (*Do you like this restaurant?*)

¿Vienen hoy? (*Are they coming today?*)

REMEMBER

Unlike in English, when you want to write a question in Spanish, you put an upside-down question mark (¿) at the beginning of the sentence and a standard question mark (?) at the end:

¿Tiene Ud. sed? (*Are you thirsty?*)

Asking Yes/No Questions

It's very easy to form a question in Spanish that requires a yes or no answer. You use the three simple methods that follow.

Intonation

Intonation is by far the easiest way to ask a question in Spanish. If you're speaking, all you need to do is raise your voice at the end of what was a statement and add an imaginary question mark at the end of your thought. When writing, you just write down your thought and put question marks before and after it. It's that simple. Here's an example:

Statement: **Ud. Quiere tomar algo.** (*You want to drink something.*)

Question: **¿Ud. quiere tomar algo?** (*Do you want to drink something?*)

TIP

To form a negative question, you simply put **no** before the conjugated Spanish verb:

¿Ud. no quiere tomar algo? (*Don't you want to drink something?*)

The tags "¿No es verdad?" "¿Verdad?"and "¿No?"

¿No es verdad? or simply ¿Verdad? or **¿No?** are *tags* (questions added to statements or questions for emphasis) that can have a variety of meanings:

>> *Isn't that so?*

>> *Right?*

>> *Isn't/doesn't he/she?*

>> *Aren't/don't they?*

>> *Aren't/don't we?*

>> *Aren't/don't you?*

You generally place **¿No es verdad? ¿Verdad?** or **¿No?** at the end of a statement — especially when *yes* is the expected answer:

> **Ud. quiere tomar algo. ¿(No es) Verdad?** (*You want to drink something, don't you?*)

> **Tenemos jugo. ¿No?** (*We have juice. right?*)

Inversion

Inversion means that you turn something around, whether it's a picture or words in a sentence. When forming a yes or no question in Spanish, you may invert the word order of the pronoun or the subject noun and its accompanying verb form. The following list details some different considerations when using inversion:

>> Spanish shows a lot of flexibility when it comes to question formation. When using inversion, the subject pronoun generally, but not necessarily, follows the conjugated verb. Note the position of the subject pronoun and the verb in the following questions:

- Intonation:
- **¿Ud. tiene sed?** (*Are you thirsty?*)
- **¿Ana habla inglés?** (*Does Ana speak English?*)
- Inversion:
- **¿Tiene Ud. sed? ¿Tiene sed Ud.?** (*Are you thirsty?*)
- **¿Habla Ana inglés? ¿Habla inglés Ana?** (*Does Ana speak English?*)

>> If the subject noun or pronoun is followed by two consecutive verbs, put the subject noun or pronoun after the conjugated verb or after the phrase containing the second verb (remember to keep the meaning of the phrase intact):

- Intonation
- **¿Uds. quieren comer?** (*Do you want to eat?*)
- **¿Pablo sabe nadar?** (*Does Pablo know how to swim?*)
- Inversion:
- **¿Quieren comer Uds.? ¿Quieren Uds. comer?** (*Do you want to eat?*)
- **¿Sabe nadar Pablo? ¿Sabe Pablo nadar?** (*Does Pablo know how to swim?*)

REMEMBER

>> In most instances, the subject pronoun is omitted in Spanish when the subject is obvious:

- **¿Quieres comer algo ahora?** (*Do you want to eat something now?*)

Apply the rules in this section to ask questions. You are with friends and you are hungry.

Q. Ask whether they are hungry using ¿ **Verdad?**

A. (Uds.) **Tienen hambre ¿Verdad?** The expression **tener hambre** means *to be hungry.* Use the **Uds.** form of **tener** to express the plural *you*: change **-e** to **-ie** and add the **-en** ending for **Uds.** Add the tag **¿No es verdad?** to form the question.

1. Ask whether they want to drink something using inversion.

   _____

2. Ask whether they can eat now using **¿No?**

   _____

3. Ask whether they eat chicken using inversion.

   _____

4. Ask whether they generally have lunch at one o'clock using **¿Verdad?**

   _____

Answering Questions with Yes and No

All speakers of a new language spend a lot of time asking questions, but many struggle to answer them. Where you can really shine and impress others is by providing information properly. You undoubtedly know how to answer *yes* in Spanish, because the word for *yes* (**sí**) is common in pop culture. Answering *no* requires a bit more work, because a simple *no* doesn't always suffice. Sometimes you need to express *nothing, nobody,* or other negative ideas. The following sections cover these topics in detail.

Saying yes

Saying *yes* in Spanish is really quite easy. You use **sí** to answer *yes* to a question:

> **¿Quieres salir conmigo?** (*Do you want to go out with me?*)
>
> **Sí, con mucho gusto.** (*Yes, I'd be delighted.*)

Saying no

The most common negative response to a question is a plain and simple **no** (*no, not*).

To make a sentence negative, you put **no** before the conjugated verb. **No** is often repeated for emphasis:

¿Tocas la guitarra? (*Do you play the guitar?*)

(No,) No toco la guitarra. (*[No,] I don't play the guitar.*)

Using other negatives

Other common negatives, which you may or may not use in conjunction with **no,** include the following:

Spanish	Negative English Equivalent
ni . . . ni	*neither . . . nor*
tampoco	*neither, not either*
jamás, nunca	*never, (not) ever*
nadie	*no one, nobody*
ninguno (-a)	*no, none, (not) any*
nada	*nothing*

The following details some general considerations when answering negatively in Spanish:

>> You generally place the negatives **nunca** (most commonly in poetic language only), **tampoco** and **nadie** before the conjugated verb. However, when a double negative is used, **ninguno** and **nada** tend to be placed after the verb and **no** is placed before the conjugated verb:

- **Nunca comprendo lo que Miguel dice.** (*I never understand what Michael says.*)

- **No tengo nada en el bolsillo.** (*I don't have anything in my pocket.*)

>> When you have two verbs in the negative answer, place **no** before the conjugated verb and put the other negative word after the infinitive:

- **No puedo comer ninguna comida picante.** (*I can't eat any spicy food.*)

>> You may also use negatives alone (without **no**):

- **¿Qué buscas?** (*What do you want?*) **Nada.** (*Nothing.*)

- **¿Dice mentiras ese muchacho?** (*Does that boy tell lies?*) **Nunca.** (*Never.*)

REMEMBER

Unlike in English, it's perfectly acceptable — and sometimes even necessary in common usage — for a Spanish sentence to contain a double negative. If **no** is one of the negatives, it precedes the conjugated verb and the second negative follows it. When **no** is omitted, the negative precedes the conjugated verb. Here are some examples of both:

- **No fumo nunca / Nunca fumo.** (*I never smoke.*)

- **No viene nadie / Nadie viene.** (*No one is coming.*)

Using nadie

Nadie can be the subject or the object of the verb. When **nadie** is the object of the verb, a preposition precedes it:

(Subject)	**Nadie habla.**	**No habla nadie.**	*No one speaks.*
(Object)	**No habla a nadie.**	**A nadie habla.**	*He speaks to no one.*
(Object)	**No habla de nadie.**	**De nadie habla.**	*He doesn't speak about anyone.*

Using ni . . . ni

In a **ni . . . ni** construction (*neither . . . nor*), the sentence usually begins with the word **no.** Each part of the **ni . . . ni** construction precedes the word or words being stressed. Each **ni,** therefore, may be used before a noun, an adjective, or an infinitive:

No nos gusta ni el café ni el té. (*We don't like coffee or tea.*)

Su coche no es ni grande ni pequeño. (*His car is neither big nor little.*)

No puedo ni cocinar ni coser. (*I can neither cook nor sew.*)

Using ninguno

Ninguno (*no, none [not] any*), when used before a masculine singular noun, drops the final **-o** and adds an accent to the **-u** (**ningún**). The feminine singular form is **ninguna.** No plural forms exist. Here are some examples of its usage:

¿Tiene algunos problemas? (*Do you have any problems?*)

No tengo problema ninguno. (*I don't have a problem.*)

No tengo ningún problema. (*I don't have a problem.*)

Question words requiring their opposite in the negative answers

When used in questions, some words require that you use negative words of opposite meaning in the responses. The following table presents these words:

If the Question Contains . . .	The Answer Should Contain . . .
alguien (*someone, anyone*)	**nadie** (*no one, nobody*)
siempre (*always*)	**jamás/nunca** (*never*)
algo (*something*)	**nada** (*nothing*)
también (*also*)	**tampoco** (*neither*)
alguno(a) (*some, any*)	**ninguno(a)** (*none, [not] any*)

Here's an example question and answer:

¿Ves algo? (*Do you see something?*)

No veo nada. (*I don't see anything.*)

Write a note to your parents explaining what you and your siblings don't do around the house (in other words, you skip out on your chores!). Use the clues provided to fill in the appropriate negative responses.

Q. (*not*) **Clarita _____ limpió la casa.**

EXAMPLE

A. **Clarita no limpió la casa.**

Queridos Paders,

(5. not) Yo _____ cocino porque tengo dolor de estómago.

(6. nobody) _____ no rega el jardin.

(7. not any) Diana no lava _____ plato.

(8. neither … nor) Enrique no da de comer _____ al perro _____ al gato.

(9. nothing) Ernesto no hace _____.

(10. either) _____ Esteban no arregla su cuarto.

(11. never) Rosa _____ plancha la ropa.

(12. never, anybody) Virginia _____ ayuda a _____.

Asking for Information

When a simple yes or no won't satisfy your curiosity, you need to know how to ask for more information in Spanish. Although the names sound a bit formidable, interrogative adjectives, interrogative adverbs, and interrogative pronouns are the tools that allow you to get all the facts you want and need. Find out how in the following sections.

Interrogative adjectives

The interrogative adjectives **¿Cuánto (-a, -os, -as)?** and **¿Qué?** precede nouns.

¿Cuánto (-a, -os, -as)?

You use the interrogative adjective **¿cuánto?** (*how much?/how many?*) before a noun when that noun may be counted or measured. **¿Cuánto?** varies and must agree in number and gender with the noun it describes: (Note that **cuánto, cuánta, cuántos,** and **cuántas** may also be used as interrogative pronouns. See the following table.)

	Masculine	Feminine
Singular	¿cuánto?	¿cuánta?
Plural	¿cuántos?	¿cuántas?

Here are some examples of **¿cuánto?** in use:

¿Cuánto dinero necesitas? (*How much money do you need?*)

¿Cuántos dólares ganan por hora? (*How many dollars do they earn per hour?*)

¿Cuánta energia te queda? (*How much energy do you have*)

¿Cuántas horas trabajan? (*How many hours do they work?*)

¿Qué?

The interrogative adjective **¿qué?** (*what?/which?*), on the other hand, is invariable (it doesn't change) and refers to a noun that isn't being counted.

¿Qué idiomas sabes hablar? (*What [Which] languages do you know how to speak?*)

REMEMBER

Prepositions are used before interrogative adjectives where logical:

¿De cuántos hombres hablan? (*How many men are you speaking about?*)

¿A qué hora sale el tren? (*At what time does the train leave?*)

Practice using the correct form of **¿cuánto? ¿qué?** in the following exercise.

PRACTICE

You are planning a party and discussing it with some friends, who are asking you questions. Complete each question with **¿qué?** or the correct form of **¿cuánto?**

Q. ¿_____ invitaciones envías?

A. **Cuántas.** Words that end in **-ción** are generally feminine. The **-es** ending indicates the plural. Use the feminine plural interrogative adjective **¿cuántas?** to express *how many?*

13 ¿_____ dinero puedes gastar?

14 ¿_____ personas vienen?

15 ¿_____ música piensas tocar?

16 ¿_____ refrescos tienes que comprar?

17 ¿_____ fruta vas a servir?

Interrogative adverbs

You use interrogative adverbs before verbs. You often use the following interrogative adverbs with an inverted subject and verb:

English Adverb	Spanish Interrogative Adverb
How?	**¿cómo?**
When?	**¿cuándo?**
Where (to)?	**¿dónde?**
Why? (for what reason)	**¿por qué?**

Here are a couple of these adverbs at work:

> **¿Cómo va Ud. a la oficina?** (*How do you get to work?*)

> **¿Dónde vive tu hermana?** (*Where does your sister live?*)

¿Dónde?

The prepositions **a** (*to*) and **de** (*from*) may be used with **¿dónde?** as follows:

> **¿Adónde quieren ir los niños?** (*Where do the children want to go?*)

> **¿De dónde es Ud.?** (*Where are you from?*)

¿Por qué?

¿Por qué? asks about a reason and, therefore, requires an answer with **porque** (*because*):

> **¿Por qué llora el niño?** (*Why [For what reason] is the boy crying?*)

> **Llora porque está enfermo.** (*He's crying because he is sick.*)

PRACTICE

Your Spanish pen pal is coming to visit you. Express each of the questions your friends are asking about him by following the example.

Q. Guillermo llega *mañana.*

A. **¿Cuándo llega Guillermo?** Guillermo is arriving tomorrow. Use **¿cuándo?** to ask when he will arrive and invert the subject and the verb.

18 Es *de Madrid.* _____

19 Llega a Boston *en avión.* _____

20 El avión aterriza *mañana.* _____

21 Pasa dos semanas *en mi casa.* _____

22 Viene *porque quiere perfeccionar su inglés.* _____

23 También va *a Nueva York.* _____

Interrogative pronouns

An interrogative pronoun asks a question. The following table presents the Spanish equivalents to English pronouns:

English Pronoun	Spanish Interrogative Pronoun
Who?	**¿quién(es)**
What? (Which one[s])	**¿cuál(es)?**
What?	**¿qué?**
How much?	**¿cuánto?**
How many?	**¿cuántos(as)?**

The following sections break down the characteristics of these interrogative pronouns.

¿Quién(es)?

¿Quién? (*who*) is used when asking about one person (irrespective of gender) while **¿Quiénes?** (*who*) anticipates a plural answer (irrespective of gender):

> **¿Quién llega?** (*Who is arriving?*)
>
> **Raquel llega.** (*Raquel is arriving.*)
>
> **¿Quiénes llegan?** (*Who is arriving?*)
>
> **Raquel y Domingo llegan.** (*Raquel and Domingo are arriving.*)

Prepositions may be used before **¿quién?** and **¿quiénes?** to ask questions:

> **¿A quiénes escribes?** (*To whom are you writing?*)
>
> **A mis padres.** (*To my parents.*)
>
> **¿De quién hablas?** (*About whom are you speaking?*)
>
> **De Luis.** (*About Luis*)
>
> **¿Con quién viajas?** (*With whom are you traveling?*)
>
> **Con mi novio.** (*With my boyfriend.*)
>
> **¿Para quién trabajas?** (*For whom do you work?*)
>
> **Para mi tío.** (*For my uncle.*)

Using **¿quién?** can be a little tricky, so see how well you can do with the exercise below.

PRACTICE

Ask what people are doing by using **¿quién?** and a preposition, if needed. Follow the example.

Q. Teodoro lee a sus abuelos.

A. **¿A quiénes lee?** Use the preposition **a** to express *to*. Use **¿quiénes?** to speak about more than one person.

24 Javier estudia *con esas muchachas.* _____

25 *Gloria y Susana* juegan al tenis. _____

26 Vicente telefonea a *Gloria.* _____

27 La señora Robles prepara la comida *para sus niños.* _____

28 *El señor Machado* repara su coche. _____

29 Estela habla *de su familia.* _____

¿Cuál(es)?

¿Cuál? (*which one, what*) is used when a singular answer is expected (irrespective of gender) while **¿Cuáles?** (*which ones*) anticipates a plural answer (irrespective of gender). Each asks about a choice or a selection, as illustrated in the following examples:

¿Cuál de las dos prefieres? (*Which of the two do you prefer?*)

Prefiero la roja. (*I prefer the red one.*)

¿Cuáles de estas blusas prefieres? (*Which of these blouses do you prefer?*)

Prefiero las rojas. (*I prefer the red ones.*)

¿Cuál es tu número de teléfono? (*What is your phone number?*)

Mi número de teléfono es 555-1234 (cinco, cinco, cinco, uno. dos, tres, cuatro).

(*My phone number is 555-1234.*)

¿Cuáles son los días de la semana? (*What are the days of the week?*)

Los días de la semana son lunes, martes, miércoles, jueves, viernes, sábado, y domingo. (*The days of the week are Monday, Tuesday, Wednesday, Thursday, Friday, Saturday, and Sunday.*)

¿Qué?

¿Qué? means *what* when it precedes a verb and asks about a definition, description, or an explanation. When **¿qué?** precedes a noun, it expresses *which*.

¿Qué es un gato? (*What is a cat?*)

¿Qué significa esto? (*What does that mean?*)

¿Qué hacen durante el verano? (*What are they doing during the summer?*)

TIP

As an adjective, **¿qué?** is generally used instead of **¿cuál(es)?**

¿Qué camisa deseas? (*What [Which] shirt do you want?*)

Prepositions may be used before **¿qué?** to ask questions:

¿Con qué trabaja Ud.? (*What are you working with?*)

¿De qué hablan? (*What are they talking about?*)

It's a good idea to practice when to use **¿qué?** and when to use **¿cuál(es)?**

PRACTICE

Imagine that you have a very curious young family member who is asking you questions to annoy you. Complete his questions to you using **¿qué?** or **¿cuál(es)?**

Q. ¿_____ estás haciendo?

A. Qué. Use ¿qué? to ask for an explanation.

30 ¿_____ es esto?

31 ¿_____ es la fecha de hoy?

32 ¿_____ día es hoy?

33 ¿_____ son los meses del año?

34 ¿_____ es tu deporte preferido?

35 ¿_____ tiempo hace hoy?

36 ¿_____ comes cuando tienes hambre?

37 ¿_____ son tus películas favoritas?

38 ¿_____ canción quieres escuchar?

¿Cuánto?

¿Cuánto? when it means *how much*, remains invariable.

¿Cuánto cuesta el boleto? (*How much does the ticket cost?*)

¿Cuánto? when it means *how many*, agrees in both number and gender with the noun being replaced:

¿Cuántos pasan el examen? (*How many are passing the test?*)

Try your hand at determining which form of **¿cuánto?** to use.

You are in a furniture store trying to purchase things for your new apartment. Complete the questions you might ask by using **¿cuánto(-a)(-s)?**

Q. Muchos clientes compran muebles. ¿_____ compran muebles nuevos?

A. Cuántos. When **¿cuánto?** means *how many,* it agrees in number and gender with the noun being replaced.

(39) ¿Estas mesas? ¿_____ cuestan?

(40) Muchas personas compran muebles. ¿_____ pagan en efectivo (*cash*)?

(41) ¿Los vendedores? ¿_____ ganan una gran comisión?

(42) ¿Este sofà? ¿_____ vale?

Hay

Hay (*there is/are?* or *is/are there?*) is the third-person singular present-tense form of the aux-iliary verb **haber** (*to have*). You use this verb impersonally (there is no specific subject, so **hay** remains invariable) both to ask and to answer the question you ask. You can use **hay** by itself or with a preceding question word:

> **¿(No) Hay un buen restaurante por aquí?** (*Is[n't] there a good restaurant nearby?*)

> **¿Dónde hay un buen restaurante por aquí?** (*Where is there a good restaurant nearby?*)

You will find that **hay** is very easy to use. Here's a quick practice exercise that should be a snap.

You are asking about a hotel room. Ask whether the following things are available.

Q. aire acondicionado

A. **¿Hay aire acondicionado?** Use **hay** to express *is there* and place it before the noun.

(43) un salón de belleza _____

(44) un centro de negocios _____

(45) cuidado de niños _____

(46) un gimnasio _____

Answering Information Questions

This section is chock-full of tips on how to answer questions that ask you for information in Spanish. Carefully consider what's being asked so you answer each question in an appropriate manner.

¿Cuánto(-a)(-s)?

When you see a question with **¿Cuánto(a)(s)** (*how much/many*), you answer with a number, an amount, or a quantity:

¿Cuánto cuesta este coche? (*How much does this car cost?*)

Diez mil dólares. (*10,000 dollars.*)

¿Cuántas horas me está esperando? (*How long have you been waiting for me?*)

Dos horas. (*Two hours.*)

¿Cuántos huevos necesitas? (*How many eggs do you need?*)

Una docena. (*A dozen.*)

¿Qué?

When you see a question with **¿Qué?** (*what*), answer according to the situation. As with the previous section, if the question contains a preposition, you must use that same preposition in the answer:

¿Qué estás haciendo? (*What are you doing?*)

Estoy escribiendo algo. (*I'm writing something.*)

¿Qué escribes? (*What are you writing?*)

Una carta. (*A letter.*)

¿Con qué escribes? (*With what are you writing?*)

Con un bolígrafo. (*With a ballpoint pen.*)

¿Cómo?

When you see a question with **¿Cómo?** (*how, what*), give the information or the explanation that's requested:

¿Cómo te llamas? (*What's your name?*)

Susana. (*Susan.*)

¿Cómo estás? (*How are you?*)

Muy bien, gracias. (*Very well, thank you.*)

¿Cómo prepara Ud. este plato? (*How do you prepare that dish?*)

Con mantequilla y crema. (*With butter and cream.*)

¿Cuándo?

When you see a question with **¿Cuándo?** (*when*), you answer with a specific time or an expression of time:

¿Cuándo empieza la película? (*When does the film begin?*)

En diez minutos. (*In 10 minutes.*)

A las tres y media. (*At 3:30.*)

Enseguida. (*Immediately.*)

¿Dónde?

When you see a question with **¿Dónde?** (*where*), you answer with the name of a place. You use the preposition **en** to express *in*:

¿Dónde vive Ud.? (*Where do you live?*)

En Nueva York. (*In New York.*)

¿Quién(es)?

When you see a question with **¿Quién(-es)?** (*who, whom*), answer with the name of a person.

REMEMBER

If the question contains a preposition — **a, de, con, para,** and so on — you must use that same preposition in the answer:

¿Quién te acompaña al espectáculo? (*Who is going with you to the show?*)

Isabel. (*Isabel.*)

¿A quién espera Ud.? (*Whom are you waiting for?*)

A mi novio. (*For my boyfriend.*)

¿Con quién vives? (*With whom do you live?*)

Con mis padres. (*With my parents.*)

Hay

When **hay** is used in the question, use **hay** to answer the question.

¿Hay un cine por aquí? (*Is there a movie theater nearby?*)

(No) Hay un cine por aquí. (*There is [isn't] a theater nearby.*)

Your friend has sent you an email to ask questions about your plans to go to a restaurant. Respond to his email by choosing the best answer from the following table.

(A) **cinco**	(D) **los tamales y los tacos**	(G) **en la Avenida Sexta**
(B) **ir al cine**	(E) **en taxi**	(H) **a eso de las siete**
(C) **porque sirve comida mexicana**	(F) **mi tío**	(I) **treinta dólares**

Q. ¿Cuánto cuesta una comida típica?

A. I. **treinta dólares.** The question is asking how much a meal costs. The answer must contain an amount in dollars.

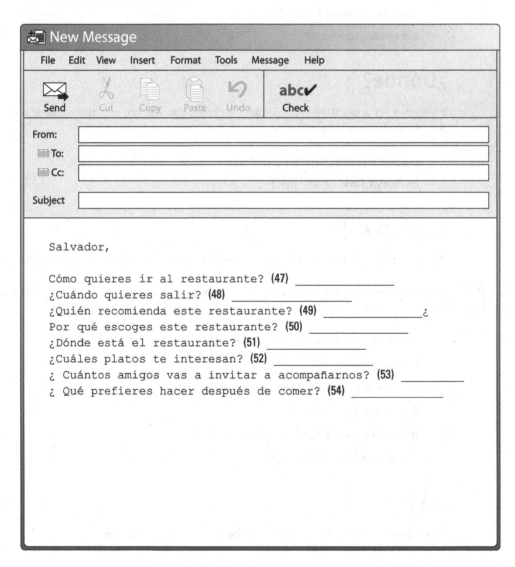

New Message

File   Edit   View   Insert   Format   Tools   Message   Help

Send   Cut   Copy   Paste   Undo   **abc✔** Check

From:
To:
Cc:
Subject

Salvador,

Cómo quieres ir al restaurante? **(47)** _____
¿Cuándo quieres salir? **(48)** _____
¿Quién recomienda este restaurante? **(49)** _____ ¿
Por qué escoges este restaurante? **(50)** _____
¿Dónde está el restaurante? **(51)** _____
¿Cuáles platos te interesan? **(52)** _____
¿ Cuántos amigos vas a invitar a acompañarnos? **(53)** _____
¿ Qué prefieres hacer después de comer? **(54)** _____

PRACTICE

Gisela has a new boyfriend, and her friend Elena is curious about him. Write Elena's questions based on Gisela's answers.

Q. Se llama *Guillermo*.

A. **¿Cómo se llama?** Use **¿Cómo?** to express *how*. (The literal meaning is *How is he called?*) Place **¿Cómo?** before the verb.

55 Tiene *veinticinco* años. _____

56 Es *grande, moreno* y *muy guapo.* _____

57 Es *de Perú.* _____

58 Hay *cinco* personas en su familia. _____

59 Ahora vive *en Boston.* _____

60 Vive *con sus hermanos.* _____

61 Estudia *la medicina.* _____

62 Estudia la medicina *porque quiere ser doctor.* _____

63 Su educación vale *mucho.* _____

64 Habla mucho *de sus estudios.* _____

65 *Sus hermanos* estudian la informática. _____

66 Sus deportes favoritos son *el fútbol y el tenis.* _____

67 Va *a Perú* en el verano. _____

68 Va a la universidad cada día *a las siete de la mañana.* _____

Answers to "Getting Answers with the Right Questions" Practice Questions

The following are the answers to the practice questions presented in this chapter.

(1) **¿Quieren Uds. beber algo?** Always invert with the first verb in the sentence. Use the **Uds.** form of **querer** to express the plural *you*: change **-e** to **-ie** and add the **-en** ending for **Uds.** Put an upside-down question mark at the beginning of the question. Invert the form of querer with **Uds.** Use the infinitive of **beber** (*to drink*). Use algo to express something. Put a question mark at the end of the sentence.

(2) **Uds. pueden comer ahora. ¿Está bien?** Use the **Uds.** form of **poder** to express the plural *you*: change **-o** to **-ue** and add the **-en** ending for **Uds.** Use the infinitive of **comer** (*to eat*). Use **ahora** to express *now*. Use the tag **¿Está bien?** to form the question.

(3) **¿Comen Uds. pollo?** Use the **Uds.** form of **comer** to express *Do you eat?* Put an upside-down question mark at the beginning of the question. Use **pollo** to express *chicken*.

(4) **Uds. almuerzan generalmente a la una. ¿Verdad?** Use the **Uds.** form of **almorzar** to express the plural *you*: change **-o** to **-ue** and add the **-an** ending for **Uds.** Use the adverb **generalmente** after the verb it modifies. Use **a la una** to express *at one o'clock*. Use the tag **¿Verdad?** to form the question.

(5) **no.** Use **no** to express *not*.

(6) **nadie.** Use **nadie** to express *not*.

(7) **ningún.** Use **ningún** to express *not any*. Drop the **-o** from **ninguno** and add an accent to the **-u** before a masculine singular noun.

(8) **ni . . . ni.** Use **ni . . . ni** to express *neither . . . nor* before each noun.

(9) **nada.** Use **nada** to express *nothing*.

(10) **tampoco.** Use **tampoco** to express *either*.

(11) **nunca.** Use **nunca** to express *never*.

(12) **nunca . . . nadie.** Use **nunca** to express *never* and **nadie** to express *anybody*.

(13) **Cuánto.** Words that end in **-o** are generally masculine. Use the masculine singular interrogative adjective **¿cuánto?** to express *how many?*

(14) **cuántas.** Words that end in **-a** are generally feminine. The **-as** ending indicates the plural. Use the feminine plural interrogative adjective **¿cuántas?** to express *how many?*

(15) **qué.** Because the amount or quantity of music isn't being measured, use the invariable **¿qué?** to express *what?*

(16) **cuántos.** Words that end in **-o** are generally masculine. The **-os** ending indicates the plural. Use the masculine plural interrogative adjective **¿cuántos?** to express *how many?*

(17) **cuánta.** Words that end in **-a** are generally feminine. Use the feminine singular interrogative adjective **¿cuánta?** to express *how many?*

(18) **¿De dónde es?** Use the preposition **de** before **¿dónde?** to replace **de Madrid** and to express *from where?*

(19) **¿Cómo llega a Boston?** Use **¿Cómo?** to express *how?* and to replace **en avión.**

(20) **¿Cuándo aterriza el avión?** Use **¿Cuándo?** to replace **mañana** and to express *when?* Invert the subject and the verb.

(21) **¿Dónde pasa dos semanas?** Use **¿Dónde?** to express *where?* and to replace **en mi casa.**

(22) **¿Por qué viene?** Use **¿Por qué?** to express *why?* and to replace the reason: **porque quiere perfeccionar su inglés.**

(23) **¿Adónde va también?** Use **¿Adónde?** to express *to where?* and to replace **a Nueva York.**

(24) **¿Con quiénes estudia?** Use the preposition **con** to express *with.* Use **¿quiénes?** to speak about more than one person.

(25) **¿Quiénes juegan al tenis?** Replace the plural subject with **¿quiénes?** to express *who?*

(26) **¿A quién telefonea Vicente?** Use the preposition **a** to express that Vicente calls Gloria. Use **¿quién?** to speak about one person, Gloria.

(27) **¿Para quiénes prepara la comida?** Use the preposition **para** (because it expresses a direction) to express *for.* Use **¿quiénes?** to speak about more than one person.

(28) **¿Quién repara su coche?** Replace the singular subject with **¿quién?** to express *who?*

(29) **¿De quién habla?** Use the preposition **de** to express *about.* Use **¿quién?** to speak about the collective noun, **la familia.**

(30) **qué.** Use **¿qué?** to ask for an explanation.

(31) **cuál.** Use **¿cuál?** when a singular answer is expected and when asking about a choice.

(32) **qué.** Use **¿qué?** to ask for an explanation.

(33) **cuáles.** Use **¿cuáles?** when a plural answer is expected and when asking about a selection.

(34) **cuál.** Use **¿cuál?** when a singular answer is expected and when asking about a choice.

(35) **qué.** Use **¿qué?** to ask for an explanation.

(36) **qué.** Use **¿qué?** when asking for an explanation.

(37) **cuáles.** Use **¿cuáles?** when a plural answer is expected and when asking about a selection.

(38) **qué.** As an adjective, **¿qué?** is used generally instead of **¿cuál?**

(39) **Cuánto. ¿Cuánto?** when it means *how much,* remains invariable.

(40) **Cuántas. ¿Cuánto?** when it means *how many,* agrees in both number and gender with the noun being replaced. **Personas** is feminine plural, therefore, **¿Cuántas?** is needed.

(41) **Cuántos, ¿Cuánto?** when it means *how many*, agrees in both number and gender with the noun being replaced. **Vendedores** is masculine plural, therefore, **¿Cuántos?** is needed.

(42) **Cuánto. ¿Cuánto?** when it means *how much*, remains invariable.

(43) **¿Hay un salón de belleza?** Use **hay** to express *is there* and place it before the noun.

(44) **¿Hay un centro de negocios?** Use **hay** to express *is there* and place it before the noun.

(45) **¿Hay cuidado de niños?** Use **hay** to express *is there* and place it before the noun.

(46) **¿Hay un gimnasio?** Use **hay** to express *is there* and place it before the noun.

(47) **E. en taxi.** The question is asking how to get to the restaurant. The answer must give a means of transportation.

(48) **H. a eso de las siete.** The question is asking when you want to leave. The answer must give a time.

(49) **F. mi tío.** The question is asking who recommends this restaurant. The answer must name a person.

(50) **C. porque sirve comida mexicana.** The question is asking why he recommends this restaurant. The answer must contain a reason preceded by *because* (**porque**).

(51) **G. en la Avenida Sexta.** The question is asking for the location of the restaurant. The answer must contain the name of a place.

(52) **D. los tamales y los tacos.** The question is asking what dishes he prefers. The answer must contain the names of foods.

(53) **A. cinco.** The question is asking how many friends will accompany them. The answer must contain a number.

(54) **B. ir al cine.** The question is asking what he prefers to do after dinner. The answer must contain an activity.

(55) **¿Cuántos años tiene?** Use **¿Cuántos?** to express *how many?* before the masculine plural noun **años.** Place **¿Cuántos?** before the verb.

(56) **¿Cómo es?** Use **¿Cómo?** to express *how?* Place **¿Cómo?** before the verb.

(57) **¿De dónde es?** Use the preposition **de** to express *from*. Use **¿dónde?** to express *where?* Place **¿De dónde?** before the verb.

(58) **¿Cuántas personas hay en su familia?** Use **¿Cuántas?** to express *how many?* before the feminine plural noun **personas.** Place **¿Cuántas?** before the verb.

(59) **¿Dónde vive ahora?** Use **¿dónde?** to express *where?* Place **¿Dónde?** before the verb.

(60) **¿Con quiénes vive?** Use the preposition **con** to express *with*. Use **¿quiénes?** to express *whom* before the feminine plural noun personas. Place **¿Con quiénes?** before the verb.

(61) **¿Qué estudia?** Use **¿Qué?** to express *what?* Place **¿Qué?** before the verb.

(62) **¿Por qué estudia la medicina? Porque** (*because*) is giving a reason. Use **¿Por qué?** to express *why?* Place **¿Por qué?** before the verb.

Chapter 9

Being Clear and Concise with Object Pronouns

magine that you're sitting in the food court of your local mall, eating a fabulous-looking hot-fudge sundae with mint chocolate chip ice cream. A friend stops to chat and says: "Wow! What a delicious-looking sundae! Can I see your sundae? Can I taste your sundae? Give me the sundae. Where can I buy that sundae? Do they make that sundae every day? I want that sundae!" Overly fixated on what you're consuming, your friend uses the word *sundae* to the point of being boring and downright annoying. Can you help your friend expand their horizons? Sure you can.

If you want to speak freely and naturally, and if you want to sound as if Spanish comes quite naturally to you, you must step up and master the use of direct and indirect object pronouns. You'll be glad you did, because your Spanish will sound more colloquial and more fluent. In the previous example, the trick is to use the direct object pronoun *it* to avoid repetition of the direct object noun *sundae*. Can an indirect object pronoun also substitute for an indirect object noun? Of course. Here's an example: "My grandfather is old. I read to my grandfather. I send cards to my grandfather. I write emails to my grandfather." You can vary your wording by substituting the indirect object pronoun "him" for the indirect object noun "my grandfather."

In this chapter, you see the difference between direct and indirect object nouns and pronouns, and you find out how to use them properly in the sentences you want to create. You'll know which verbs require a direct or indirect object pronoun so that selecting the one you need isn't a guessing game. You also discover how to place these words correctly within your sentences. By the end of this chapter, you'll be writing and speaking a much clearer and more concise sentence in Spanish.

Dealing Directly with Direct Object Pronouns

A direct object pronoun is a replacement word for a direct object noun. This pronoun helps you avoid unnecessary, continuous repetition of the noun, which allows for a more colloquial, free-flowing conversational tone when you're speaking or writing. Don't be tricked by these pronouns. Remember that the verb in your sentence must always agree with the subject pronoun.

Understanding direct object pronouns

Direct object nouns or *pronouns* answer the question, "Whom or what is the subject acting upon?" Direct objects may refer to people, places, things, or ideas. A direct object pronoun simply replaces a direct object noun and agrees with it in number and gender.

WARNING

In both English and Spanish, a direct object noun follows the subject and its verb:

> **Yo veo la casa.** (*I see the house.*)

Unlike in English, however, you usually place a Spanish direct object pronoun before the conjugated verb:

> **Yo la veo.** (*I see it.*)

Table 9-1 lists the direct object pronouns in Spanish.

Table 9-1   **Spanish Direct Object Pronouns**

Singular Pronouns	Meaning	Plural Pronouns	Meaning
me	*me*	**nos**	*us*
te	*you* (familiar)	**os**	*you* (polite)
lo	*him, it, you*	**los**	*them, you*
la	*her, it, you*	**las**	*them, you*

Here are some example sentences that show you how to use Spanish direct object pronouns:

> **Él me comprende.** (*He understands me.*)
>
> **¿Nos ve Ud.?** (*Do you see us?*)
>
> **¿Los periódicos? Yo los leo cada día.** (*The newspapers? I read them every day.*)

REMEMBER In certain areas of Spain, people may incorrectly use the indirect object **le** rather than the direct object **lo** to express *him/her/them*. This is known as *leísmo*. In South America, however, **Lo** is used as the direct object pronoun. The plural of **lo** and **le** is **los,** which means *them* or *you*. Here are some examples:

> **Cuido al niño.** (*I watch the child.*)
>
> **Lo [Le] cuido.** (*I watch him.*)
>
> **Cuido a los niños.** (*I watch the children.*)
>
> **Los cuido.** (*I watch them.*)
>
> **Ayudé a la niña.** (*I helped the child.*)
>
> **La [Le] ayudé.** (*I helped her.*)
>
> **Ayudé a las niñas.** (*I helped the children.*)
>
> **Las ayudé.** (*I helped them.*)

PRACTICE Complete the following journal entries in which you explain what you bought during your travels and what you did with these items. To complete your entries, you must insert the correct direct object pronoun. Here's an example to get you started:

Q. Compré un poster y _____ admiré.

A. Compré un poster y <u>lo</u> admiré.

1. Compré una chaqueta y _____ llevé.

2. Compré tarjetas postales y _____ envié a mis amigos.

3. Compré un libro y _____ leí.

4. Compré recuerdos y _____ guardé.

5. Compré camisetas y _____ mostré a mi amiga.

6. Compré una guía y _____ estudié.

7. Compré sombreros y _____ usé.

8. Compré un plano de la ciudad y _____ miré.

Getting personal with the personal "a"

In Spanish, the personal **a** conveys absolutely no meaning and is used only before a direct object noun (not before a direct object pronoun or any indirect objects) to indicate that it refers to a person or a beloved pet. (I hope you aren't too surprised by this!) The following list explains in more detail how to use the personal **a**:

>> You use the personal **a** before a common or proper noun that refers to a person or persons. The personal **a** combines with the definite article **el** (see Chapter 3) to form the contraction **al,** but it doesn't combine with the other definite articles:

- **No conozco a las niñas.** (*I don't know the children.*)
- **Busco al señor Gómez.** (*I'm looking for Mr. Gómez.*)
- **Visitamos a la señora Perón.** (*We visited Mrs. Perón.*)

>> You use the personal **a** before the name of your pooch, tabby, hamster, turtle, or other pet:

- **Adiestró a Fido.** (*She tamed Fido.*)
- **Llamé a Boots.** (*I called Boots.*)

>> You use the personal **a** before an indefinite pronoun that refers to a person:

- **No espero a nadie.** (*I'm not waiting for anyone.*)

WARNING

You don't, however, use the personal **a** with the verb **tener** (*to have*):

Tengo dos hermanos. (*I have two brothers.*)

PRACTICE

Write a journal entry in which you express what you and your family members intend to do by using the verb **pensar** as shown in the example. when you take a trip to Argentina. For each question, I provide the subject, the verb, and the direct object noun. You must combine the elements between the slashes by conjugating the verb in the present tense and by correctly adding the personal **a.**

Q. nosotros/ver/nuestros primos

A. **Nosotros** <u>**pensamos**</u> **ver a nuestros primos. Pensar** is a stem-changing **-ar** verb. Change **-e** to **-ie** in all forms except **nosotros** and **vosotros** and add the **-ar** verb endings. Follow the conjugated form of **pensar** with the infinitive, **ver.** Add the personal **a** before **nuestros primos** (*our cousins*).

9 yo/ver/mi familia

_____

10 mis hijos/conocer/alcalde de Buenos Aires

_____

11 nosotros/invitar/las primas de nuestros amigos

_____

12 José/visitar/Carlota Hernández

_____

13 tú/buscar/señor Rueda

_____

14 vosotros/admirar/todos los niños

_____

I'm sure you found that exercise rather easy. Now try an exercise where you get to put all the direct object pronouns to use.

PRACTICE

Express what the following people and their acquaintances do by completing the sentences according to the model, writing the reciprocal action.

Q. Clarita saluda a sus amigos y ellos _____ también.

A. **la saludan.** Use **la** to express _her._ Conjugate **saludar** to agree with the new subject, **ellos.** Put the pronoun before the verb.

15 Yo veo a Claudio y él _____ también.

16 Las muchachas conocen a los muchachos y ellos _____ también.

17 Guillermo adora a Gisela y ella _____ también.

18 Tú buscas a León y él _____ también.

19 Nosotros ayudamos a nuestros amigos y ellos _____ también.

20 Vosotros visitáis a vuestros abuelos y ellos _____ también.

Using Indirect Object Pronouns

Indirect object nouns or _pronouns_ refer only to people (and to beloved pets); they answer the question _to_ or _for_ whom the subject is doing something. An indirect object pronoun can replace an indirect object noun but can also be used in Spanish when the indirect object noun is included in the sentence. (In the second example below, the indirect object noun, **Gloria**, is used in addition to the indirect object pronoun, **le.**) Just like with direct object pronouns, indirect object pronouns are generally placed before the conjugated verb. For example:

Le escribo un email. (_I'm writing an email to him._)

Le escribo a Gloria un email. (_I'm writing an email to Gloria._)

Table 9-2 presents the indirect object pronouns in Spanish.

Table 9-2 Spanish Indirect Object Pronouns

Singular Pronouns	Meaning	Plural Pronouns	Meaning
me	*to/for me*	nos	*to/for us*
te	*to/for you* (familiar)	os	*to/for you* (familiar)
le	*to/for him, her, you* (formal)	les	*to/for them, you* (formal)

The following sentences show you how to use indirect object pronouns:

¿Me dices la verdad? (*Are you telling me the truth?*)

La mujer nos ofrece un refresco. (*The lady offers us a drink.*)

Les doy un abrazo. (*I give them a hug.*)

TIP

A clue that may indicate that you need an indirect object pronoun is the use of the preposition **a** (**al, a la, a los,** or **a las**), which means *to* or *for* (unlike the personal **a,** which has no meaning [see the previous section]), followed by the name of or reference to a person. You may use **a él, a ella,** or **a Ud.** or the person's name to clarify to whom you're referring:

Yo le escribo a Rosa. (*I write to Rosa.*)

Yo le escribo. (*I write to her.*)

Ella le habla al niño. (*She speaks to the child.*)

Ella le habla. (*She speaks to him.*)

Ella le habla a Juan. (*She speaks to Juan.*)

Ella le habla a él. (*She speaks to him.*)

WARNING

Although you may use the prepositions *to* and *for* in English, you can omit these prepositions in Spanish sentences before an indirect object pronoun:

Te compro un regalo. (*I'm buying a present for you / I'm buying you a present.*)

Me escriben. (*They are writing to me / They are writing me.*)

PRACTICE

Write a text message to a friend explaining what's happening at Linda's party by combining all the elements I provide (remember to conjugate the verb in the present tense) and inserting the proper indirect object pronoun. Here's an example:

Q. Linda/leer una carta/a sus padres.

A. **Linda les lee una carta a sus padres.** Use the indirect object pronoun **les** to reinforce the indirect object **a sus padres.** Put **les** before the conjugated form of the **-er** verb **leer** that agrees with the subject, **Linda.**

21 Carlos/pedir una rebanada del pastel/a vosotros

_____

22 yo/contar todo/a tí

_____

23 tú/telefonear/a tus amigos

_____

24 Juana y yo/dar un regalo/a Linda

_____

25 Linda/servir refrescos/a nosotros

_____

26 Gloria/ofrecer un sándwich/a mí

_____

Selecting a Direct or an Indirect Object Pronoun

Sometimes people get confused when trying to figure out whether to use a direct object pronoun or an indirect object pronoun. The good news is you'll have absolutely no problem with **me, te, nos,** and **os** because they act as both direct and indirect object pronouns. They're also reflexive pronouns (see Chapter 10):

> **Me respeta.** (_He respects me._) (_direct object pronoun_)
>
> **Me dice un secreto.** (_He tells me a secret./He tells a secret to me._) (_indirect object pronoun_)
>
> **Nos visita.** (_She visits us._) (_direct object pronoun_)
>
> **Nos trae flores.** (_She brings us flowers./She brings flowers to us._) (_indirect object pronoun_)

TIP

If you can somehow use the word _to_ or _for_ in an English sentence before a reference to a person — no matter how awkward the construction may seem — you must use an indirect object pronoun in your Spanish sentence.

> **Quiero mostrarte esta foto.** (_I want to show [to you] this photo._)

The following sections give you some more "insider" tips that will help you decide whether to use a direct or an indirect object.

Common Spanish verbs requiring a direct object

Verbs that require an indirect object in English may require a direct object in Spanish because *to* or *for* is included in the meaning of the infinitive. (Remember that any **a** you see will be the personal **a** [see the earlier section on this topic].) Some of these high-frequency verbs include the following:

>> **buscar** (*to look for*)

>> **escuchar** (*to listen to*)

>> **esperar** (*to wait for*)

>> **llamar** (*to call*)

>> **mirar** (*to look at*)

The following examples illustrate how you use these verbs:

Nosotros esperamos a nuestros amigos. (*We are waiting for our friends.*)

Nosotros los esperamos. (*We are waiting for them.*)

Busco a mi perro. (*I'm looking for my dog.*)

Lo busco. (*I'm looking for it.*)

Common Spanish verbs requiring an indirect object

Verbs that require a direct object in English don't necessarily require a direct object in Spanish. The verbs that follow take indirect objects in Spanish, regardless of the object used in English. This is because *to* or *for* is implied when speaking to a person or because the verb generally is followed by the preposition **a:**

acompañar (*to accompany*)	**obedecer** (*to obey*)
aconsejar (*to advise*)	**ofrecer** (*to offer*)
contar (*to relate, tell*)	**pedir** (*to ask*)
contestar (*to answer*)	**preguntar** (*to ask*)
dar (*to give*)	**presentar** (*to introduce*)
decir (*to say, tell*)	**prestar** (*to lend*)
enviar (*to send*)	**prohibir** (*to forbid*)
escribir (*to write*)	**prometer** (*to promise*)
explicar (*to explain*)	**regalar** (*to give a gift*)
llamar (*to call*)	**telefonear** (*to call*)
mandar (*to send*)	

Here are a few examples:

Te aconsejo practicar más. (*I advise you to practice more.*)

Ella le pide disculpa a su amiga. (*She asks her friend for an apology.*)

Me regala un reloj. (*He is giving me a watch as a gift.*)

PRACTICE

Your friend Marta is having problems. Complete the following email to another friend with the proper direct or indirect object pronoun to explain what you do to help. Here's an example:

Q. Yo _____ telefoneo a menudo.

A. Yo <u>le</u> telefoneo a menudo. **Telefonear** takes an indirect object pronoun.

27 Yo _____ short llamo.

28 Yo _____ aconsejo.

29 Yo _____ busco todo el tiempo.

30 Yo _____ escucho.

31 Yo _____ doy mi opinión.

32 Yo _____ digo francamente lo que pienso.

33 Yo _____ ofrezco ayuda.

34 Yo _____ espero cuando quiere hablarme.

Placing Object Pronouns Correctly

How do you decide where to place a direct or indirect object pronoun in a Spanish sentence? Generally, you place these pronouns before the conjugated verb:

> **Nosotros los necesitamos.** (*We need them.*)

> **Siempre les cuentas chistes.** (*You always tell them jokes.*)

In sentences with two verbs (the second being the infinitive) that follow one subject or in sentences with a gerund (the **-ando** or **-iendo** forms; see Chapter 5), you have the choice of placing the object pronoun before the conjugated verb or after and attached to the infinitive or the gerund. The following examples demonstrate this construction.

REMEMBER

When you attach the pronoun to the gerund, an accent is required on the stressed vowel. In general, to correctly place the accent, you count back three vowels and add the accent. Also, remember that negatives go before the pronoun when it precedes the verb.

>> With an infinitive:

- **(No) Lo quiero hacer.** (*I [don't] want to do it.*)

- **(No) Quiero hacerlo.** (*I [don't] want to do it.*)

➤ With a gerund:

- **(No) Lo estoy haciendo.** (*I'm [not] doing it.*)
- **(No) Estoy haciéndolo.** (*I'm [not] doing it.*)

PRACTICE

For this exercise, write out what your plans are with an acquaintance. Place the indirect or direct object pronoun (provided in parentheses) in its proper place in each sentence. You must decide whether to use a direct or indirect object pronoun to replace the indicated noun and then you must put the pronoun in its proper place in the sentence. Where appropriate, provide both correct responses. Here's are some examples to get you started:

Q. (las muchachas) necesito telefonear.

A. **Necesito telefonearles. (Les necesito telefonear.) Telefonear** takes an indirect object. Use **les** to refer to **las muchachas**. Place **les** after the infinitive (**telefonear**) and attached to it. Alternatively, put **les** before the conjugated verb (**necesito**).

Q. (el césped) no quiero cortar.

A. No quiero cortarlo. (**No lo** quiero cortar.) **Cortar** takes a direct object. Use **lo** to refer to **el césped**. Place **lo** after the infinitive (**cortar**) and attached to it. Alternatively, put **lo** before the conjugated verb (**quiero**).

35 (los muebles) puedo sacudir

_____

36 (a María) no debo decir nuestros planes

_____

37 (la aspiradora) no prefiero pasar

_____

38 (a mi padre) deseo pedir dinero

_____

39 (a Ramón y a Jorge) pienso dar consejos

_____

40 (a mis primos) quiero llamar

_____

PRACTICE

Now do the same, using direct and indirect object pronouns, by asking your friend questions.

Q. (la cena) ¿estás comiendo?

A. **¿Estás comiéndola? (¿La estás comiendo?) Comer** takes a direct object. Use **la** to refer to **la cena.** Place **la** after the gerund (**comiendo**) and attached to it. Count back three vowels and add an accent. Alternatively, put **la** before the conjugated verb (**estás**).

Q. (a tu novio) ¿estás explicando tus sentimientos?

A. **¿Estás explicándole tus sentimientos? (¿Le estás explicando tus sentimientos?) Explicar** takes an indirect object. Use **le** to refer to **a tu novio.** Place **le** after the gerund (**explicando**) and attached to it. Count back three vowels and add an accent. Alternatively, put **le** before the conjugated verb (**estás**).

41 (las noticias) ¿por qué estás mirando?

_____

42 (a Julia) ¿no estás hablando?

_____

43 (ejercicios) ¿estás haciendo?

_____

44 (el piano) ¿estás tocando?

_____

45 (a tu amigo por correspondencia) ¿no estás escribiendo?

_____

46 (a sus hermanas) ¿estás leyendo?

_____

Doing Double Duty with Double Object Pronouns

It's quite common in Spanish that a sentence requires both a direct and an indirect object pronoun. You have many rules to consider when creating these sentences, as the following list shows:

>> When the verb has two object pronouns, the indirect object pronoun (a person) precedes the direct object pronoun (usually a thing):

- **Ella nos muestra las revistas.** (*She shows us the magazines.*)

- **Ella nos las muestra.** (*She shows them to us.*)

- **Nosotros te damos el boleto.** (*We give you the ticket.*)

- **Nosotros te lo damos.** (*We give it to you.*)

» When a sentence has two third-person object pronouns, the indirect object pronouns **le** and **les** change to **se** before the direct object pronouns **lo, la, los,** and **las:**

- **Él les lee las revistas a sus abuelos.** (*He reads the magazines to his grandparents.*)

- **Él se las lee.** (*He reads them to you [him, her].*)

TIP

To clarify the meaning of **se** — because it can mean *to/for you, him, her,* and *them* — you may include the phrases **a Ud. (Uds.), a él (ellos), a ella (ellas)** or the specific noun:

- **Yo se lo explico a él (a ella) (a Uds.) (a mi[s] amigo[s]), (a mi[s] prima[s]) (a Juan [y a Ana]).** (*I explain it to him [her] [you][my friend(s), [my cousin[s])], [Juan (and Ana)].*)

The same rules for the positioning of single object pronouns apply for double object pronouns. (See the previous section.) The following examples show how you use and place double object pronouns:

TIP

» With an infinitive, you may place the two separate pronouns before the conjugated verb, or you may connect and attach them to the end of the infinitive and add an accent to the stressed syllable.

To find the stressed vowel, you generally count back three vowels and add an accent.

- **(No) Te los quiero mostrar.** (*I [don't] want to show them to you.*)

- **(No) Quiero mostrártelos.** (*I [don't] want to show them to you.*)

TIP

» With a gerund, you may place the two separate pronouns before the conjugated form of **estar,** or you may connect and attach them to the end of the gerund and attach an accent to the stressed vowel.

To find the stressed vowel, you generally count back four vowels and add an accent.

- **(No) Se la estoy leyendo a él.** (*I'm [not] reading it to him.*)

- **(No) Estoy leyéndosela.** (*I'm [not] reading it to him.*)

PRACTICE

You're helping your younger brother do his homework, in which he must discuss the jobs people perform. Make his sentences shorter by replacing the direct and indirect object nouns with pronouns. I provide the subject and the conjugated verb forms as well as the indirect and object nouns in parentheses. You must replace the nouns with pronouns and place them properly within the sentence. Here's an example:

Q. el peluquero corta (el pelo/a tí)

A. **El peluquero *te lo* corta.** Replace the masculine singular direct object noun, **el pelo** with **lo.** Use the indirect object pronoun **te** to replace **a tí.** The indirect object precedes the direct object noun. Place both before the conjugated verb.

47 el cartero trae (el correo/a la gente)

_____

48 la profesora enseña (la gramática/a los alumnos)

_____

49 el dentista quiere extraer (los dientes/a tí)

_____

50 el cajero está dando (la moneda/a nosotros)

_____

51 el comerciante no vende (las mercancías/a sus competidores)

_____

52 el banquero no va a cambiar (dinero/a todos los turistas)

_____

53 el juez está explicando (las leyes/a los criminales)

_____

54 el poeta escribe (poemas/a su novia)

_____

55 el artista muestra (sus obras/a vosotros)

_____

56 el panadero puede vender (pasteles/a mí)

_____

57 el doctor está recetando (medicina/a los enfermos)

_____

58 la secretaria no escribe (cartas/a Uds.)

_____

Getting by with Gustar

During any average day, most people have occasion to express their likes and dislikes. To do so in Spanish, you have to use the verb **gustar** (*to please*). **Gustar** requires special attention because although you can say *I like* in English, in Spanish, you have to say that something is pleasing to you. This means that Spanish sentences appear somewhat backward to English speakers. This also means (since something is pleasing *to* the subject) that **gustar** always requires the use of an indirect object pronoun. Note how the English and Spanish sentences convey the same meaning but are expressed in a totally different fashion:

> English: *I like chocolate.*

> Spanish: **Me gusta el chocolate**. (*Chocolate is pleasing to me.*)

As you can see, in English, the subject *I* is followed by the verb *like,* which in turn is followed by the direct object *chocolate.* In Spanish, however, *chocolate* becomes the subject. The verb *is pleasing* agrees with the subject *chocolate,* and *to me* is the indirect object. So your sentence in Spanish reads as follows: **Me gusta el chocolate.** Using **gustar** is a little confusing at first, but you'll quickly get the hang of it.

Here are more examples to show you how **gustar** works:

> **¿Te gustan los deportes?** (*Do you like sports?*)

> **A nosotros nos gusta esa película.** (*We like that film.*)

> **A ella no le gustan las frutas.** (*She doesn't like fruits.*)

Other high-frequency verbs that work exactly like **gustar** are:

>> **encantar** (*to love*)

>> **faltar** (*to need, to be lacking*)

>> **fascinar** (*to fascinate*)

>> **interesar** (*to inter*est).

Here are some examples using: **encantar and faltar**

> **Me encanta la ópera.** (*I love the opera.*)

> **Le faltan cien dólares.** (*He [She] need $100.*)

You use the third-person singular form of any verb from the previous list with one or more infinitives:

> **Me gusta cantar (y bailar).** (*I like to sing [and dance].*)

The following list presents some more details you should know about using these verbs:

>> An indirect object pronoun must be preceded by the preposition **a** + the corresponding prepositional pronoun — **mí, ti, él, ella, Ud., nosotros, vosotros, ellos, ellas, Uds.** — for stress or clarification (see Chapter 12):

- **A ellas les gusta esa música.** (*They like that music*)

>> An indirect object pronoun may be preceded by the preposition **a** + the indirect object noun:

- **A Miguel no le gusta trabajar.** (*Michael doesn't like to work.*)
- **A las niñas les gusta el helado.** (*The girls like ice cream.*)

PRACTICE

For this exercise, write a letter to your pen pal in which you state what you and your friends like by using the verb **gustar.** This example gets you started:

Q. a nosotros/leer

A. **A nosotros nos gusta leer.** (*We like to read.*) Use **a nosotros** (*to us*) at the beginning of the sentence for emphasis and clarity. Use the indirect object pronoun **nos** to express *to us*. The verb **gustar** must agree with the subject, which happens to be a verb, **leer,** in its infinitive form.

59 a Julio/los deportes

_____

60 a mí/el ballet y la opera

_____

61 a Roberto y a mí/la natación

_____

62 a las muchachas/levantar pesas

_____

63 a Carmen/tocar la guitarra y jugar al fútbol

_____

64 a tí/las películas

_____

Answers to "Being Clear and Concise with Object Pronouns" Practice Questions

The following are the answers to the practice questions presented in this chapter.

1. **la. Chaqueta** is feminine singular.

2. **las. Tarjetas postales** is feminine plural.

3. **lo. Libro** is masculine singular.

4. **los. Recuerdos** is masculine plural.

5. **las. Camisetas** is feminine plural.

6. **la. Guía** is feminine singular.

7. **los. Sombreros** is masculine plural.

8. **lo. Plano** is masculine singular.

9. **Yo pienso ver a mi familia. Pensar** is a stem-changing **-ar** verb. Change **-e** to **-ie** in all forms except **nosotros** and **vosotros** and add the **-ar** verb endings. Follow the conjugated form of **pensar** with the infinitive, **ver.** Add the personal **a** before **mi familia** (*my family*).

10. **Mis hijos piensan conocer al alcalde de Buenos Aires. Pensar** is a stem-changing **-ar** verb. Change **-e** to **-ie** in all forms except **nosotros** and **vosotros** and add the **-ar** verb endings. Follow the conjugated form of **pensar** with the infinitive, **conocer.** Contract the personal **a** with the definite article **el** to form **al** before **alcalde** (*mayor*).

11. **Nosotros pensamos invitar a las primas de nuestros amigos. Pensar** is a stem-changing **-ar** verb. Change **-e** to **-ie** in all forms except **nosotros** and **vosotros** and add the **-ar** verb endings. Follow the conjugated form of **pensar** with the infinitive, **invitar.** Add the personal **a** before **las primas de nuestros amigos** (*our friends' cousins*).

12. **José piensa visitar a Carlota Hernández. Pensar** is a stem-changing **-ar** verb. Change **-e** to **-ie** in all forms except **nosotros** and **vosotros** and add the **-ar** verb endings. Follow the conjugated form of **pensar** with the infinitive, **visitar.** Add the personal **a** before **Carlota Hernández.**

13. **Tú piensas buscar al señor Rueda. Pensar** is a stem-changing **-ar** verb. Change **-e** to **-ie** in all forms except **nosotros** and **vosotros** and add the **-ar** verb endings. Follow the conjugated form of **pensar** with the infinitive, **buscar.** Contract the personal **a** with the definite article **el** to form **al** before **señor Rueda.**

14. **Vosotros pensáis admirar a todos los niños. Pensar** is a stem-changing **-ar** verb. Change **-e** to **-ie** in all forms except **nosotros** and **vosotros** and add the **-ar** verb endings. Follow the conjugated form of **pensar** with the infinitive, **admirar.** Add the personal **a** before **todos los niños.**

(15) **me ve.** Use **me** to express *me*. Conjugate **ver** to agree with the new subject, **él.** Put the pronoun before the verb.

(16) **las conocen.** Use **las** to express *them* (feminine). Conjugate **conocer** to agree with the new subject, **ellos.** Put the pronoun before the verb.

(17) **lo adora.** Use **lo** to express *him*. Conjugate **adorar** to agree with the new subject, **ella.** Put the pronoun before the verb.

(18) **te busca.** Use **te** to express *you*. Conjugate **buscar** to agree with the new subject, **él.** Put the pronoun before the verb.

(19) **nos ayudan.** Use **nos** to express *us*. Conjugate **ayudar** to agree with the new subject, **ellos.** Put the pronoun before the verb.

(20) **os visitan.** Use **os** to express *you*. Conjugate **visitar** to agree with the new subject, **ellos.** Put the pronoun before the verb.

(21) **Carlos os pide una rebanada del pastel a vosotros.** Use the indirect object pronoun **os** to reinforce the indirect object **a vosotros.** Put **os** before the conjugated form of the **-ir** verb **pedir,** that agrees with the subject, Carlos. **Pedir** undergoes an **-e** to **-i** stem change in all forms except **nosotros** and **vosotros.**

(22) **Yo te cuento todo a tí.** Use the indirect object pronoun **te** to reinforce the indirect object noun **a tí.** Put **te** before the conjugated form of the **-ar** verb **contar,** that agrees with the subject, **yo. Contar** undergoes an **-o** to **-ue** stem change in all forms except **nosotros** and **vosotros.**

(23) **Tú les telefoneas a tus amigos.** Use the indirect object pronoun **les** to reinforce the indirect object noun **a tus amigos.** Put **les** before the conjugated form of the **-ar** verb **telefonear,** that agrees with the subject, **tú.**

(24) **Juana y yo le damos un regalo a Linda.** Use the indirect object pronoun **le** to reinforce the indirect object noun **a Linda.** Put **le** before the conjugated form of the **-ar** verb **dar,** that agrees with the subject, **Juana y yo (nosotros).**

(25) **Linda nos sirve refrescos a nosotros.** Use the indirect object pronoun **nos** to reinforce the indirect object noun **a nosotros.** Put **nos** before the conjugated form of the **-ir** verb **servir,** that agrees with the subject, **Linda. Servir** undergoes an **-e** to **-i** stem change in all forms except **nosotros** and **vosotros.**

(26) **Gloria me ofrece un sándwich a mí.** Use the indirect object pronoun **me** to reinforce the indirect object noun **a mí.** Put **me** before the conjugated form of the **-er** verb **ofrecer,** that agrees with the subject, **Gloria.**

(27) **la. Llamar** takes a direct object pronoun.

(28) **le. Aconsejar** takes an indirect object pronoun.

(29) **la. Buscar** takes a direct object pronoun.

(30) **la. Escuchar** takes a direct object pronoun.

(31) **le. Dar** takes an indirect object pronoun.

(32) **le. Decir** takes an indirect object pronoun.

(33) **le. Ofrecer** takes an indirect object pronoun.

(34) **la. Esperar** takes an direct object pronoun.

(35) **Puedo sacudirlos. (Los puedo sacudir.) Sacudir** takes a direct object. Use **los** to refer to **los muebles.** Place **los** after the infinitive (**sacudir**) and attached to it. Alternatively, put **los** before the conjugated verb (**puedo**).

(36) **No debo decirle nuestros planes. (No le debo decir nuestros planes.) Decir** takes an indirect object. Use **le** to refer to **a María.** Place **le** after the infinitive (**decir**) and attached to it. Alternatively, put **le** before the conjugated verb (**debo**).

(37) **No prefiero pasarla. (No la prefiero pasar.) Pasar** takes a direct object. Use **la** to refer to **la aspiradora.** Place **la** after the infinitive (**pasar**) and attached to it. Alternatively, put **la** before the conjugated verb (**prefiero**).

(38) **Deseo pedirle dinero. (No le deseo pedir dinero.) Pedir** takes an indirect object. Use **le** to refer to **a mi padre.** Place **le** after the infinitive (**pedir**) and attached to it. Alternatively, put **le** before the conjugated verb (**deseo**).

(39) **Pienso darles consejos. (No les pienso dar consejos.) Dar** takes an indirect object. Use **les** to refer to **a Ramón y a Jorge.** Place **les** after the infinitive (**dar**) and attached to it. Alternatively, put **les** before the conjugated verb (**pienso**).

(40) **Quiero llamarlos. (Los quiero llamar.) Llamar** takes a direct object. The **a** is the personal **a.** Use **los** to refer to **a mis primos.** Place **los** after the infinitive (**llamar**) and attached to it. Alternatively, put **los** before the conjugated verb (**quiero**).

(41) **¿Por qué estás mirándolas? (¿Por qué las estás mirando?) Mirar** takes a direct object. Use **las** to refer to **las noticias.** Place **las** after the gerund (**mirando**) and attached to it. Count back three vowels and add an accent. Alternatively, put **las** before the conjugated verb (**estás**).

(42) **¿No estás hablándole? (¿No le estás hablando?) Hablar** takes an indirect object. Use **le** to refer to **a Julia.** Place **le** after the gerund (**hablando**) and attached to it. Count back three vowels and add an accent. Alternatively, put **le** before the conjugated verb (**estás**).

(43) **¿Estás haciéndolos? (¿Los estás haciendo?) Hacer** takes a direct object. Use **los** to refer to **los ejercicios.** Place **los** after the gerund (**haciendo**) and attached to it. Count back three vowels and add an accent. Alternatively, put **los** before the conjugated verb (**estás**).

(44) **¿Estás tocándolo? (¿Lo estás tocando?) Tocar** takes a direct object. Use **lo** to refer to **el piano.** Place **lo** after the gerund (**tocando**) and attached to it. Count back three vowels and add an accent. Alternatively, put **lo** before the conjugated verb (**estás**).

(45) **¿No estás escribiéndole? (¿No le estás escribiendo?) Escribir** takes an indirect object. Use **le** to refer to **a tu amigo por correspondencia.** Place **le** after the gerund (**escribiendo**) and attached to it. Count back three vowels and add an accent. Alternatively, put **le** before the conjugated verb (**estás**).

(46) **¿Estás leyéndoles? (¿Les estás leyendo?) Leer** takes an indirect object. Use **les** to refer to **a sus hermanas.** Place **les** after the gerund (**leyendo**) and attached to it. Count back three vowels and add an accent. Alternatively, put **les** before the conjugated verb (**estás**).

(47) **El cartero se lo trae.** Replace the masculine singular direct object noun, **el correo** with **lo.** When two third-person object pronouns are used together, the indirect object **le,** which would have replaced **a la gente** (a collective noun) becomes **se.** The indirect object pronoun precedes the direct object pronoun. Place both pronouns before the conjugated verb.

(48) **La profesora se la enseña.** Replace the feminine singular direct object noun, **la gramática** with **la.** When two third-person object pronouns are used together, the indirect object **les,** which would have replaced **a los alumnos** becomes **se.** The indirect object pronoun precedes the direct object pronoun. Place both pronouns before the conjugated verb.

(49) **El dentista quiere extraértelos. (El dentista te los quiere extraer.)** Replace the masculine plural direct object noun, **los dientes** with **los.** Use the indirect object pronoun **te** to replace **a tí.** The indirect object pronoun precedes the direct object pronoun. Place both after the infinitive and attached to it. Count back three vowels and add an accent. Alternatively, place both pronouns before the conjugated verb.

(50) **El cajero está dándonosla. (El cajero nos la está dando.)** Replace the feminine singular direct object noun, **la moneda** with **la.** Use the indirect object pronoun **nos** to replace **a nosotros.** The indirect object pronoun precedes the direct object pronoun. Place both after the gerund and attached to it. Count back four vowels and add an accent. Alternatively, place both pronouns before the conjugated verb.

(51) **El comerciante no se las vende.** Replace the feminine plural direct object noun, **las mercancías** with **las.** When two third-person object pronouns are used together, the indirect object **le,** which would have replaced **a sus competidores,** becomes **se.** The indirect object pronoun precedes the direct object pronoun. Place both pronouns before the conjugated verb.

(52) **El banquero no va a cambiárselo. (El banquero no se lo va a cambiar.)** Replace the masculine singular direct object noun, **dinero** with **lo.** When two third-person object pronouns are together, the indirect object **les,** which would have replaced **a todos las turistas,** becomes **se.** The indirect object pronoun precedes the direct object pronoun. Place both after the infinitive and attached to it. Count back three vowels and add an accent. Alternatively, place both pronouns before the conjugated verb.

(53) **El juez está explicándoselas. (El juez se las está explicando.)** Replace the feminine plural direct object noun, **las leyes** with **las.** When two third-person object pronouns are used together, the indirect object **les,** which would have replaced **a los criminales,** becomes **se.** The indirect object pronoun precedes the direct object pronoun. Place both after the gerund and attached to it. Count back four vowels and add an accent. Alternatively, place both pronouns before the conjugated verb.

(54) **El poeta se los escribe.** Replace the masculine plural direct object noun, **los poemas** with **los.** When two third-person object pronouns are used together, the indirect object **le,** which would have replaced **a su novia,** becomes **se.** The indirect object pronoun precedes the direct object pronoun. Place both pronouns before the conjugated verb.

(55) **El artista os las muestra.** Replace the feminine plural direct object noun, **sus obras** with **las.** Use the indirect object pronoun **os** to replace **a vosotros.** The indirect object pronoun precedes the direct object pronoun. Place both pronouns before the conjugated verb.

(56) **El panadero puede vendérmelos. (El panadero me los puede vender.)** Replace the masculine singular direct object noun, **los pasteles** with **los.** Use the indirect object pronoun **te** to replace **a ti.** The indirect object precedes the direct object noun. Place both after the infinitive and attached to it. Count back three vowels and add an accent. Alternatively, place both pronouns before the conjugated verb.

(57) **El doctor está recentándosela. (El doctor se la está recetando.)** Replace the feminine singular direct object noun, **medicina** with **la.** When two third-person object pronouns are used together, the indirect object **les,** which would have replaced **a los enfermos,** becomes **se.** The indirect object pronoun precedes the direct object pronoun. Place both after the gerund and attached to it. Count back four vowels and add an accent. Alternatively, place both pronouns before the conjugated verb.

(58) **La secretaria no se las escribe.** Replace the feminine plural direct object noun, **cartas** with **las.** When two third-person object pronouns are used together, the indirect object **le,** which would have replaced **a Uds.,** becomes **se.** The indirect object pronoun precedes the direct object pronoun. Place both pronouns before the conjugated verb.

(59) **A Julio le gustan los deportes.** Use **a Julio** (*to Julio*) at the beginning of the sentence for emphasis and clarity. Use the indirect object pronoun **le** to express *to him.* The verb **gustar** must agree with the plural subject, **los deportes.**

(60) **A mí me gustan el ballet y la ópera.** Use **a mí** (*to me*) at the beginning of the sentence for emphasis and clarity. Use the indirect object pronoun **me** to express *to me.* The verb **gustar** must agree with the plural subject, **el ballet y la ópera.**

(61) **A Roberto y a mí (A nosotros) nos gusta la natación.** Use **a Roberto y a mí** (*to Robert and me*) or **A nosotros** (*to us*) at the beginning of the sentence for emphasis and clarity. Use the indirect object pronoun **nos** to express *to us.* The verb **gustar** must agree with the singular subject, **la natación.**

(62) **A las muchachas les gusta levantar pesas.** Use **a las muchachas** (*to the girls*) at the beginning of the sentence for emphasis and clarity. Use the indirect object pronoun **les** to express *to them.* The verb **gustar** must agree with the singular subject, which happens to be a verb, **levantar pesas**.

(63) **A Carmen le gusta tocar la guitarra y jugar al fútbol.** Use **a Carmen** (*to Carmen*) at the beginning of the sentence for emphasis and clarity. Use the indirect object pronoun **le** to express *to her.* The verb **gustar** must agree with the subject, which happen to be verbs, **tocar la guitarra y jugar al fútbol.** The singular form of **gustar** is used with one or more infinitives.

(64) **A tí te gustan las películas.** Use **a tí** (*to you*) at the beginning of the sentence for emphasis and clarity. Use the indirect object pronoun **te** to express *to you.* The verb **gustar** must agree with the plural subject, **las películas.**

Chapter **10**

Reflecting on Reflexive Pronouns and Verbs

'm willing to wager that if you've ever heard of reflexive verbs, it's because your foreign language teacher explained them to you. Most assuredly, your English teachers haven't covered them at all. *A reflexive verb* shows that the subject is acting upon itself and, therefore, requires a reflexive pronoun that expresses *myself, yourself, himself, herself, ourselves, yourselves,* or *themselves.*

Are you thinking, "Oh no, not more pronouns"? Don't worry; reflexive pronouns act as either direct or indirect object pronouns and are almost exactly the same as the pronouns I discuss in Chapter 9. So if you've mastered object pronouns, reflexive pronouns will be a snap.

In this chapter, I explain how to recognize and use reflexive verbs in Spanish, as well as which pronouns are used for different subjects. The placement of reflexive pronouns in different types of sentences should come as no surprise if you've practiced the materials in the preceding chapters. I also cover the special meaning of some reflexive verbs so that you can use them properly when speaking and writing Spanish.

Recognizing and Using Reflexive Verbs

Reflexive verbs have several applications. They're used not only to express how an action is performed by a subject on itself but also to show how subjects act toward one another.

Recognizing a reflexive verb is quite easy. If an **-ar, -er,** or **-ir** infinitive has an **-se** attached to its end, you know you have a reflexive verb (**lavarse** [*to wash oneself*]; **bañarse** [*to bathe oneself*]). That **-se** ending shows that the reflexive verb has a reflexive pronoun as its direct or indirect object. (See Chapter 9.)

Using reflexive pronouns

You always conjugate a reflexive verb with the reflexive pronoun that agrees with the subject (which may be omitted, as with other verbs). Generally, these pronouns, like the direct and indirect object pronouns I discuss in Chapter 9, precede the conjugated verbs. Table 10-1 shows example verbs, the reflexive pronoun for each subject, and how you place the pronoun before the conjugated verb.

TIP

Because you use **se** when double object pronouns appear in a sentence (see Chapter 9), it should be relatively easy to remember to use it as the reflexive pronoun:

Table 10-1   Properly Using Reflexive Pronouns

Infinitive	Subject	Reflexive Pronoun	Verb
bañarse (*to bathe oneself*)	**yo**	**me**	**baño**
lavarse (*to wash oneself*)	**tú**	**te**	**lavas**
levantarse (*to get up*)	**él, ella, Ud.**	**se**	**levanta**
cansarse (*to become tired*)	**nosostros**	**nos**	**cansamos**
callarse (*to become silent*)	**vosotros**	**os**	**calláis**
marcharse (*to go away*)	**ellos, ellas, Uds.**	**se**	**marchan**

Here are some examples that show you how to use these reflexive pronouns:

¿A qué hora te levantas? (*At what time do you get up?*)

Me acuesto temprano. (*I go to bed early.*)

Los alumnos se callan. (*The students become silent.*)

PRACTICE

You're writing a journal entry in which you talk about your bad habits and those of your acquaintances. I provide the subject and the reflexive verb and you provide the reflexive pronoun and conjugate the verb.

Q. yo/acostarse tarde

A. **Yo me acuesto tarde.** The reflexive pronoun for **yo** is **me**. **Acostar** is a stem changing **-ar** verb that changes **-o** to **-ue**. Drop **-ar** and add the **-o** ending for **yo**.

1   Isabel y yo/preocuparse (*worry*) de todo

2   Gloria/aburrirse (*to become bored*) fácilmente

_____

3   mis hermanos/equivocarse (*to be mistaken*) a menudo

_____

4   yo/enfadarse (*to become angry*) con mis amigos

_____

5   tú/ponerse (*to become*) triste de vez en cuando

_____

6   vosotros/olvidarse (*to forget*) de vuestras obligaciones

_____

Common reflexive verbs

This section looks closer at high-frequency Spanish verbs that are often used reflexively. Table 10-2 presents these verbs. (The letters in parentheses indicate a spelling change.)

Table 10-2   Common Reflexive Verbs

Verb	Meaning	Verb	Meaning
abrazarse	to hug each other	irse	to go away
aburrirse	to become bored	lavarse	to wash oneself
acostarse (-o to -ue)	to go to bed	levantarse	to get up
afeitarse	to shave	llamarse	to be called, named
bañarse	to bathe oneself	maquillarse	to put on makeup
callarse	to be silent	marcharse	to go away
cansarse	to become tired	olvidarse (de)	to forget
casarse	to get married	peinarse	to comb one's hair
cepillarse	to brush (hair, teeth)	ponerse	to put on, become
despedirse (-e to -i)	to say goodbye	preocuparse (de)	to worry
despertarse (-e to -ie)	to wake up	quedarse	to remain
Desvestirse (-e to -i)	to get undressed	quejarse (de)	to complain
divertirse (-e to -i)	to have fun	quitarse	to take off (clothing)
ducharse	to take a shower	relajarse	to relax
encontrarse (-o to -ue)	to be located, meet	romperse	to break (body part)
enfadarse (con)	to get angry	secarse	to dry oneself
engañarse	to deceive	sentarse (-e to -ie)	to sit down
enojarse	to become angry	sentirse (-e to -ie)	to feel
equivocarse	to be mistaken	vestirse (-e to -i)	to get dressed
hacerse	to become	volverse (-o to -ue)	to become

PRACTICE

Each person has certain reactions in different situations. Use the clues provided to express what they do.

Q. Gloria no quiere hablar con Estela. (callarse)

A. **Gloria se calla.** Use the reflexive pronoun **se** to refer to Gloria. **Callar** is a regular –ar verb. Drop the –**ar** infinitive ending and add –**a** for Gloria.

7 El señor Morales tiene una barba larga. (afeitarse)

8 Tú tienes calor. (quitarse el suéter)

9 Nosotros estamos cansados. (sentarse)

10 Los alumnos reciben buenas notas. (hacerse contentos)

11 Vosotros tenéis sueño. (acostarse)

12 Yo tengo frío. (ponerse un abrigo)

Considering verbs with special reflexive meanings

Some verbs may throw you off a bit. Depending on what you want to say, a verb may have both a reflexive and a non-reflexive form. How's that possible? Well, a reflexive verb requires that the subject act upon itself. What if, however, that subject acts upon someone or something else? In that case, the sentence doesn't need a reflexive pronoun.

Look carefully at the examples that follow:

Ella se lava. (*She washes herself.*)

Ella lava a su perro. (*She washes her dog.*)

In the first example, the verb requires a reflexive pronoun (**se**) because the subject, *she,* is washing *herself.* In the second example, however, the subject, *she,* is washing *her dog.* Because the subject isn't acting upon herself in this case, you don't use the reflexive pronoun. You simply use the possessive adjective **su** before the noun **perro.** (See Chapter 3.)

Conversely, some verbs that generally aren't used reflexively can be made reflexive (if the subject is acting upon itself) by adding a reflexive pronoun:

Él prepara la comida. (*He prepares the meal.*)

Él se prepara. (*He prepares himself.*)

In the first example, the verb doesn't require a reflexive pronoun because the subject, *he*, is preparing someone or something else (*the meal*). In the second example, however, the subject, *he*, is preparing *himself*, which requires a reflexive pronoun.

Table 10-3 shows a list of high-frequency verbs that have a different meaning when they're used reflexively. (The letters in parentheses indicate a spelling change.)

Table 10-3   Spanish Verbs with Different Reflexive Meanings

General Form	General Meaning	Reflexive Form	Reflexive Meaning
aburrir	to bore	aburrirse	to become bored
acordar (-o to -ue)	to agree	acordarse de	to remember
acostar (-o to -ue)	to put to bed	acostarse	to go to bed
bañar	to bathe (someone)	bañarse	to bathe oneself
cansar	to tire	cansarse	to become tired
dormir (-o to -ue)	(to sleep)	dormirse	to fall asleep
engañar	to deceive	engañarse	to be mistaken
esconder	to hide (something)	esconderse	to hide oneself
ir	to go	irse	to go away
levantar	to raise (something)	levantarse	to get up
llamar	to call	llamarse	to be called, to call oneself
poner	to put (something)	ponerse	to put (something on), to become
sentar (-e to -ie)	to seat	sentarse	to sit down

Here are two examples that show you how the meanings of these verbs differ when you use them reflexively and non-reflexively:

La profesora se sienta después de sentar a los alumnos por orden alfabético. (*The teacher sits after seating the students in alphabetical order.*)

Ella llama a su amiga que se llama Emilia. (*She calls her friend whose name is Emilia.*)

PRACTICE

You're spending the day at the movies with your friend Juan. Complete the following sentences with the correct form of the verb I provide and a reflexive pronoun, if necessary.

Q. (levantar/levantarse) Yo _____ tarde.

A. **Yo me levanto tarde.** Because I am getting myself up, the reflexive pronoun *me* is needed.

13 (llamar/llamarse) Yo _____ a Juan.

14 (ir/irse) Él quiere _____ al cine.

15 (bañar/bañarse) Antes, yo tengo que _____.

16 (acordar/acordarse) Nosotros _____ tomar el autobús.

17 (sentar/sentarse) Nosotros _____ enfrente de la pantalla.

18 (dormir/dormirse) Cuando empieza la película Juan _____.

You and some of your friends are getting into some mischief today. Read what everyone is doing in the following exercise sentences and insert the reflexive pronoun **se** only if it's necessary because the subject is performing an action upon itself. Here's an example to get you started.

PRACTICE

Q. **Las muchachas_____ lavan el coche con agua sucia y después _____ lavan.**

A. **Las muchachas lavan el coche con agua sucia y después se lavan.** The first verb isn't used reflexively because the girls are washing the car. The reflexive pronoun **se** is needed for the second verb because the girls are washing themselves.

19 **Julio_____ afeita y después _____ al perro.**

20 **Yo _____ pongo un impermeable y después _____ mi gato en la bañera.**

21 **Tú _____ maquillas a tu hermana menor y después _____ maquillas.**

22 **Uds. _____ despiertan a las tres de la mañana y después _____ despiertan a su familia.**

23 **Nosotros _____ vestimos a nuestra prima con ropa de bebé y después nosotros _____ vestimos.**

24 **Manuela rompe _____ el juguete de su hermana y después _____ rompe la pierna.**

Expressing reciprocal actions

Some situations in Spanish call for special reflexive constructions, such as when there's reciprocal action.

In Spanish, it's common to use a plural reflexive construction if you want to convey an English reciprocal action that expresses *one another* or *each other*. Here's the simple way to construct this:

Nos respetamos. (*We respect one another [each other].*)

Se abrazan. (*They hug one another [each other].*)

Guillermo and Gisela will be married soon. Express how they're acting by creating reciprocal constructions based on the information I provide.

Q. respetarse

A. **Ellos se respetan.** Use the reflexive pronoun **se** to show that they respect each other. Use the **-an** ending for the **-ar** verb **respetar**.

25 amarse

_____

26 hablarse todo el tiempo

_____

27 abrazarse a menudo

_____

28 mirarse con cariño

_____

29 besarse mucho

_____

30 casarse dentro de poco

_____

Properly Placing Reflexive Pronouns

Just like with direct and indirect object pronouns (see Chapter 9), you generally place reflexive pronouns before the conjugated verbs:

Me aplico en la clase de español. (*I apply myself in Spanish class.*)

¿Por qué te pones enojado? (*Why are you becoming angry?*)

Ella no se siente bien. (*She doesn't feel well.*)

To negate a reflexive verb, you put **no** or the proper negative word (see Chapter 6) before the reflexive pronoun:

¿Se enoja Ud. a menudo? (*Do you often get angry?*)

No, no me enojo a menudo. (*No, I don't get angry often.*)

Nunca me enojo. (*I never get angry.*)

No me enojo nunca. (*I never get angry.*)

Likewise, in sentences with two verbs that follow one subject (as in the first two following examples) or in sentences with a gerund (as in the second two examples), you have the choice of placing the reflexive pronoun before the conjugated verb or after and attached to the infinitive or the gerund. When you attach the pronoun to a gerund, an accent is required on the stressed vowel. (Count back three vowels and add the accent.)

(No) Voy a maquillar*me*. (*I'm [not] going to put on my makeup.*)

(No) *Me* voy a maquillar. (*I'm [not] going to put on my makeup.*)

(No) Estoy maquillándo*me*. (*I am [not] putting on my makeup.*)

(No) *Me* estoy maquillando. (*I am [not] putting on my makeup.*)

TIP

A negative goes before the pronoun when it precedes the verb:

(No) Voy a maquillar*me*. (*I'm [not] going to put on my makeup.*)

(No) *Me* voy a maquillar. (*I'm [not] going to put on my makeup.*)

PRACTICE

Write a journal entry in which you state what each person wants to do under the given circumstances. Conjugate the first verb in the present tense. Leave the second verb in its infinitive form. In your first sentence, place the correct reflexive pronoun before the conjugated present tense verb form. In your second sentence, place the correct reflexive pronoun after the infinitive and attached to it.

Q. Ella tiene miedo. (querer/esconderse)

A. **Se quiere esconder. Quiere esconderse.** The reflexive pronoun for **ella** is **se. Querer** is a stem-changing **-er** verb that changes **-e** to **-ie** in all forms except **nosotros** and **vosotros**. Place **se** before the conjugated form of **querer** for **ella: quiere** and add the infinitive. Alternatively, conjugate **querer** and add the reflexive pronoun to the end of the infinitive.

31 Yo tengo sueño. (querer/acostarse)

_____

32 Tú estás sucio. (ir a/bañarse)

_____

33 Alberto está mojado. (pensar/secarse)

_____

34 Las muchachas están cansadas. (poder/sentarse)

_____

35 Uds. están enfermos. (preferir/quedarse en casa)

_____

36 Julia tiene hambre. (deber/prepararse un sándwich)

_____

PRACTICE Did you see what just happened? Write down in your journal what the people around you are doing. Conjugate **estar** (*to be*) in the present tense. Put the second verb in its gerund form. In your first sentence, place the correct reflexive pronoun before the conjugated present tense form of **estar**. In your second sentence, place the correct reflexive pronoun after the gerund and attached to it.

Q. **Ellos acaban de discutir con su amigo. (pelearse)**

A. **Se están peleando. Están peleándose.** Conjugate **estar** to agree with the subject, **ellos**. The reflexive pronoun for **ellos** is **se**. Put **se** before the conjugated form of **estar**. Form the gerund of **pelear** by dropping the **-ar** ending and adding **-ando**. Alternatively, use the conjugated form of **estar** followed by the gerund. Attach **se** to the gerund. Count back three vowels and add an accent.

37 Yo acabo de oír truenos y de ver relámpagos. (esconderse)

_____

38 Susana acaba de recibir una invitación al cine. (vestirse)

_____

39 Los muchachos acaban de jugar al fútbol en el lodo. (ducharse)

_____

40 Tú acabas de derramar jugo de uva en tus pantalones. (cambiarse de ropa)

_____

41 Nosotros acabamos de oír sonar el timbre de la puerta. (levantarse)

_____

42 Uds. acaban de terminar su tarea. (relajarse)

_____

Answers to "Reflecting on Reflexive Pronouns and Verbs" Practice Questions

The following are the answers to the practice questions presented in this chapter.

1. **Isabel y yo** *nos preocupamos* **de todo.** The reflexive pronoun for **Isabel y yo (nosotros)** is **nos. Preocupar** is an **-ar** verb. Drop **-ar** and add the **-amos** ending for **nosotros.**

2. **Gloria** *se aburre* **fácilmente.** The reflexive pronoun for **Gloria** is **se. Aburrir** is an **-ir** verb. Drop **-ir** and add the **-e** ending for **Gloria.**

3. **Mis hermanos** *se equivocan* **a menudo.** The reflexive pronoun for **mis hermanos** is **se. Equivocar** is an **-ar** verb. Drop **-ar** and add the **-an** ending for **mis hermanos.**

4. **Yo** *me enfado* **con mis amigos.** The reflexive pronoun for **yo** is **me. Enfadar** is an **-ar** verb. Drop **-ar** and add the **-o** ending for **yo.**

5. **Tú** *te pones* **triste vez en cuando.** The reflexive pronoun for **tú** is **te. Poner** is an **-er** verb. Drop **-er** and add the **-es** ending for **tú.**

6. **Vosotros** *os olvidáis* **de vuestras obligaciones.** The reflexive pronoun for **vosotros** is **os** Olvidar is an **-ar** verb. Drop the **-ar** ending and add **-áis** for **vosotros.**

7. **El señor Morales se afeita.** Use the reflexive pronoun **se** to refer to **el señor Morales. Afeitar** is an **-ar** verb. Drop the **-ar** ending and add **-a** for **el señor Morales.**

8. **Tú te quitas el suéter.** Use the reflexive pronoun **te** to refer to **tú. Quitar** is an **-ar** verb. Drop the **-ar** ending and add **-as** for **tú.**

9. **Nosotros nos sentamos.** Use the reflexive pronoun **nos** to refer to **nosotros. Sentar** is an **-ar** verb. Drop the **-ar** ending and add **-amos** for **nosotros.**

10. **Los alumnos se hacen contentos.** Use the reflexive pronoun **se** to refer to **los alumnos. Hacer** is an **-er** verb that is sregular in its third-person plural form. Drop the **-er** ending and add **-en** for **los alumnos.**

11. **Vosotros os acostáis.** Use the reflexive pronoun **os** to refer to **vosotros. Acostar** is an **-ar** verb. Drop the **-ar** ending and add **-áis** for **vosotros.**

12. **Carmela se pone un abrigo.** Use the reflexive pronoun **se** to refer to **Carmela. Poner** is an **-er** verb that is regular in its third-person singular form. Drop the **-er** ending and add **-e** for **Carmela.**

13. **llamo.** The subject isn't acting upon itself.

14. **ir.** The subject isn't acting upon itself.

15. **bañarme.** The subject is acting upon itself and the reflexive pronoun **me** is needed.

16. **acordamos.** The subject isn't acting upon itself.

17. **nos sentamos.** The subject is acting upon itself and the reflexive pronoun **nos** is needed.

18. **se duerme.** The subject is acting upon itself and the reflexive pronoun **se** is needed. **Dormir** is a verb with an **-o** to **-ue** stem change in all forms except **nosotros** and **vosotros.**

(19) **se/.**— In the first action, she's shaving herself and the reflexive pronoun **se** is required. In the second action, she's shaving the dog.

(20) **me/.** In the first action, I'm putting on my raincoat and the reflexive pronoun **me** is required. In the second action, I'm putting my cat in the bathtub.

(21) —/**te.** In the first action, you're putting makeup on your younger sister. In the second action, you're putting makeup on yourself and the reflexive pronoun **te** is required.

(22) **se/.** In the first action, you're waking up at 3 a.m. and the reflexive pronoun **se** is required. In the second action, you're waking your family.

(23) —/**nos.** In the first action, we're dressing our female cousin in baby clothing. In the second action, we're dressing ourselves and the reflexive pronoun **nos** is required.

(24) —/**se.** In the first action, she's breaking her sister's toy. In the second action, she's breaking her own leg and the reflexive pronoun **se** is required.

(25) **Ellos** *se aman.* Use the reflexive pronoun **se** to show that they love each other. Use the **-an** ending for the **-ar** verb **amar.**

(26) **Ellos** *se hablan* **todo el tiempo.** Use the reflexive pronoun **se** to show that they speak to each other. Use the **-an** ending for the -ar verb **hablar.**

(27) **Ellos** *se abrazan* **a menudo.** Use the reflexive pronoun **se** to show that they hug each other. Use the **-an** ending for the -ar verb **abrazar.**

(28) **Ellos** *se miran* **con cariño.** Use the reflexive pronoun **se** to show that they look at each other. Use the -**an** ending for the -ar verb **mirar.**

(29) **Ellos** *se besan* **mucho.** Use the reflexive pronoun **se** to show that they kiss each other. Use the -**an** ending for the -ar verb **besar.**

(30) **Ellos** *se casan* **dentro de poco.** Use the reflexive pronoun **se** to show that they get married to each other. Use the **-an** ending for the -ar verb **casar.**

(31) **Me quiero acostar. Quiero acostarme. Querer** is a verb with an **-e** to **-ie** stem change. **Quiero acostarme.** The reflexive pronoun for **yo** is **me. Querer** is a stem-changing **-er** verb that changes **-e** to **-ie** in all forms except **nosotros** and **vosotros.** Place **me** before the conjugated form of **querer** for **yo: quiero** and add the infinitive. Alternatively, conjugate **querer** and add the reflexive pronoun to the end of the infinitive.

(32) **Te vas a bañar. Vas a bañarte. Ir** is an irregular verb. The reflexive pronoun for **tú** is **te. Ir** is an irregular verb. Place **te** before the conjugated form of **ir** for **tú: vas** and add the infinitive. Alternatively, conjugate **ir** and add the reflexive pronoun to the end of the infinitive.

(33) **Se piensa secar. Piensa secarse. Pensar** is a verb with an **-e** to **-ie** stem change. The reflexive pronoun for **Alberto** is **se. Pensar** is a stem-changing **-ar** verb that changes **-e** to **-ie** in all forms except **nosotros** and **vosotros.** Place **se** before the conjugated form of **pensar** for **Alberto: piensa** and add the infinitive. Alternatively, conjugate **pensar** and add the reflexive pronoun to the end of the infinitive.

(34) **Se pueden sentar. Pueden sentarse.** The reflexive pronoun for **las muchachas** is **se. Poder** is a stem-changing **-er** verb that changes **-o** to **-ue** in all forms except **nosotros** and **vosotros.** Place **se** before the conjugated form of **poder** for **las muchachas: pueden** and add the infinitive. Alternatively, conjugate **poder** and add the reflexive pronoun to the end of the infinitive.

(35) **Se prefieren quedar en casa. Prefieren quedarse en casa.** The reflexive pronoun for **Uds.** is **se. Preferir** is a stem-changing **-ir** verb that changes **-e** to **-ie** in all forms except **nosotros** and **vosotros**. Place **se** before the conjugated form of **preferir** for **Uds.: prefieren** and add the infinitive. Alternatively, conjugate **preferir** and add the reflexive pronoun to the end of the infinitive.

(36) **Se debe preparar un sándwich. Debe prepararse un sándwich.** The reflexive pronoun for **Julia** is **se. Deber** is an **-er** verb. Place **se** before the conjugated form of **deber** for **Julia: debe** and add the infinitive. Alternatively, conjugate **deber** and add the reflexive pronoun to the end of the infinitive.

(37) **Me estoy escondiendo. Estoy escondiéndome.** Conjugate **estar** to agree with the subject, **yo.** The reflexive pronoun for **yo** is **me.** Put **me** before the conjugated form of **estar.** Form the gerund of **esconder** by dropping the **-er** ending and adding **-iendo.** Alternatively, use the conjugated form of **estar** followed by the **gerund.** Attach **me** to the gerund. Count back three vowels and add an accent.

(38) **Se está vistiendo. Está vistiéndose.** Conjugate **estar** to agree with the subject, **Susana.** The reflexive pronoun for **Susana** is **se.** Put **se** before the conjugated form of **estar. Vestir** is a verb with an **e** to **i** stem change Form the gerund of **vestir** by changing **-e** to **-i** and dropping the **-ir** ending and adding **-iendo.** Alternatively, use the conjugated form of **estar** followed by the gerund. Attach **se** to the gerund. Count back three vowels and add an accent.

(39) **Se están duchando. Están duchándose.** Conjugate **estar** to agree with the subject, **los muchachos.** The reflexive pronoun for **ellos** is **se.** Put **se** before the conjugated form of **estar.** Form the gerund of **duchar** by dropping the **-ar** ending and adding **-ando.** Alternatively, use the conjugated form of **estar** followed by the gerund. Attach **se** to the gerund. Count back three vowels and add an accent.

(40) **Te estás cambiando de ropa. Estás cambiándote de ropa.** Conjugate **estar** to agree with the subject, **tú.** The reflexive pronoun for **tú** is **te.** Put **te** before the conjugated form of **estar.** Form the gerund of **cambiar** by dropping the **-ar** ending and adding **-ando.** Alternatively, use the conjugated form of **estar** followed by the gerund. Attach **te** to the gerund. Count back three vowels and add an accent.

(41) **Nos estamos levantando. Estamos levantándonos.** Conjugate **estar** to agree with the subject, **nosotros.** The reflexive pronoun for **nosotros** is **nos.** Put **nos** before the conjugated form of **estar.** Form the gerund of **levantar** by dropping the **-ar** ending and adding **-ando.** Alternatively, use the conjugated form of **estar** followed by the gerund. Attach **nos** to the gerund. Count back three vowels and add an accent.

(42) **Se están relajando. Están relajándose.** Conjugate **estar** to agree with the subject, **Uds.** The reflexive pronoun for **Uds.** is **se.** Put **se** before the conjugated form of **estar.** Form the gerund of **relajar** by dropping the **-ar** ending and adding **-ando.** Alternatively, use the conjugated form of **estar** followed by the gerund. Attach **se** to the gerund. Count back three vowels and add an accent.

Chapter **11**

Getting Attention with Commands

Can you guess how many times you've had to give people directions to your home or to a restaurant? Perhaps you often give instructions on how to do something, like how to fix a broken object, how to lose weight, or how to succeed at a job interview. Maybe, if you're a cook and baker like me, you've had to explain recipes and procedures. And at different points in life, we all have to ask others for help or for favors.

In all these situations, you've had to use the *imperative,* which is a fancy way of saying that you've given a command. Just like in English, the imperative isn't a tense in Spanish because it doesn't show time. It's called a *mood* because it indicates the manner in which the action occurs.

In this chapter, you explore the different ways to give a command in Spanish so that whatever needs to get done gets done. Finally, you discover how to shorten your commands by using direct and indirect object pronouns.

TIP

You will, in all probability, have to refer to Chapter 6 when reading this chapter because some of the imperative forms are based on or are identical to subjunctive forms. If you've success-fully mastered the subjunctive, the imperative will be a piece of cake for you.

The Imperative Mood

When something is imperative, it just *has* to be done — and right away at that. In such an instance, it's only logical to command someone to do something to ensure that the job gets done. When you talk about the imperative in Spanish, you're talking about giving a command. And, just like in English, the subject of most commands in Spanish is *you.*

In Spanish, you have four ways to express *you:* two formal (**Ud.** and **Uds.**) and two informal (**tú** and **vosotros**).

In Spanish, it's common to place an inverted exclamation mark (¡) at the beginning of an emphasized command and a regular exclamation mark (!) at the end:

¡Abra la ventana! (*Open the window!*)

¡No discutan! (*Don't argue!*)

Forming Formal Commands

You give formal (or polite) commands to people who are older and wiser or to people who are unfamiliar to you. Of course, in a formal situation, you don't want to be rude, so you'll use the Spanish words for *please:* **por favor.**

The subjects of formal commands are **Ud.** (if you're addressing only one person) and **Uds.** (if you're addressing more than one person):

Abra (Ud.) la puerta, por favor. (*Open the window, please.*)

Por favor, hablen (Uds.) más despacio. (*Please speak more slowly.*)

In English, you never actually say the word *you* when you give a command or make a request. In Spanish, the use of a subject pronoun (**Ud., Uds., tú, or vosotros**) in a command is optional and not used all that frequently. You can identify the subject by a quick look at the verb ending being used (see below):

Pase (Ud.) la sal, por favor. (*Pass the salt, please.*)

Presten (Uds.) atención. (*Pay attention.*)

Commanding with regular verbs and irregular yo form verbs

The subjunctive comes in handy when you want to give a formal command, because all formal commands are expressed by the present subjunctive. Here's a quick refresher course on forming the present subjunctive:

1. Drop the final **-o** from the **yo** form of the present tense.

2. For infinitives ending in **-ar,** add **-e** for **Ud.** and **-en** for **Uds.**

3. For infinitives ending in **-er** or **-ir,** add **-a** for **Ud.** and **-an** for **Uds.**

4. To form the negative, simply put **no** before the verb.

Here's a chart to help you see these changes in action:

-ar Verbs	-er Verbs	-ir Verbs
firmar (*to sign*)	**comer** (*to eat*)	**subir** (*to go up*)
yo firmo (*I sign*)	**yo como** (*I eat*)	**yo subo** (*I go up*)
¡[No] Firme (Ud.)! ([*Don't*] *Sign.*)	**¡[No] Coma (Ud.)!** ([*Don't*] *Eat.*)	**¡[No] Suba (Ud.)!** ([*Don't*] *Go up.*)
¡[No]Firmen (Uds.)! ([*Don't*] *Sign.*)	**¡[No]Coman (Uds.)!** ([*Don't*] *Eat.*)	**¡[No] Suban (Uds.)!** ([*Don't*] *Go up.*)

The following sentences show some regular verbs in commands:

¡(No) Mire la televisión! (*[Don't] Watch television!*)

¡(No) Lea en voz alta! (*[Don't] Read aloud!*)

¡(No) Escriba una carta! (*[Don't] Write a letter!*)

PRACTICE

You don't feel well and decide to go to the doctor for a checkup. Complete the doctor's written instructions to you by giving the formal singular command form of the verbs provided in parentheses. Here's an example:

Q. (hablar) No _____ demasiado.

A. **No hable demasiado.** (*Don't talk too much.*) For **-ar** verbs, drop **-a** and add **-e.**

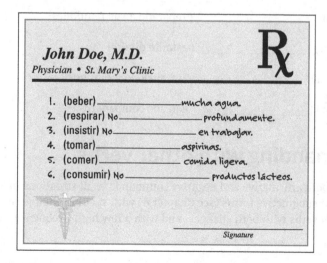

REMEMBER

The formula discussed in this section also works for verbs with irregular **yo** forms, as shown in Table 11-1.

Table 11-1   **Verbs with Irregular Yo Forms**

Spanish Verbs	Commands	Meaning
decir	(no) diga(n)	*(don't) tell*
hacer	(no) haga(n)	*(don't) do*
poner	(no) ponga(n)	*(don't) put*
salir	(no) salga(n)	*(don't) leave*
tener	(no) tenga(n)	*(don't) have (be)*
traer	(no) traiga(n)	*(don't) bring*
venir	(no) venga(n)	*(don't) come*

Here are a couple of examples:

> **Digan la verdad siempre.** (*Always tell the truth.*)
>
> **No tenga miedo.** (*Don't be afraid.*)

PRACTICE

You are going on a business trip. Express the advice you receive from others by filling in the correct command form.

Q. (poner) ¡_____ los documentos importantes en su maletín!

A. **ponga.** Take the **yo** form of the present tense. Drop the **-o** and add **-a**.

7.   (tener) ¡ _____ cuidado!

8.   (decir) ¡ _____ la verdad!

9.   (venir) ¡ _____ preparado a sus reuniones!

10.   (traer) ¡ _____ bastante dinero!

11.   (hacer) ¡ _____ su trabajo lo mejor posible!

12.   (salir) ¡ _____ con sus compañeros.

Commanding with other verbs

To create both affirmative and negative commands in all situations in Spanish, you have to use the present subjunctive forms (see Chapter 6) with spelling change verbs, with stem-changing verbs, with verbs with both changes, and with a few high-frequency irregular verbs.

Verbs with spelling changes

Verbs with spelling changes have the following changes in the present subjunctive:

>> **-car** changes **-c** to **-qu**

>> **-gar** changes **-g** to **-gu**

>> **-zar** changes **-z** to **-c**

These examples show how to use verbs with spelling changes in commands:

Saque su carta de crédito. (*Take out your credit card.*)

Pague la cuenta, por favor. (*Pay the bill, please.*)

No utilice esto. (*Don't use this.*)

Verbs with stem changes

In Chapter 6, I point out the following about verbs with stem changes in the subjunctive:

>> **-ar, -er,** and **-ir** verbs change their internal **-e** to **-ie.**

>> **-ar, -er,** and **-ir** verbs change their internal **-o** to **-ue.**

>> **Jugar** changes its internal **-u** to **-ue.**

>> Certain **-ir** verbs: **medir** (*to measure*), **pedir** (*to ask*), **repetir** (*to repeat*) and **servir** (*to serve*) change internal **-e** to **-i.**

>> **-iar** verbs add an accent to the **-i: í.**

>> **-uar** verbs add an accent to the **-u: ú.**

>> **-uir** verbs (but not **-guir** verbs, which change **-gu** to **-g**) add **-y** after the **-u.**

Here are some examples that show how to use these verbs in commands:

Cierre la puerta, por favor. (*Please close the door.*)

Cuente la historia. (*Tell the story.*)

No pierda sus llaves. (*Don't lose your keys.*)

No vuelva tarde. (*Don't return late.*)

Envíe ese paquete inmediatamente. (*Send this package immediately.*)

No destruya ese documento. (*Don't destroy that document.*)

Verbs with spelling and stem changes

Some Spanish verbs undergo both spelling and stem changes when used in commands as shown in Table 11-2.

Table 11-2   Verbs with Spelling and Stem Changes

Spanish Verbs	Commands	Meaning
colgar (o to ue/g to gu)	**(no) cuelgue(n)**	*(don't) hang*
jugar (u to ue/g to gu)	**(no) juegue(n)**	*(don't) play*
comenzar (e to ie/z to c)	**(no) comience(n)**	*(don't) begin*
empezar (e to ie/z to c)	**(no) empiece(n)**	*(don't) begin*
almorzar (o to ue/z to c)	**(no) almuerce(n)**	*(don't) eat lunch*
corregir (e to i/g to j)	**(no) corrija(n)**	*(don't) correct*
seguir (e to i/gu to g)	**(no) siga(n)**	*(don't) follow*

Here are some sample commands containing verbs with both spelling and stem changes:

No jueguen allá. (*Don't play there.*)

Empiecen inmediatamente. (*Begin immediately.*)

Siga ese auto. (*Follow that car.*)

Irregular verbs

To close things out, Table 11-3 shows the irregular verbs you have to memorize in order to use them in commands.

Table 11-3   Irregular Verbs

Spanish Verbs	Commands	Meaning
dar	**(no) dé/(no) den**	*(don't) give*
estar	**(no) esté(n)**	*(don't) be*
ir	**(no) vaya(n)**	*(don't) go*
saber	**(no) sepa(n)**	*(don't) know*
ser	**(no) sea(n)**	*(don't be)*

Here's how you use these irregular verbs in commands:

Estén listos a las siete. (*Be ready at seven o'clock.*)

Vaya a la tienda ahora. (*Go to the store now.*)

PRACTICE

You have some family members from out of town who are staying at your house for an extended time. How about you put them to work! Leave them a list explaining what they should and shouldn't do. Use the plural, formal command form of the verbs provided in parentheses. Here's an example:

Q. (almorzar) No _____ en la sala.

A. No almuercen en la sala.

13 (destruir) No _____ nada.

14 (cerrar) No _____ las ventanas.

15 (mentir) Si hay un problema, no _____.

16 (decir) Siempre _____ la verdad.

17 (perder) No _____ nada.

18 (pedir) _____ ayuda si es necesario.

19 (hacer) _____ las camas.

20 (poner) _____ la mesa.

21 (llegar) No _____ tarde al trabajo.

22 (organizar) _____ los gabinetes.

23 (tener) _____ cuidado.

24 (ir) _____ al supermercado.

25 (colgar) No _____ nada afuera.

26 (empezar) _____ su trabajo inmediatamente.

27 (apagar) _____ todas las luces.

28 (sacar) _____ la basura.

29 (recoger) _____ la ropa del suelo.

30 (seguir) _____ todas las instrucciones.

Issuing Informal Commands

You give informal (or familiar) commands to people you know: friends, peers, family members, or pets. The subject of an informal Spanish command is **tú** (if you're addressing one person) or **vosotros** (if you're addressing more than one person).

REMEMBER

The **vosotros** (second-person plural) command is used primarily in Spain. In Spanish American countries, people use the **Uds.** form for plural informal commands.

Giving affirmative commands with tú

Singular, affirmative, familiar commands are very easy to form. For all verbs except those that are completely irregular, you just take the present tense **tú** form of the verb and drop the final **-s**.

Let's take a look at how easy this is. The following table shows how to form **tú** commands by dropping the final **-s** from the present tense.

Infinitive	Present Tense tú form	Tú Command	Meaning
hablar	hablas	habla	*speak*
leer	lees	lee	*read*
escribir	escribes	escribe	*write*
explicar	explicas	explica	*explain*
pagar	pagas	paga	*pay*
organizar	organizas	organiza	*organize*
obedecer	obedeces	obedece	*obey*
conducir	conduces	conduce	*drive*
cerrar	cierras	cierra	*close*
mostrar	muestras	muestra	*show*
enviar	envías	envía	*send*
continuar	continúas	continúa	*continue*
defender	defiendes	defiende	*defend*
volver	vuelves	vuelve	*return*
advertir	adviertes	advierte	*warn*
dormir	duermes	duerme	*sleep*
contribuir	contribuyes	contribuye	*contribute*

Here are a couple of examples to show you how easy this can be:

Habla español. (*Speak Spanish.*)

Escribe tu nombre. (*Write your name.*)

Explica las reglas. (*Explain the rules.*)

Advierte a los demás. (*Warn the others.*)

A few verbs, however, have irregular command forms in the affirmative only and must be memorized.

Table 11-4 displays irregular affirmative **tú** command verbs.

Table 11-4   Irregular Verbs

Spanish Verbs	Affirmative	Meaning
decir	di	*say*
hacer	haz	*do, make*
ir	ve	*go*
poner	pon	*put*
salir	sal	*leave*
ser	sé	*be*
tener	ten	*have*
venir	ven	*come*

Here are a couple of examples of these irregular verbs in commanding action:

Pon el libro en la mochila. (*Put the book in the backpack.*)

Ven aquí. (*Come here.*)

PRACTICE

Your friend wants to help you cook. Write down instructions for her, using the singular familiar command form. I provide the regular verbs in parentheses and you insert the proper command form. Here's an example:

Q. (abrir) _____ el saco de legumbres.

A. **Abre el saco de** For regular **-er** verbs, drop **-s** from the present tense form.

31 (proceder) _____ lentamente.

32 (leer) _____ la receta.

33 (ser) _____ diligente.

34 (limpiar) _____ las verduras.

35 (pelar) _____ las zanahorias.

36 (mezclar) _____ los guisantes con las zanahorias.

37 (cortar) _____ cebollas.

38 (poner) _____ todos los ingredientes en una cacerola.

39 (anadir) _____ mantequilla y aqua.

40 (cubrir) _____ la cacerola.

41 (tener) _____ paciencia.

42 (dejar) _____ cocinar por treinta minutos.

Giving negative commands with tú

To form a singular, negative, familiar command with any verb when **tú** is the subject, you use the present subjunctive **tú** form. Follow these steps to form the present subjunctive (for a more in depth, look see Chapter 6):

1. Drop the final **-o** from the **yo** form of the present tense.

2. For infinitives ending in **-ar,** add **-es** for the **tú** form.

3. For infinitives ending in **-er** or **-ir,** add **-as** for the **tú** form.

4. To form the negative, put **no** before the verb.

The following table shows how to form negative **tú** commands using the present subjunctive of the **tú** form.

Infinitive	Present Subjunctive	Negative Command	Meaning
hablar	hables	no hables	*don't speak*
leer	leas	no leas	*don't read*
escribir	escribas	no escribas	*don't write*
explicar	expliques	no expliques	*don't explain*
pagar	pagues	no pagues	*don't pay*
organizar	organices	no organices	*don't organize*
obedecer	obedezcas	no obedezcas	*don't obey*
conducir	conduzcas	no conduzcas	*don't drive*
cerrar	cierres	no cierres	*don't close*
mostrar	muestres	no muestres	*don't show*
enviar	envíes	no envíes	*don't send*
continuar	continúes	no continúes	*don't continue*
defender	defiendas	no defiendas	*don't defend*
volver	vuelvas	no vuelvas	*don't return*
advertir	adviertas	no adviertas	*don't warn*
dormir	duermas	no duermas	*don't sleep*
contribuir	contribuyas	no contribuyas	*don't contribute*
traer	traigas	no traigas	*don't bring*
escoger	escojas	no escojas	*don't choose*
distinguir	distingas	no distingas	*don't distinguish*
pedir	pidas	no pidas	*don't ask*

Here are some examples that show how negative singular familiar commands should look:

No hables tan rápidamente. (*Don't speak so fast.*)

No leas ese libro. (*Don't read that book.*)

No pagues la cuenta. (*Don't pay the bill.*)

No obedezcas a esa mujer. (*Don't obey that woman.*)

No traigas el periódico. (*Don't bring the newspaper.*)

Table 11-5   Verbs with Spelling and Stem Changes

Spanish Verbs	Present Subjunctive	Negative Command	Meaning
colgar (-**o** to -**ue**/-**g** to -**gu**)	**cuelgues**	**no cuelgues**	(*don't*) hang
jugar (-**u** to- **ue**/-**g** to -**gu**)	**juegues**	**no juegues**	(*don't*) play
comenzar (-**e** to -**ie**/-**z** to -**c**)	**comiences**	**no comiences**	(*don't*) begin
empezar (-**e** to- **ie**/-**z** to -**c**)	**empieces**	**no empieces**	(*don't*) begin
almorzar (-**o** to -**ue**/-**z** to -**c**)	**almuerces**	**no almuerces**	(*don't*) eat lunch
corregir (-**e** to -**i**/-**g** to -**j**)	**corrijas**	**no corrijas**	(*don't*) correct
seguir (-**e** to -**i**/-**gu** to -**g**)	**sigas**	**no sigas**	(*don't*) follow

Verbs with both spelling and stem changes can be quite tricky. Table 11-5 lists some high-frequency Spanish verbs that undergo two changes in the negative:

The examples here show these verbs in the negative singular familiar command form:

No cuelgues. (*Don't hang up.*)

No juegues con el gato. (*Don't play with the cat.*)

PRACTICE

Your friend Verónica wants to lose weight. Write out your suggestions for her by using the singular, familiar, affirmative, and negative command form of the verb I provide in parentheses. Take your time with this exercise. It requires a lot of attention to detail.

Q. (exigir) No _____ helado, _____ ensalada.

A. No exijas helado, exige ensalada.

43 (tener) No _____ dudas, _____ confianza.

44 (salir) _____ del gimnasio contenta, no _____ triste.

45 (pedir) No _____ una porción grande, _____ una porción pequeña.

46 (poner) No _____ mayonesa en tu sándwich, _____ mostaza.

47 (hacer) _____ ejercicios físicos frecuentemente, no _____ ejercicios raramente.

48 (jugar) No _____ a las damas, _____ a un deporte.

(49) (almorzar) _____ cuando tengas hambre, no _____ después de comer algo.

(50) (seguir) _____ tu régimen concienzudamente, no _____ tu régimen solamente de vez en cuando.

(51) (perder) No _____ diez libras, _____ veinte libras.

(52) (continuar) _____ el régimen cuando estés bien, no _____ el régimen cuando estés enferma.

(53) (ser) _____ optimista, no _____ pesimista.

(54) (mostrar) No _____ tu menú a tus amigas, _____ tu menú a tu entrenadora.

(55) (escoger) Siempre _____ verduras, no _____ nunca postres.

(56) (ir) No _____ al cine, _____ al gimnasio.

(57) (gozar) _____ de la comida saludable, no _____ de la comida poco saludable.

Giving plural commands with vosotros

Because the **vosotros** commands are used primarily in Spain, you may not have occasion to use them. But just in case you need them, this section's got you covered.

Using affirmative vosotros commands

Forming plural, affirmative, familiar commands is a cinch. For all Spanish verbs, including irregular verbs, you just drop the final **-r** of the infinitive and add **-d,** as illustrated in the following table.

Infinitive	Vosotros Command	Meaning
hablar	hablad	*speak*
leer	leed	*read*
escribir	escribid	*write*
explicar	explicad	*explain*
hacer	haced	*do*
ir	id	*go*
ser	sed	*be*

Here are some example commands:

Hablad más despacio. (*Speak more slowly.*)

Venid acá. (*Come here.*)

PRACTICE

Your two nieces are coming over to babysit your children. Write them a note to tell them what to do. Use the affirmative, plural, familiar form of the verb I provide for each question to form a full sentence. Here's an example:

Q. hablar/con ellos.

A. Hablad con ellos. To form the **vosotros** affirmative command, drop **-r** from the infinitive and add **-d**.

58 mirar/la televisión con ellos. _____

59 insistir/en comer temprano._____

60 ayudar/a los niños con sus tareas. _____

61 leer/historias a los niños. _____

62 prometer/ acostar a los niños a las ocho. _____

63 escribir/una nota si hay problemas. _____

Using negative vosotros commands

You form all plural, negative, familiar commands by using the present subjunctive **vosotros** form of the verb, even for irregular verbs. (See Chapter 6).

To form a negative command with any verb when **vosotros** is the subject, use the present subjunctive **vosotros** form:

1. Drop the final **-o** from the **yo** form of the present tense.

2. For infinitives ending in **-ar,** add **-éis** for the **vosotros** form.

3. For infinitives ending in **-er** or **-ir,** add **-áis** for the **vosotros** form.

4. To form the negative, put **no** before the verb.

Table 11-6 shows how to form negative **vosotros** commands using the present subjunctive of the **vosotros** form. Note the following:

REMEMBER

>> Verbs with spelling changes, change **-car**, **-gar**, and **-zar**, change **-c** to **-qu, -g** to **-gu,** and **-z** to **-c** in all present subjunctive forms. (See **buscar, pagar,** and **utilizar.**)

>> The stem vowel of certain **-ir** stem-changing verbs change **-e** to **-i** and **-o** to **-u** in the **nosotros** and **vosotros** forms. (See **dormir, pedir,** and **seguir.**)

WARNING

>> Stem-changing **-ar, -er,** and **-ir** verbs have stem changes in the present subjunctive in all forms *except* **nosotros** and **vosotros.** For the plural, familiar command construction, when a verb has both a spelling and a stem change, only the spelling change occurs, and it occurs only in the negative form. (See **jugar.**)

Table 11-6　　Negative Vosotros Commands

Regular Verbs	Present Subjunctive	Negative	Meaning
firmar	firméis	no firméis	*don't sign*
comer	comáis	no comáis	*don't eat*
subir	subáis	no subáis	*don't go up*
buscar	busquéis	no busquéis	*don't look for*
pagar	paguéis	no paguéis	*don't pay*
utilizar	utilicéis	no utilicéis	*don't use*
cerrar	cerréis	no cerréis	*don't close*
volver	volváis	no volváis	*don't return*
pedir	pidáis	no pidáis	*don't ask*
dormir	durmáis	no durmáis	*don't sleep*
jugar	juguéis	no juguéis	*don't play*
seguir	sigáis	no sigáis	*don't follow*
ir	vayáis	no vayáis	*don't go*

Here's how your negative **vosotros** commands should look:

No tiréis la cuerda. (*Don't pull the cord.*)

No bebáis café. (*Don't drink coffee.*)

No restistáis. (*Don't resist.*)

No pidáis ayuda. (*Don't ask for help.*)

No colguéis la noticia aquí. (*Don't hang the notice here.*)

No comencéis. (*Don't begin.*)

No vayáis allá. (*Don't go there.*)

No seáis pesimistas. (*Don't be pessimistic.*)

PRACTICE

Your friends will be doing some traveling and you want to give them some advice so they don't make any big mistakes. Use the plural, negative, familiar form of the verbs provide in parentheses. Here's an example:

Q. (caminar) No _____ solos.

A. **No caminéis solos.** To form the negative **vosotros** command, use the **vosotros** form of the present subjunctive.

64　(ir) No _____al aeropuerto tarde.

65　(pagar) No _____en efectivo.

66 (dar) No _____ vuestros nombres a un desconocido.

67 (hacer) No _____ vuestras maletas a última hora.

68 (llevar) No _____ ningún artículo peligroso en vuestro equipaje.

69 (olvidar) No _____ vuestros pasaportes.

You need advice, so you seek help from a friend and a teacher. Both say the same things to you, but your friend uses the **tú** command form and your teacher uses the **Ud.** command form. I provide verb phrases in parentheses. You write each command of the verb in the familiar and in the polite command form. Here's an example:

Q. Yo no salgo bien en mi clase. (estudiar más)

A. *Friend*: **Estudia más.** Drop **-s** from the present tense **tú** form of the verb.

Teacher: **Estudie más.** For **-ar** verbs, drop **-a** from the **Ud.** form of the verb and add **-e.**

Q. Mis padres no están contentos de mis notas. (no salir tan frecuentemente)

A. *Friend*: **No salgas tan frecuentemente.** Use the **tú** form of the present subjunctive.

Teacher: **No salga tan frecuentemente.** Drop **-o** from the present tense **yo** form of the verb and add **-a.**

70 Estoy enfermo. (no venir a la escuela)

Friend: _____

Teacher: _____

71 Tengo una cita con mi profesor. (no llegar tarde)

Friend: _____

Teacher: _____

72 Quiero comprar un abrigo muy caro. (pagar con una tarjeta de crédito)

Friend: _____

Teacher: _____

73 Quiero regresar tarde a casa. (pedir permiso)

Friend: _____

Teacher: _____

74 No sé nadar. (no ir a la playa)

Friend: _____

Teacher: _____

75 No me gustan los perros. (no tener miedo de Fido)

Friend: _____

Teacher: _____

76 Cometo muchos errores. (corregir el trabajo)

Friend: _____

Teacher: _____

77 Estoy cansado. (cerrar los ojos)

Friend: _____

Teacher: _____

Using Object Pronouns in Commands

Object pronouns (including reflexive pronouns) have different positions in affirmative and negative commands. It's also quite common in Spanish that a sentence requires both a direct and an indirect object pronoun.

Single object pronouns

In affirmative commands, object pronouns follow the verb and are attached to it. You place an accent on the stressed vowel. Usually, you count back three vowels and add the accent.

Here are some examples with single object pronouns:

Direct object: **¡Ayúdeme (Ud.)!** (*Help me!*)

Indirect object: **¡Escríbanles (Uds.)!** (*Write to them!*)

Reflexive verb: **¡Levántate (tú)!** (*Get up!*)

REMEMBER

For the following command, count back four vowels and add an accent to maintain proper stress:

¡Tráiganlos! (*Bring them!*)

In negative commands, object pronouns precede the verb. These examples show you how it's done:

!No lo hagas (tú)! (*Don't do it!*)

¡No nos escuchen (Uds.)! (*Don't listen to us!*)

¡No se duerma (Ud.) (*Don't fall asleep!*)

Double object pronouns

When the command has two object pronouns, the indirect object pronoun (a person) precedes the direct object pronoun (usually a thing):

¡Dígamelo! (*Tell it to me!*)

¡No me lo diga! (*Don't tell it to me!*)

¡Muéstrasela! (*Show it to her!*)

¡No se la muestres! (*Don't show it to her!*)

PRACTICE

You are at a bridal shower. Express the commands that are given. Follow the example.

Q. (**Uds./el champán**) *Serve it to me.*

A. ¡**Sírvanmelo!** The verb **servir** expresses *to serve*. Use the **Uds.** command form: change **-en** to **-an**. **Servir** has an **-e** to **-i** stem change. The indirect object **me** (*to me*) precedes the direct object **lo,** which refers to the masculine noun, **el champán.**

78 (**tú/los regalos**) (*Show them to her.*) _____

79 (**Ud./el rumor**) (*Don't tell it to us.*) _____

80 (**vosotros/las cartas**) (*Give them to me.*) _____

81 (**tú/el postre**) (*Don't bring it to them.*)_____

82 (**Uds./ayuda**) (*Offer it to them*)_____

Answers to "Getting Attention with Commands" Practice Questions

The following are the answers to the practice questions presented in this chapter.

1. **Beba.** For **-er** verbs, drop **-e** and add **-a.**

2. **Respire.** For **-ar** verbs, drop **-a** and add **-e.**

3. **Insista.** For **-ir** verbs, drop **-e** and add **-a.**

4. **Tome.** For **-ar** verbs, drop **-a** and add **-e.**

5. **Coma.** For **-er** verbs, drop **-e** and add **-a.**

6. **Consuma.** For **-ir** verbs, drop **-e** and add **-a.**

7. **Tenga.** Take the **yo** form of the present tense. Drop the **-o** and add **-a.**

8. **Diga.** Take the **yo** form of the present tense. Drop the **-o** and add **-a.**

9. **Venga.** Take the **yo** form of the present tense. Drop the **-o** and add **-a.**

10. **Traiga.** Take the **yo** form of the present tense. Drop the **-o** and add **-a.**

11. **Haga.** Take the **yo** form of the present tense. Drop the **-o** and add **-a.**

12. **Salga.** Take the **yo** form of the present tense. Drop the **-o** and add **-a.**

13. **destruyan. Destruir** is stem-changing verb that adds a **-y** after the **-u.** Add the **-an** ending for the plural.

14. **cierren. Cerrar** is a stem-changing verb that changes **-e** to **-ie.** Add the **-en** ending for the plural.

15. **mientan. Mentir** is a stem-changing verb that changes **-e** to **-ie.** Add the **-an** ending for the plural.

16. **digan.** Take the **yo** form of the present tense. Drop the **-o** and add **-an** for the plural.

17. **pierdan. Perder** is a stem-changing verb that changes **-e** to **ie.** Add the **-an** ending for the plural.

18. **pidan. Pedir** is a stem-changing verb that changes **-e** to **i** (**-ir**). Add the **-an** ending for the plural.

19. **haga.** Take the **yo** form of the present tense. Drop the **-o** and add **-an.**

20. **pongan.** Take the **yo** form of the present tense. Drop the **-o** and add **-an.**

21. **estén. Estar** is an irregular verb. Add the **-en** ending for the plural.

22. **organicen. Organizar** is a **-z** to **-c** spelling change verb. Add the **-en** ending for the plural.

23. **tengan.** Take the **yo** form of the present tense. Drop the **-o** and add **-an.**

(24) **vayan. Ir** is an irregular verb. Add the **-an** ending for the plural.

(25) **cuelguen. Colgar** is a stem-changing verb that changes **-o** to **-ue**. It is also a **-g** to **-gu** spelling change verb. Add the **-en** ending for the plural.

(26) **empiece. Empezar** is a stem-changing verb that changes **-e** to **-ie**. It is also a **-z** to **-c** spelling change verb. Add the **-en** ending for the plural.

(27) **apaguen. Apagar** is a **-g** to **-gu** spelling change verb. Add the **-en** ending for the plural.

(28) **saquen. Sacar** is a **-c** to **-qu** spelling change verb. Add the **-en** ending for the plural.

(29) **recoja. Recoger** is a **-g** to **-j** spelling change verb. Add the **-an** ending for the plural.

(30) **siga. Seguir** is a stem-changing verb that changes **-e** to **-i**. It is also a **-gu** to **-g** spelling change verb. Add the **-en** ending for the plural.

(31) **Procede.** For regular **-er** verbs, drop **-s** from the present tense form.

(32) **Lee.** For regular **-er** verbs, drop **-s** from the present tense form.

(33) **Sé. Ser** is an irregular verb.

(34) **Limpia.** For regular **-ar** verbs, drop **-s** from the present tense form.

(35) **Pela.** For regular **-ar** verbs, drop **-s** from the present tense form.

(36) **Mezcla.** For regular **-ar** verbs, drop **-s** from the present tense form.

(37) **Corta.** For regular **-ar** verbs, drop **-s** from the present tense form.

(38) **Pon. Poner** is an irregular verb.

(39) **Añade.** For regular **-ir** verbs, drop **-s** from the present tense form.

(40) **Cubre.** For regular **-ir** verbs, drop **-s** from the present tense form.

(41) **Ten. Tener** is an irregular verb.

(42) **Deja.** For regular **-ar** verbs, drop **-s** from the present tense form.

(43) **tengas/ten.** For the negative, use the **tú** form of the subjunctive and add **-as. Tener** is irregular in an affirmative command.

(44) **sal/salgas. Salir** is irregular in an affirmative command. For the negative, use the **tú** form of the subjunctive.

(45) **pidas/pide. Pedir** is a stem-changing **-e** to **-i** verb. For the negative, use the **tú** form of the subjunctive and add **-as**. For the affirmative, drop **-s** from the present tense **tú** form.

(46) **pongas/pon. Poner** is irregular in an affirmative command. For the negative, use the **tú** form of the subjunctive and add **-as**.

(47) **haz/hagas. Hacer** is irregular in an affirmative command. For the negative, use the **tú** form of the subjunctive and add **-as**.

(48) **juegues/juega. Jugar** is a stem-changing **-u** to **-ue** and a verb with a **-g** to **-gu** spelling change. For the negative, use the **tú** form of the subjunctive and add **-es**. For the affirmative, drop **-s** from the present tense **tú** form.

(49) **almuerza/almuerces. Almorzar** is a stem-changing **-o** to **-ue** verb and a verb with a **-z** to **-c** spelling change. For the affirmative, drop **-s** from the present tense **tú** form. For the negative, use the **tú** form of the subjunctive and add **-es.**

(50) **sigue/sigas. Seguir** is a stem-changing **-e** to **-i** verb and a verb with **-gu** to **-g** spelling change. For the affirmative, drop **-s** from the present tense **tú** form. For the negative, use the **tú** form of the subjunctive and add **-as.**

(51) **pierdas/pierde. Perder** is a stem-changing **-e** to **-ie** verb. For the negative, use the **tú** form of the subjunctive and add **-as.** For the affirmative, drop **-s** from the present tense **tú** form.

(52) **continúa/continúes. Continuar** is a verb with **-u** to **-ú** stem change. For the affirmative, drop **-s** from the present tense **tú** form. For the negative, use the **tú** form of the subjunctive and add **-es.**

(53) **sé/seas. Ser** is an irregular verb.

(54) **muestres/muestra. Mostrar** is a stem-changing **-o** to **-ue** verb. For the negative, use the **tú** form of the subjunctive and add **-es.** For the affirmative, drop **-s** from the present tense **tú** form.

(55) **escoge/escojas. Escoger** is a verb with **-g** to **-j** spelling change. For the affirmative, drop **-s** from the present tense **tú** form. For the negative, use the **tú** form of the subjunctive and add **-as.**

(56) **vayas/ve. Ir** is an rregular verb.

(57) **goza/goces. Gozar** is a verb with a **-z** to **-c** spelling change. For the affirmative, drop **-s** from the present tense **tú** form. For the negative, use the **tú** form of the subjunctive and add **-es.**

(58) **Mirad la televión con ellos.** To form the **vosotros** affirmative command, drop **-r** from the infinitive and add **-d.**

(59) **Insistid en comer temprano.** To form the **vosotros** affirmative command, drop **-r** from the infinitive and add **-d.**

(60) **Ayudad a los niños con sus tareas.** To form the **vosotros** affirmative command, drop **-r** from the infinitive and add **-d.**

(61) **Leed historias a los niños.** To form the **vosotros** affirmative command, drop **-r** from the infinitive and add **-d.**

(62) **Prometed acostar a los niños a las ocho.** To form the **vosotros** affirmative command, drop **-r** from the infinitive and add **-d.**

(63) **Escribid una nota si hay problemas.** To form the **vosotros** affirmative command, drop **-r** from the infinitive and add **-d.**

(64) **vayáis. Ir** is an irregular verb in the subjunctive.

(65) **paguéis. Pagar** is a verb with **-g** to **-gu** spelling change.

(66) **deis.** To form the negative **vosotros** command, use the **vosotros** form of the present subjunctive.

(67) **hagáis.** To form the negative **vosotros** command, use the **vosotros** form of the present subjunctive.

68 **llevéis.** To form the negative **vosotros** command, use the **vosotros** form of the present subjunctive.

69 **olvidéis.** To form the negative **vosotros** command, use the **vosotros** form of the present subjunctive.

70 Friend: **No vengas a la escuela.** Use the **tú** form of the present subjunctive.

Teacher: **No venga a la escuela.** Drop **-o** from the **yo** form of the verb and add **-a,** which is the same as the present subjunctive **Ud.** form.

71 Friend: **No llegues tarde. Llegar** is a spelling change **-g** to **-gu** verb. Use the **tú** form of the present subjunctive.

Teacher: **No llegue tarde. Llegar** is a spelling change **-g** to **-gu** verb. Add **-e** for the singular.

72 Friend: **Paga con una tarjeta de crédito.** Drop **-s** from the present tense **tú** form of the verb.

Teacher: **Pague con una tarjeta de crédito. Pagar** is a spelling change **-g** to **-gu** verb. Add **-e** for the singular.

73 Friend: **Pide permiso. Pedir** is a spelling change **-e** to **-i** verb. Drop **-s** from the present tense **tú** form of the verb.

Teacher: **Pida permiso. Pedir** is a spelling change **-e** to **-i** verb. Drop **-e** from the **Ud.** form of the verb and add **-a.**

74 Friend: **No vayas a la piscina. Ir** is an irregular verb. Use the **tú** form of the present subjunctive.

Teacher: **No vaya a la piscina. Ir** is an irregular verb. Use the present subjunctive **Ud.** form.

75 Friend: **No tengas miedo de Fido.** Use the **tú** form of the present subjunctive.

Teacher: **No tenga miedo de Fido.** Drop **-o** from the present tense **yo** form of the verb and add **-a,** which is the same as the present subjunctive **Ud.** form.

76 Friend: **Corrige el trabajo.** Drop **-s** from the present tense **tú** form of the verb.

Teacher: **Corrija el trabajo. Corregir** is a verb with a **-g** to **-j** spelling change. Drop **-o** from the present tense **yo** form of the verb and add **-a,** which is the same as the present subjunctive **Ud.** form.

77 Friend: **Cierra los ojos. Cerrar** is a spelling change **-e** to **-ie** verb. Drop **-s** from the present tense **tú** form of the verb.

Teacher: **Cierre los ojos. Cerrar** is a spelling change **-e** to **-ie** verb. Drop **-o** from the present tense **yo** form of the verb and add **-e,** which is the same as the present subjunctive **Ud.** form.

(78) **¡Muéstraselos!** The verb **mostrar** expresses *to show.* Use the **tú** command form: change **-as** to **-a. Mostrar** has an **-o** to **-ue** stem change. The indirect object **se** (*to her*) precedes the direct object **los,** which refers to the masculine plural noun, **los regalos.** In an affirmative command the pronouns follow the verb and are attached to it. Count back four vowels and add an accent.

(79) **¡No nos lo diga!** The verb **decir** expresses *to tell.* Use the **Ud.** command form, **diga,** which is irregular. The indirect object **nos** (*to us*) precedes the direct object **lo,** which refers to the masculine singular noun, **el rumor.** In a negative command the pronouns precede the verb.

(80) **¡Dádmelas!** The verb **dar** expresses *to give.* Use the **vosotros** command form: drop **-a** from the infinitive and add **-d.** The indirect object **me** (*to me*) precedes the direct object **las,** which refers to the feminine plural noun, **las cartas.** In an affirmative command the pronouns follow the verb and are attached to it. Count back three vowels and add an accent.

(81) **¡No se lo traigas!** The verb **traer** expresses *to bring.* Use the **tú** command negative form, **traigas,** which is irregular. The indirect object **se** (*to them*) precedes the direct object **lo,** which refers to the masculine singular noun, **el postre.** In a negative command the pronouns precede the verb.

(82) **¡Ofrézcansela!** The verb **ofrecer** expresses *to offer.* **Ofrecer** has a **-c** to **-zc** spelling change. Use the **Uds.** command form, **ofrezcan,** which reflects this change. The indirect object **se** (*to them*) precedes the direct object **la,** which refers to the feminine singular noun, **ayuda.** In an affirmative command the pronouns follow the verb and are attached to it.

Chapter **12**

Preparing to Connect with Prepositions

Prepositions are words used before nouns or pronouns to relate them to other words in the sentence. Think of prepositions as words that join different words, clauses, or phrases. Have you ever heard of a dangling preposition? Writing a sentence with one is a big no-no among grammarians. Here's an example: "That's the car I'm dreaming *about.*" Why is this sentence grammatically incorrect? Because prepositions should always be followed by objects to create prepositional phrases. How should the sentence read? "That's the car *about* which I'm dreaming." Yes, it definitely sounds awkward, but that's the proper way to express that thought.

In this chapter, I introduce you to common Spanish prepositions, and I explain how to select the most appropriate preposition for your sentences. Certain Spanish verbs require a preposition before an infinitive, so being familiar with them will enhance your speaking and writing skills. Also, you'll discover the special pronouns that follow prepositions. By the time you finish this chapter, the quality of your Spanish connections should be excellent!

Using Common Spanish Prepositions

Prepositions are important because they're frequently used in speaking and writing. They connect and relate vocabulary words and pronouns to other words in the sentence. A preposition with its object and any modifiers is called a *prepositional phrase.* In Spanish, prepositions also may contract with articles: **a + el = al, de + el = del,** and so on. (See Chapter 3 for more on articles.)

Here are some examples of Spanish prepositions at work:

> **Necesito esa hoja *de* papel.** (*I need that piece **of** paper.*)
>
> **El niño empieza *a* reír.** (*The child begins **to** laugh.*)
>
> **Ella estudia *con* sus amigas.** (*She studies **with** her friends.*)
>
> **¿Qué piensas *de* esto?** (*What do you think **about** that?*)

High-frequency Spanish prepositions are listed in Table 12-1.

Table 12-1   Common Spanish Prepositions

Preposition	Meaning	Preposition	Meaning
a	to, at	detrás de	behind
a eso de (+ time)	about (time)	durante	during
a fuerza de	by persevering	en	in, on, by
a pesar de	in spite of	en cambio	on the other hand
a tiempo	on time	en casa de	at the house of
a través (de)	across, through	en lugar de	instead of
acerca de	about	en vez de	instead of
además de	besides	encima de	above, on top of
alrededor de	around	enfrente de	opposite, in front of
antes (de)	before	entre	between
cerca de	near	frente a	in front of
con	with	fuera de	outside of
contra	against	hacia	toward
de	of, from, about	hasta	until
de otro modo	otherwise	lejos de	far
debajo de	beneath, under	por	for, by
delante de	in front of	para	for
dentro de	inside, within	según	according to
desde	since	sin	without
después (de)	after	sobre	over, above, on, upon

Here are more examples to show you prepositions at work in Spanish:

> **La farmacia está *cerca del* supermercado.** (*The pharmacy is **near the** supermarket.*)
>
> **A *fuerza de* estudiar Ud. saldrá bien.** (*By studying you will succeed.*)

Manuel is writing an email to a friend. In the email, he states what he does when he leaves the office. Complete his email with the missing prepositions: **a, al, antes de, cerca de, con, de, dentro de, después de, en, enfrente de, entre, para**. Use each preposition only once.

Q. Hay un banco _____ mi oficina.

A. cerca de. Use **cerca de** to express *near*.

No vivo _____ (1) mi oficina. Por eso, _____ (2) ir _____ (3) casa tomo el autobús. Afortunadamente, el autobús se para _____ (4) de mi casa. Cuando llego y _____ (5) entrar, saco mis llaves _____ (6) mi bolsillo y abro la puerta. _____ (7) de entrar, pongo todo lo que llevo _____ (8) la mesa y hablo _____ (9) mi hermano. Entonces voy _____ (10) comedor que está situado _____ (11) la cocina y la sala. _____ (12) cinco minutos ceno.

Distinguishing One Preposition from Another

Sometimes, selecting the correct preposition to use in a sentence can be tricky, because some prepositions have more than one meaning. Take **a**, for example, which can mean *to* or *at*; **en**, which can mean *at*, *on*, or *in*; and **por** and **para**, which can both mean *for*. I'm sure you can see the dilemma. Fortunately, Spanish has some rules that will help you understand when the more common prepositions are appropriate.

A

I'll start with the preposition **a** (which contracts with the definite article **el** to become **al**). You use **a** to show:

>> Time: **Te llamo a las tres.** (*I'll call you at three o'clock.*)

>> Movement: **Vamos a la playa.** (*We're going to the beach.*)

>> Location: **Espere a la entrada.** (*Wait at the entrance.*)

>> Means/manner: **Hágalo a mano.** (*Do it by hand.*) **Se prepara a la española.** (*It's prepared the Spanish way.*)

>> Price: **Puede comprarlo a cien pesos.** (*You can buy it for 100 pesos.*)

>> Speed: **Iba a cien kilómetros por hora.** (*He was going 1,000 kilometers per hour.*)

You use the preposition **a** before a direct object alluding to a person; this is referred to as the *personal a* (see Chapter 11):

Buscamos al señor Nuñez. (*We are looking for Mr. Nuñez.*)

De

Another preposition with several meanings is **de** (which contracts with the definite article **el** to become **del**). You use **de**, which means *of, from,* or *about,* to show:

>> Possession: **Es el coche de Julio.** (*It's Julio's car.*)

>> Origin: **Soy de Panamá.** (*I'm from Panama.*)

>> Time: **No duerme de noche.** (*He doesn't sleep at night.*)

>> Cause: **Fracasa de no estudiar.** (*He is failing from not studying.*)

>> Material: **Es un anillo de oro.** (*It's a gold ring.*)

>> Characteristics: **Es de buena calidad.** (*It's of a good quality.*)

>> Contents: **Bebo una taza de café.** (*I'm drinking a cup of coffee.*)

>> Relationship: **Madrid es la capital de España.** (*Madrid is the capital of Spain.*)

>> Part of a whole: **Toma un trozo de pan.** (*She's taking a piece of bread.*)

>> A subject: **No encuentro mi libro de arte.** (*I can't find my art book.*)

>> A superlative: **Es el más alto de todos.** (*He's the tallest of them all.*)

En

Now I'll move on to the preposition **en,** which can mean *in, by at,* or *on.* You use **en** to show:

>> Time: **Estamos en el otoño.** (*It's [We're in] the fall.*)

>> Location: **Está en esta calle.** (*It's on that street.*) **Trabajo en esta tienda.** (*I work at that store.*)

>> Means/manner: **Hable en voz baja.** (*Speak in a low voice.*) **Está escrita en español.** (*It's written in Spanish.*)

>> Movement: **Entran en el banco.** (*They enter the bank.*)

>> Means of transportation: **Viajan en avión.** (*They are traveling by plane.*)

TIP

If you're speaking about a means of transportation for a passenger, use **en** rather than **por** to express *by:*

> **Van a la capital en tren.** (*They are going to the capital by train.*)

Hasta

The preposition **hasta,** which means *until* (but which can also have the meaning *to*), shows the following:

>> Place/location: **Conduzca hasta el semáforo.** (*Drive to the traffic light.*)

>> Time: **Hasta luego.** (*See you later. [Until then.]*)

Para vs. Por

Now you come to two prepositions that can cause much confusion among students of Spanish. **Por** and **para** both mean *for* in English, which is what causes the problem.

The preposition **para** shows the following:

>> Destination/place: **Salimos para Madrid.** (*We are leaving for Madrid.*)

>> Destination/person: **Esto es para Ud.** (*This is for you.*)

>> A future time limit: **Es para mañana.** (*It's for tomorrow.*)

>> Purpose/goal: **Nado para divertirme.** (*I swim to have fun.*)

>> Use/function: **Es un cepillo para el pelo.** (*It's a hairbrush.*)

>> Comparisons: **Para su edad, lee bien.** (*For her age, she reads well.*)

>> Opinion: **Para mí es demasiado crudo.** (*For me it's too rare.*)

The preposition **por** shows the following:

>> Motion/place: **Caminan por las calles.** (*They walk through the streets.*)

>> Means/manner: **Lo envío por correo aéreo.** (*I'm sending it by airmail.*)

>> In exchange for/substitution: **Voy a hacerlo por tí.** (*I'm going to do it for you.*)

>> Duration of an action: **Trabajo por una hora.** (*I'm working for an hour.*)

>> Indefinite time period: **Duerme por la tarde.** (*He sleeps in the afternoon.*)

>> On behalf of: **La firmo por Ud.** (*I am signing it on your behalf.*)

>> Per: **Me pagan por día.** (*They pay me per day.*)

REMEMBER

You use **por** to express *for* after the verbs **enviar** (*to send*), **ir** (*to go*), **mandar** (*to order, send*), **preguntar** (*to ask*), **regresar** (*to return*), **venir** (*to come*), and **volver** (*to return*). Here are two examples:

> **Voy (Envío, Pregunto) por la factura.** (*I am going [sending, asking] for the bill.*)

> **Ven (Regresa, Vuelve) por tu libro.** (*Come [Return, Come back] for your book.*)

You also use **por** in the following adverbial expressions:

>> **por eso** (*therefore, so*)

> • **Trabaja mucho y por eso gana mucho dinero.** (*He works a lot and therefore he earns a lot of money.*)

>> **por lo general** (*generally*)

> • **Por lo general me acuesto a las diez.** (*Generally, I go to bed at ten o'clock.*)

>> **por supuesto** (*of course*)

> • **¿Puede Ud. ayudarme? ¡Por supuesto!** (*Can you help me? Of course!*)

PRACTICE

You're on vacation in Puerto Rico, and you're writing a postcard home to a friend. Complete the postcard with the correct proposition: **a (al), de, en, hasta, para, por.**

Q. Vivo _____ Puerto Rico.

A. **en** Use **en** to express *in* and a location.

This is a handmade post-card from the art studio of
Fernando

Postcard

Place
Stamp
Here

Rodrigo,

Estoy_____(13) San Juan. Es la capital
_____(14) Puerto Rico. Voy_____(15) la
playa todos los días._____(16)
divertirme hablo_____(17) todo el
mundo. No me quedo_____(18) sol
porque no quiero sufrir_____(19) una
quemadura de sol. Compré dos botellas_____
(20) bronceador_____(21) diez dólares
cada una. Nado_____(22) el mar
cada día_____(23) una hora _____
(24) hacer ejercicio. Cada noche salgo_____
(25) las nueve y no regreso_____(26) el
dos_____(27) la mañana. Voy_____
(28) quedarme aquí en San Juan _____
(29) el tres de junio._____(30) luego.

Fernando

Focusing on Prepositions Used with Infinitives

The only verb form in the Spanish language that may follow a preposition is an infinitive. Some Spanish verbs require the preposition **a, de, en,** or **con** before the infinitive. Other Spanish verbs that are followed immediately by the infinitive don't require a preposition. The following sections break down all the categories for you.

Spanish verbs requiring a

How can you tell which verbs require the preposition **a** before the infinitive? Generally, verbs that express beginning, motion, teaching, or learning take **a.** However, many other verbs use this preposition before an infinitive, so the best answer to the question is that you have to memorize these verbs. After you've used them often enough, you'll develop the instinctive feeling that **a** is the preposition of choice. Table 12-2 shows which Spanish verbs call for the use of **a** before the infinitive.

Table 12-2   Spanish Verbs Requiring A

Infinitive	Meaning
acercarse	to approach
acostumbrarse	to become accustomed to
aprender	to learn to
apresurarse	to hurry to
atreverse	to dare to
ayudar	to help to
comenzar (-ie)	to begin to
correr	to run to
decidirse	to decide to
dedicarse	to devote oneself to
disponerse	to get ready to
empezar (-ie)	to begin to
enseñar	to teach to
ir	to go
llegar	to succeed in
negarse (-ie)	to refuse to
obligar	to force to
ponerse	to begin to
resignarse	to resign oneself to
salir	to go out to
venir (-ie)	to come to
volver (-ue)	to return (again) to

Here are some examples that show how you use the preposition **a**:

> **Los niños se apresuran a llegar a tiempo.** (*The children hurry to arrive on time.*)

> **No empieces a llorar.** (*Don't start to cry.*)

Spanish verbs requiring de

The list of verbs requiring **de** before an infinitive is much shorter than the list for those verbs requiring **a.** I can't give you any hard and fast rules to help you with these. You simply have to memorize them and use them as much as possible. Table 12-3 lists the Spanish verbs that are followed by **de** before an infinitive.

Table 12-3   Spanish Verbs Requiring De

Infinitive	Meaning
acabar	to have just
acordarse (ue)	to remember to
alegrarse	to be glad
dejar	to stop
encargarse	to take charge of
olvidarse	to forget
tratar	to try to

Here are some examples showing you how to use **de** before an infinitive:

> **Mi mejor amiga dejó de fumar.** (*My best friend stopped smoking.*)

> **Mi esposo siempre se olvida de sacar la basura.** (*My husband always forgets to take out the garbage.*)

Spanish verbs requiring en

The list of verbs that require **en** before an infinitive is even shorter than the others, thankfully! Again, you must commit them to memory to know when to use them. Table 12-4 lists the Spanish verbs that are followed by **en** before an infinitive.

Table 12-4   Spanish Verbs Requiring En

Infinitive	Meaning
consentir (ie)	to agree to
consistir	to consist of
insistir	to insist on
tardar	to delay in

These examples illustrate how you use **en** before an infinitive:

> **Yo consiento en ir al teatro con Ramón.** (*I agree to go to the theater with Ramón.*)

> **¿Por qué insistes en partir ahora?** (*Why do you insist on leaving now?*)

Spanish verbs requiring con

The good news? As you move through all the preposition tables, your memorization duties get shorter and shorter! Table 12-5 shows the two Spanish verbs that use **con** before an infinitive.

Table 12-5   Spanish Verbs Requiring Con

Infinitive	Meaning
contar (-ue)	to count on
soñar (-ue)	to dream of

Here are examples with verbs that require **con** before the infinitive:

>**Él cuenta con trabajar con nosotros.** (*He is counting on working with us.*)

>**Yo sueño con salir con él.** (*I am dreaming about going out with him.*)

Verbs requiring no preposition

Bet you thought your memorization duties were over! I'm sorry to say that there's one more list you'll need to study. Table 12-6 shows verbs that don't require a preposition and are followed immediately by the infinitive.

Table 12-6   Verbs That Require No Preposition

Infinitive	Meaning
deber	to must (have to)
dejar	to allow to
desear	to want, wish to
esperar	to hope to
hacer	to make (have something done)
necesitar	to need to
pensar	to intend to
poder	to be able to
preferir	to prefer to
pretender	to attempt to
prometer	to promise to
querer	to want, to wish to
saber	to know how to

Here are example sentences containing verbs that require no preposition before the infinitive:

>**Pensamos hacer un viaje pronto.** (*We plan to take a trip soon.*)

>**Sé tricotar.** (*I know how to knit.*)

PRACTICE

You're a conducting an interview with a famous Spanish actress for your Spanish club's newsletter. You've taken notes, but now you have to complete your sentences by conjugating the verbs and joining the elements with prepositions, if needed. (For more on verb conjugation, see Chapter 4.) Write out what the actress tells you here.

Q. querer/ser modelo para los jóvenes

A. Quiero ser modelo para los jóvenes. (*I want to be a model for young people.*)

31 insistir/dar muchas entrevistas

_____

32 acabar/hacer una nueva película

_____

33 pensar/hacer muchas películas

_____

34 consentir/leer todos los manuscritos que recibo

_____

35 aprender/bailar mejor

_____

36 saber/hablar tres lenguas extranjeras

_____

37 dedicarse/ayudar a todo el mundo

_____

38 llegar/ser muy famosa

_____

39 esperar/ganar mucho dinero

_____

40 tratar/contestar bien a sus preguntas

_____

Using Prepositional Pronouns

You must use certain special Spanish pronouns after prepositions. The prepositional pronoun is used as the object of a preposition and always follows the preposition. Table 12-7 presents these prepositional pronouns.

Table 12-7 Prepositional Pronouns

Singular	Plural
mí (*me*)	**nosotros** (**nosotras**) (*us;* pol.)
ti (*you;* familiar)	**vosotros** (**vosotras**) (*you;* familiar)
él (*him, it*)	**ellos** (*them;* masculine)
ella (*her, it*)	**ellas** (*them;* feminine)
Ud. (*you: formal/polite*)	**Uds.** (*you;* polite)

Here are some examples to show you how you'll use these pronouns:

Esta carta es para mí, no es para ella. (*This letter is for me, not for her.*)

Juego al tenis con él, no con ella. (*I play tennis with him, not with her.*)

The prepositional pronouns **mí** and **ti** combine with the preposition **con** as follows:

>> **conmigo** (*with me*)

>> **contigo** (*with you*)

The following list presents some examples that show how you use these words:

¿Puedes ir al cine conmigo? (*Can you go to the movies with me?*)

No puedo ir contigo. (*I can't go with you.*)

PRACTICE

Your friend always annoyingly says the opposite of what you say. In the following exercise, write his sentences based on what you wrote.

Q. Nosotros vivimos cerca de Uds.

A. Uds. viven cerca de nosotros. (*You live near us.*)

(41) Yo salgo con él.

_____

(42) Ellas piensan en nosotros.

_____

43 Él compra un helado para ella.

_____

44 Vosotros habláis por mí.

_____

45 Nosotros recibimos un email de él.

_____

46 Tú vas al estadio con ellas.

_____

Answers to "Preparing to Connect with Prepositions" Practice Questions

1. **cerca de.** Use **cerca de** to express *near.*

2. **para.** Use **para** to express *in order to.*

3. **a.** Use **a** to express *to.*

4. **enfrente de.** Use **enfrente de** to express *in front of.*

5. **antes de.** Use **antes de** to express *before.*

6. **de.** Use **de** to express *from.*

7. **después.** Use **después** before **de** to express *after.*

8. **en.** Use **en** to express *on,* meaning *upon.*

9. **con.** Use **con** to express *with.*

10. **al.** Use **al** to express *to the*. **A** contracts with **el** before the masculine singular noun **el comedor.**

11. **entre.** Use **entre** to express *between.*

12. **dentro de.** Use **dentro de** to express *within.*

13. **en.** Use **en** to show location.

14. **de.** Use **de** to show relationship.

15. **a.** Use **a** to show movement.

16. **para.** Use **para** to show a purpose.

17. **a.** Use **a** to express *to.*

18. **al.** **A** contracts with **el** to become **al** and expresses *in the.*

19. **de.** Use **de** to show cause.

20. **de.** Use **de** to show material.

21. **por.** Use **por** to show substitution or *in exchange for.*

22. **en.** Use **en** to show location.

23. **por.** Use **por** to show the duration of an activity.

24. **para.** Use **para** to show a purpose.

(25) **a.** Use **a** to show time.

(26) **hasta.** Use **hasta** to show *until* a time.

(27) **de.** Use **de** to show time.

(28) **a.** Use **a** to show movement.

(29) **hasta.** Use **hasta** to express *until* a time.

(30) **hasta.** Use **hasta** to express *until* a time.

(31) **Insisto en dar muchas entrevistas. Insistir** is followed by **en** before an infinitive.

(32) **Acabo de hacer una nueva película. Acabar** is followed by **de** before an infinitive.

(33) **Pienso en hacer muchas películas. Pensar** is followed by **en** before an infinitive.

(34) **Consiento en leer todos los manuscritos que recibo. Consentir** is followed by **en** before an infinitive.

(35) **Aprendo a bailar mejor. Aprender** is followed by **a** before an infinitive.

(36) **Sé hablar tres lenguas extranjeras. Saber** doesn't use a preposition before an infinitive.

(37) **Me dedico a ayudar a todo el mundo. Dedicarse** is followed by **a** before an infinitive.

(38) **Llego a ser famosa. Llegar** is followed by **a** before an infinitive.

(39) **Espero ganar mucho dinero. Esperar** doesn't use a preposition before an infinitive.

(40) **Trato de contestar bien a sus preguntas. Tratar** is followed by **de** before an infinitive.

(41) **Él sale conmigo. Mí** joins with **con** to become **conmigo.**

(42) **Nosotros pensamos en ellas.** Use **ellas** to express *them.*

(43) **Ella compra un helado para él.** Use **él** to express *him.*

(44) **Yo hablo por vosotros.** Use **vosotros** to express *you.*

(45) **Él recibe un email de nosotros.** Use **nosotros** to express *us.*

(46) **Ellas van al estadio contigo. Ti** joins with **con** to become **contigo.**

4

Reminiscing about the Past and Seeing into the Future

Chapter **13**

Leaving It Completely in the Past

S ome people remember the past with fond memories. For others, however, the past is a time they'd like to forget! No matter how you feel about it, the past is a time that can help you learn and grow. In Spanish, different tenses allow you to express past actions. One of them is the *preterit*, which expresses an action, event, or state of mind that occurred and was completed at a specific time in the past. (For example, "She closed her book" or "He caught the ball.") In other words, if you had a digital camera, it would capture that moment instantly. If you remember that the action ended at a definite moment, you'll have no trouble using the preterit.

In this chapter, I show you how to form the preterit of regular verbs, verbs with spelling changes, verbs with stem changes, and irregular verbs. Along the way, I include helpful hints on how to remember the changes and irregularities you'll have to know and memorize. I also provide a detailed explanation on when to use the preterit so you won't make mistakes when the tense is called for and appropriate. By the end of this chapter, you'll be able to express what you did or saw in the past — for better or for worse!

Forming the Preterit

Knowing how to form the preterit isn't as challenging as you may believe. All regular verbs and verbs with spelling and stem changes whose infinitive ends in **-ar** have the same preterit endings. The same holds true for those verbs whose infinitive ends in **-er** and **-ir**. All irregular verbs have the same endings, and most fall into categories that make them easy to remember.

Regular verbs

Forming the preterit of regular verbs is rather easy, because although there are three different infinitive endings — **-ar, -er,** and **-ir** — you use only two different sets of endings for the preterit. To form the preterit of regular verbs, you drop the **-ar, -er,** or **-ir** infinitive ending and add the appropriate preterit endings.

Regular -ar verbs

The following table shows the conjugation of an **-ar** verb in the preterit:

mirar (to look at)	
yo mir*e*	nosotros mir*amos*
tú mir*aste*	vosotros mir*asteis*
él, ella, Ud. mir*ó*	ellos, ellas, Uds. mir*aron*

Here are some examples:

> **Yo miré la televisión.** (*I watched television.*)
>
> **Yo estudié el español.** (*I studied Spanish.*)

Express what the following people did yesterday.

PRACTICE

Q. (estudiar) Juanita _____.

A. **estudió.** Drop the **-ar** ending and add **-ó.**

1. (patinar) Roberto y yo _____ en el parque.

2. (trabajar) La señora Robles _____ en su oficina.

3. (ayudar) Tú _____ a tu amiga.

4. (comprar) Los Gómez _____ un coche nuevo.

5. (limpiar) Yo _____ mi cuarto.

6. (visitar) Vosotros _____ a vuestros tíos.

Regular -er and -ir verbs

Now look at **-er** and **-ir** verbs. If you look at the table carefully, you'll notice that both **-er** and **-ir** verbs have the same preterit endings, which certainly makes life a lot easier.

Subject	-er Verbs Beber (to drink)	-ir Verbs Recibir (to receive)
yo	beb*í*	recib*í*
tú	beb*iste*	recib*iste*
él, ella, Ud.	beb*ió*	recib*ió*
nosotros	beb*imos*	recib*imos*
vosotros	beb*isteis*	recib*isteis*
ellos, ellas, Uds.	beb*ieron*	recib*ieron*

Here are some examples:

Él no bebió nada. (*He didn't drink anything.*)

Todos los alumnos aprendieron mucho. (*All the students learned a lot.*)

¿Qué recibiste? (*What did you receive?*)

Mi amigo ecribió un poema en español. (*My friend wrote a poem in Spanish.*)

PRACTICE

Express what each person did on a day off.

Q. **Enrique/recibir muchos paquetes.**

A. **Enrique recibió muchos paquetes.** Drop the **-ir** ending and add **-ió.**

7. Tú/comer en un restaurante peruano _____

8. Elena/asistir a un concierto _____

9. Vosotros/abrir una cuenta de ahorros _____

10. Rafael y yo/prometer estudiar más _____

11. Yo/aprender a conducir un coche _____

12. Uds./decidir estudiar italiano _____

Now see how well you do with all three regular conjugations in the preterit.

PRACTICE

You just got back from a vacation with a tour group. Express what different people did on the tour by giving the preterit of the verb indicated.

Q. **(beber) Tú _____ mucha agua y nosotros _____ mucho café.**

A. **bebiste/ bebimos.** Drop the **-er** ending and add **-iste** for **tú** and **-imos** for **nosotros.**

13. (comer) Yo _____ demasiado pero ella _____ poco.

14. (comprar) Vosotros _____ aretes y nosotros _____relojes.

(15) (correr) Nosotros _____ en el gimnasio y vosotros _____ en el campo.

(16) (escribir) Tú _____ tarjetas postales y ellos _____ cartas.

(17) (gastar) Tú _____ mucho dinero pero Juanita _____ poco.

(18) (hablar) Yo _____ con todo el mundo pero ellos no _____ con nadie.

Verbs with spelling changes

Only two categories of verbs have spelling changes in the preterit tense:

>> Those with **-car, -gar,** and **-zar** endings.

>> Those that have a vowel before their **-er** or **-ir** ending.

The following sections dive into these changes.

Verbs ending in -car, -gar, and -zar

Verbs ending in **-car, -gar,** and **-zar** have the same change that they have in the subjunctive (see Chapter 6), but only in the **yo** form of the preterit. This is necessary to preserve the original sound of the verb. The basic changes are as follows.

Vowel Stem Change	Infinitive	Preterit
-c changes to **-qu**	**buscar** (to look for)	**yo busqué** (I looked for)
-g changes to **-gu**	**pagar** (to pay)	**yo pagué** (I payed)
-z changes to **-c**	**empezar** (to begin)	**yo empecé** (I began)

Table 13-1 has more examples.

Table 13-1   The Preterit for Verbs Ending in -car, -gar, and -zar

Subject	-car Verbs Tocar (to ouch, play [an instrument])	-gar Verbs Llegar (to arrive)	-zar Verbs Empezar (to begin)
yo	to**qué**	lle**gué**	empe**cé**
yú	to**caste**	lle**gaste**	empe**zaste**
él, ella, Ud.	to**có**	lle**gó**	empe**zó**
nosotros	to**camos**	lle**gamos**	empe**zamos**
vosotros	to**casteis**	lle**gasteis**	empe**zasteis**
ellos, ellas, Uds.	to**caron**	lle**garon**	empe**zaron**

Here are some examples with other verbs that use these endings:

>> **Yo expliqué el problema.** (*I explained the problem.*)

>> **Yo apagué la luz.** (*I turned off the light.*)

>> **Yo almorcé con mis amigos.** (*I ate lunch with my friends.*)

Verbs that change -i to -y

Verbs that contain a vowel immediately preceding their **-er** or **-ir** ending change **-i** to **-y** in the third-person singular (**él, ella, Ud.**) and plural (**ellos, ellas, Uds.**) forms. All other forms have an accented **-i**: **-í.**

REMEMBER

The **-i** to **-y** change doesn't hold true for the verb **traer** (*to bring*), which is irregular:

Él no trajo su pasaporte. (*He didn't bring his passport.*)

Table 13-2 shows high-frequency Spanish verbs that require the **-i** to **-y** change:

Table 13-2 The Preterit for Verbs That Change -i to -y

Subject	Caer (to fall)	Creer (to believe)	Leer (to read)	Oír (to hear)
yo	caí	creí	leí	oí
tú	caíste	creíste	leíste	oíste
él, ella, Ud,	cayó	creyó	leyó	oyó
nosotros	caímos	creímos	leímos	oímos
vosotros	caísteis	creísteis	leísteis	oísteis
ellos, ellas, Uds.	cayeron	creyeron	leyeron	oyeron

Here are some examples of these verbs in action:

El turista se cayó al lago. (*The tourist fell in the lake.*)

Ellos no me creyeron. (*They didn't believe me.*)

¿Leyó Ud. este artículo? (*Did you read this article?*)

No oyeron nada. (*They didn't hear anything.*)

WARNING

Verbs ending in **-uir** (**concluir** [*to conclude*], **destruir** [*to destroy*], **sustituir** [*to substitute*], and so on) follow the **-i** to **-y** change but don't accent the **-i** in the **tú, nosotros,** or **vosotros** forms:

yo concluí	nosotros concluimos
tu concluiste	vosotros concluisteis
él (ella, Ud.) concluyó	ellos (ellas, Uds.) concluyeron

Here is a **-uir** verb in action:

Ellos concluyeron sus estudios. (*They finished their studies.*)

Verbs with stem changes

The only verbs with stem changes in the preterit tense are **-ir** infinitive verbs that have a stem change in the present tense. (See Chapter 5 for more on that topic.) Be careful, though! The change is different in the preterit tense than it is in the present. Here's how you form the preterit: Change **-e** to **-i** or **-o** to **-u** only in the third-person singular (**él, ella, Ud.**) and plural (**ellos, ellas, Uds.**) forms. Table 13-3 shows what these verbs look like in the preterit tense.

Table 13-3   **The Preterit for -ir Infinitive Verbs with a Stem Change in Present Tense**

Subject	Preferir (e to ie; to prefer)	Pedir (e to i; to ask)	Dormir (o to ue; to sleep)
yo	prefer**í**	ped**í**	dorm**í**
tú	prefer**iste**	ped**iste**	dorm**iste**
él, ella, Ud.	prefir**ió**	pid**ió**	durm**ió**
nostoros	prefer**imos**	ped**imos**	dorm**imos**
vosotros	prefer**isteis**	ped**isteis**	dorm**isteis**
ellos, ellas, Uds.	prefir**ieron**	pid**ieron**	durm**ieron**

Here are some examples using these verbs:

Ella prefirió quedarse en casa ese día. (*She preferred to stay home that day.*)

Nosotros pedimos su ayuda. (*We asked for his help.*)

¿Dormiste bien? (*Did you sleep well?*)

And here are some more examples that use other verbs with these changes:

Él mintió. (*He lied.*)

Ellos sirvieron vino. (*They served wine.*)

El hombre murió. (*The man died.*)

PRACTICE

Express what happened yesterday by completing the conversations you had with and about friends and others. Change the verbs I provide from the infinitive to the preterit tense:

Q.   (mentir) ¿_____Ud.? No, yo no _____.

A.   mintió/mentí. Mentir changes **-e** to **-i** only in the third-person forms. Drop **-ir** and add **-ió** for **Ud.** and **-í** for **yo.**

19   (jugar) ¿_____tú al tenis? No, yo _____al fútbol.

20   (caerse) ¿Quién _____? Nosotros _____.

21   (leer) ¿_____Ud. este artículo? No, yo no lo _____.

22. (dormir) ¿_____José una siesta? Sí, el y yo _____ una siesta.

23. (platicar) ¿_____ Ud. con sus amigos? Sí, yo _____ con ellos.

24. (sentirse) ¿_____ Uds. bien ayer? Sí, nosotros _____ bien.

25. (oír) ¿Qué chismes _____Ud.? Yo no _____ ninguno.

26. (abrazar) ¿_____tú a tus padres? Yo los _____.

27. (vestirse) ¿A qué hora _____ Uds.? Nosotros _____ a las seis y media.

28. (distribuir) ¿Qué _____ Pablo y Juan? No sé pero yo _____ folletos.

Irregular verbs

Many verbs that are irregular in the present tense also are irregular in the preterit, which makes them easier to recognize as irregular verbs. Some of these irregular verbs may be grouped according to the changes they undergo. Unfortunately, a small number of verbs are completely irregular and must be memorized. I cover both in the sections that follow.

TIP

Most irregular verbs fall into categories, which makes them easier to remember. For example, the irregular verbs in this section fall into categories that have the following endings (without accent marks) in the preterit tense:

yo	-e
tú	-iste
él, ella, Ud.	-o
nosotros	-imos
vosotros	-isteis
ellos, ellas, Uds.	-ieron (or -jeron if the stem ends in -j)

Verbs with i in the preterit stem

Some Spanish verbs with an -e or an -a in their stems change the -e or -a to -i in the preterit. Table 13-4 presents four such verbs.

Table 13-4 The Preterit of Irregular Verbs with -i in the Preterit Stem

Subject	Decir (to say)	Venir (to come)	Querer (to want)	Hacer (to make, to do)
yo	dije	vine	quise	hice
tú	dijiste	viniste	quisiste	hiciste
él	dijo	vino	quiso	hizo*
nosotros	dijimos	vinimos	quisimos	hicimos
vosotros	dijisteis	vinisteis	quisisteis	hicisteis
ellos	dijeron	vinieron	quisieron	hicieron

WARNING

In the third-person singular preterit of **hacer**, **-c** changes to **-z** to maintain the original sound of the verb.

Here are examples of these verbs in action:

> **¿Qué dijo Ud.?** (*What did you say?*)
>
> **¿A qué hora vinieron?** (*At what time did they come?*)
>
> **Yo no quise salir anoche.** (*I didn't want to go out last night.*)
>
> **Los muchachos no hicieron nada.** (*The boys didn't do anything.*)

Verbs with u in the preterit stem

Some irregular Spanish verbs with an **-a** or an **-o** in their stem change the **-a** or the **-o** to **-u.** Table 13-5 presents examples of such verbs.

Table 13-5   The Preterit of Irregular Verbs with -u in the Preterit Stem

Subject	Caber (to fit)	Saber (to find out, learn)	Poner (to put)	Poder(to be able)
yo	cupe	supe	puse	pude
tú	cupiste	supiste	pusiste	pudiste
él	cupo	supo	puso	pudo
nosotros	cupimos	supimos	pusimos	pudimos
vosotros	cupisteis	supisteis	pusisteis	pudisteis
ellos	cupieron	supieron	pusieron	pudieron

Examples with these verbs follow:

> **Nosotros no cupimos todos en el coche.** (*We didn't all fit in the car.*)
>
> **¿Supo Ud. la respuesta?** (*Did you find out the answer?*)
>
> **Lo puse en la mesa.** (*I put it on the table.*)
>
> **No pudieron hacerlo.** (*They couldn't do it.*)

TIP

The irregular verbs **conocer** (*to know, to be acquainted with*), **saber** (*to know*), **tener** (*to have*), **querer** (*to want*), and **poder** (*to be able to*) may have a different meaning in the preterit:

> **Ella lo conoció en España.** (*She met him in Spain.*)
>
> **Nunca supieron la verdad.** (*They never found out (learned) the truth.*)
>
> **Tuve un regalo de ella.** (*I received a gift from her.*)
>
> **No quise hacerlo.** (*I refused to do it.*)
>
> **Él no pudo hablarle.** (*He didn't manage to speak to him.*)

Verbs with -uv in the preterit stem

Table 13-6 shows the three Spanish verbs that use **-uv** before their preterit endings. Be careful, though, because **tener** doesn't follow the same pattern as **andar** and **estar**.

Table 13-6   The Preterit of Irregular Verbs with -uv in the Preterit Stem

Subject	Andar (to walk)	Estar(to be)	Tener(to have)
yo	anduve	estuve	tuve
tú	anduviste	estuviste	tuviste
él	anduvo	estuvo	tuvo
nosotros	anduvimos	estuvimos	tuvimos
vosotros	anduvisteis	estuvisteis	tuvisteis
ellos	anduvieron	estuvieron	tuvieron

The examples that follow demonstrate how these verbs are used in the preterit:

Nosotros anduvimos al teatro. (*We walked to the theater.*)

Ayer yo estuve en casa. (*Yesterday I was at home.*)

Ella tuve un catarro. (*She had a cold.*)

Verbs with j in the preterit stem

Some irregular Spanish verbs have a **j** in their preterit stem. This category includes all verbs that end in **-ducir** as well as the verb **decir** (*to say*; see the section "Verbs with **i** in the preterit stem"). Note that there is no **-i** in the third-person singular or plural preterit endings. Table 13-7 shows the preterit form for two separate verbs.

Table 13-7   The Preterit of Irregular Verbs with -j in the Preterit Stem

Subject	Traer (to bring)	Conducir (to drive)
yo	traje	conduje
tú	trajiste	condujiste
él	trajo	condujo
nosotros	trajimos	condujimos
vosotros	trajisteis	condujisteis
ellos	trajeron	condujeron

Here are some examples using these verbs:

Ellos no trajeron sus libros a clase. (*They didn't bring their books to class.*)

¿Quién condujo? (*Who drove?*)

The preterit of dar and ver

The Spanish verbs **dar** and **ver** have the same irregular preterit endings. You drop their respective -**ar** and -**er** infinitive endings and then add their preterit endings to **d-** and **v-**. Table 13-8 shows the preterit of **dar** and **ver**.

Table 13-8   The Preterit of Dar and Ver

Subject	Dar (to give)	Ver (to see)
to	di	vi
tú	diste	viste
él	dio	vio
nosotros	dimos	vimos
vosotros	disteis	visteis
ellos	dieron	vieron

Here are examples with **dar** and **ver** in the preterit:

> **Dimos un paseo por el parque.** (*We took a walk in the park.*)

> **¿Viste esa película?** (*Did you see that film?*)

The preterit of ser and ir

The two irregular verbs **ser** (*to be*) and **ir** (*to go*) have the exact same preterit forms. How can you tell which verb is being used in a sentence? You have to look at the context of the sentence. The highly irregular conjugations of these two verbs are as follows:

ser (to be); ir (to go)	
yo fui	**nosotros fuimos**
tú fuiste	**vosotros fuisteis**
él, ella, Ud. fue	**ellos, ellas, Uds. fueron**

The following examples show you how you can figure out the meaning of the verb in use:

> **ir: Yo fui al mercado.** (*I went to the market.*)

> **ser: Yo fui muy honesto con él.** (*I was very honest with him.*)

Using the Preterit

You can use the preterit tense in many ways to convey past actions, events, or states of mind. You use the preterit to express the following:

>> An action or event that began at a specific time in the past:

- **El avión despegó a las seis.** (*The plane took off at six o'clock.*)

>> An action or event that was completed at a specific time in the past:

- **Anoche fuimos a una fiesta.** (*Last night we went to a party.*)

>> An action or event that was completed in the past within a specific time period:

- **Preparé la cena en una hora.** (*I prepared dinner in an hour.*)

>> A series of events that were completed within a definite time period in the past:

- **Me desperté, me bañé, y me vestí antes de desayunar.** (I woke up, I bathed, and I got dressed before eating breakfast.)

PRACTICE

Last night you had a date with your special someone. Write an email to a friend to tell her all about it. Conjugate the verb in the preterit.

Querida Luz,

29. (llegar) Guillermo _____ a mi casa a las siete de la noche.

30. (ir) Nosotros _____ al cine.

31. (pedir) Yo _____ un saco de palomitas y un refresco.

32. (tener) Él _____ una caja de dulces.

33. (ser) La película _____ mala.

34. (dormirse) Guillermo casi _____.

35. (andar) Después de la película, nosotros _____ por el parque.

36. (regresar) Finalmente, nosotros _____ a mi casa.

37. (querer) Él _____ darme un beso.

38. (decir) Yo _____, "¡Por supuesto!"

Gisela

Answers to "Leaving It Completely in the Past"

(1) **patinamos.** Drop the **-ar** ending and add **-amos.**

(2) **trabajó.** Drop the **-ar** ending and add **-ó.**

(3) **ayudaste.** Drop the **-ar** ending and add **-aste.**

(4) **compraron.** Drop the **-ar** ending and add **-aron.**

(5) **limpié.** Drop the **-ar** ending and add **-é.**

(6) **visitasteis.** Drop the **-ar** ending and add **-asteis.**

(7) **comiste.** Drop the **-er** ending and add **-iste** for tú.

(8) **asistió.** Drop the **-ir** ending and add **-ió.**

(9) **abristeis.** Drop the **-ir** ending and add **-isteis.**

(10) **prometimos.** Drop the **-er** ending and add **-imos.**

(11) **aprendí.** Drop the **-er** ending and add **-í.**

(12) **decidieron.** Drop the **-ir** ending and add **-ieron.**

(13) **comí/comió.** Drop the **-er** ending and add **-í** for **yo** and **-ió** for **ella.**

(14) **comprasteis/compramos.** Drop the **-ar** ending and add **-asteis** for **vosotros** and **-amos** for **nosotros.**

(15) **corrimos/corristeis.** Drop the **-er** ending and add **-imos** for **nosotros** and **-isteis** for **vosotros.**

(16) **escribiste/escribieron.** Drop the **-ir** ending and add **-iste** for **tú** and **-ieron** for **ellos.**

(17) **gastaste/gastó.** Drop the **-ar** ending and add **-aste** for **tú** and **-ó** for **Juanita.**

(18) **hablé/hablaron.** Drop the **-ar** ending and add **-é** for **yo** and **-aron** for **ellos.**

(19) **jugaste/jugué.** Verbs ending in **-gar** change **-g** to **-gu** only in the **yo** form of the preterit. Drop the **-ar** ending and add **-aste** for **tú** and **-é** for **yo.**

(20) **se cayó/nos caímos.** Verbs that contain a vowel immediately preceding their **-er** or **-ir** endings change **-i** to **-y** in the third-person forms. All other forms have an accented i: **í. Caerse** is a reflexive verb and requires the use of a reflexive pronoun before the verb. (See Chapter 10.) Drop the **-er** ending and add **-ó** for **¿Quién?** and **-ímos** for **nosotros.**

(21) **leyó/leí.** Verbs that contain a vowel immediately preceding their **-er** or **-ir** endings change **-i** to **-y** in the third-person forms. All other forms have an accented i: **í.** Drop the **-er** ending and add **-ó** for **Ud.** and **-í** for **yo.**

(22) **durmió/dormimos.** Change **-o** to **-u** only in the third-person forms. **Dormir** changes **-o** to **-u** only in the third-person forms. Drop **-ir** and add **-ió** for **Jose** and **-imos** for **él y yo.**

(23) **platicó/platiqué.** Verbs ending in **-car** change **-c** to **-qu** only in the **yo** form of the preterit. Drop the **-ar** ending and add **-ó** for **Ud.** and **-é** for **yo.**

(24) **se sintieron/nos sentimos. Sentir** changes **-e** to **-i** only in the third-person forms. Drop **-ir** and add **-ieron** for **Uds.** and **-ímos** for **nosotros. Sentirse** is a reflexive verb and requires the use of a reflexive pronoun before the verb. (See Chapter 10.)

(25) **oyó/oí.** Verbs that contain a vowel immediately preceding their **-er** or **-ir** endings change **-i** to **-y** in the third-person forms. All other forms have an accented *i*: **í.** Drop the **-er** ending and add **-ó** for **Ud.** and **-í** for **yo.**

(26) **abrazaste/abracé.** Verbs ending in **-zar** change **-z** to **-c** only in the **yo** form of the preterit. Drop the **-ar** ending and add **-aste** for **tú** and **-é** for **yo.**

(27) **se vistieron/nos vestimos. Vestir** changes **-e** to **-i** only in the third-person forms. **Vestirse** is a reflexive verb and requires the use of a reflexive (See Chapter 10.) Drop **-ir** and add **-ieron** for **Uds.** and **-imos** for **nosotros.**

(28) **distribuyeron/distribuí.** Verbs ending in **-uir** change **-i** to **-y** but don't accent the **-i** in the **tú, nosotros,** or **vosotros** forms. Drop **-uir** and add **-eron** for **Pablo y Juan** and **-í** for **yo.**

(29) **llegó.** Verbs ending in **-gar** change **-g** to **-gu** only in the **yo** form of the preterit. Drop **-ar** and add **-ó** for **Guillermo.**

(30) **fuimos. Ir** is irregular in the preterit. Use **fuimos** for **nosotros.**

(31) **pedí.** Drop **-ir** and add **-í** for **yo.**

(32) **tuvo. Tener** is an irregular verb and uses **-uv** before its preterit ending. Drop **-er** and add **-o** for **él.**

(33) **fue. Ir** is irregular in the preterit. Use **fue** for **la película.**

(34) **se durmió. Dormirse** is a reflexive verb that changes **-o** to **-u** only in the third-person forms. (See Chapter 10.) Drop **-ir** and add **-ió** for **Guillermo.**

(35) **anduvimos. Andar** is irregular in the preterit and uses **-uv** before its preterit ending. Drop **-ar** and add **-imos** for **nosotros.**

(36) **regresamos.** Drop the **-ar** ending and add **-amos** for **nosotros.**

(37) **quiso. Querer** is an irregular verb. Some Spanish verbs with an **-e** in their stem change **-e** to **-i** in the preterit. Drop **-er** and add **-o** for **él.**

(38) **dije. Decir** is an irregular verb. Some Spanish verbs with an **-e** in their stem change the **-e** to **-i** in the preterit. Some verbs have a **-j** in their preterit stems. Drop **-ir** and add **-e** for **yo.**

Chapter **14**

Looking Back with the Imperfect

C an you describe a beautiful place you once visited? Do you remember what you used to do when you were younger? Another past tense, the *imperfect,* allows you to give descriptions and to speak about what you were in the habit of doing in the past. Whereas the preterit tense allows you to express what you did in the past (see Chapter 13), the imperfect allows you to express what was happening or what used to happen previously. To put it in a visual sense, if the preterit tense captures a snapshot of a past action with the click of the button, the imperfect tense captures the motion of a past action with a video camera. For example, "He was swimming (used to, would swim) every day." If you recall that an action extended over an indefinite period of time, you'll have no trouble using the imperfect, and you won't confuse it with the preterit.

In this chapter, you see how to form the imperfect of regular and irregular verbs. (You'll be delighted to discover that there are no verbs with spelling or stem changes in this tense!) You also work on using the imperfect, and I include plenty of explanations and clues to help you decide when the imperfect, rather than the preterit, is the tense of choice. The various exercises in this chapter, along with those in Chapter 13, give you the practice you need so that you can easily select the proper past tense for any situation.

Perfecting the Imperfect

Unless you've studied a Romance language before, the imperfect is a tense you've never worked with. That's because we have no grammatical English equivalent for this past tense. If you're unfamiliar with the imperfect, you need to know, before you work on forming it, that it expresses a continuing state or action in the past — an action that was taking place or that used to happen repeatedly over an indefinite period of time. You also use the imperfect to describe scenes, settings, situations, or states in the past. In the imperfect, beginnings and endings are unimportant; only the events taking place have significance. Here are a few examples:

Durante el verana yo viajaba. (*During the summer, I used to [would] travel.*)

¿Adónde iban? (*Where were they going?*)

La puerta estaba cerrada. (*The window was open.*)

The following sections help you form the imperfect of both regular and irregular verbs (of which there are very few).

Forming the imperfect of regular verbs

Just like the preterit, forming the imperfect of regular verbs is rather easy. Although there are three different infinitive endings for regular verbs — **-ar, -er,** and **-ir** — you use only two different sets of endings to form the imperfect of these verbs.

You form the imperfect by dropping the **-ar, -er,** or **-ir** infinitive ending and adding the proper imperfect ending. The endings for **-er** and **-ir** verbs are the same, as you'll see in the following tables.

REMEMBER

It's your lucky day! You don't have to memorize any Spanish verbs with stem or spelling changes in the imperfect tense. That's right! Except for three cases, every verb forms the imperfect in the same way.

Yo me acostaba a las diez. (*I would go to bed at ten o'clock.*)

No conocía a ese hombre. (*I didn't know that man.*)

Ella no te entendía. (*She didn't understand you.*)

The imperfect conjugation of **-ar** verbs has a bit of a twist. Because the first- and third-person singular forms are the same for all verbs in the imperfect, for clarity it is often necessary to use subject pronouns.

mirar (to look at)	
yo mir*aba*	nosotros mir*ábamos*
tú mir*abas*	vosotros mir*abais*
él, ella, Ud. Mir*aba*	ellos, ellas, Uds. mir*aban*

Yo miraba la televisión. (*I was watching television.*)

Ella miraba la televisión. (*She was watching television.*)

Here are some other examples to show you how it's done:

Los turistas admiraban a los animales. (*The tourists were admiring the animals.*)

La muchacha cantaba. (*The girl was singing.*)

A lot of adults remember the after-school jobs they had in their youth. Write what these people recall by using the imperfect.

Q. (decorar) Verónica _____ pasteles en una panadería.

A. **decoraba.** Drop the **-ar** ending and add **-aba** for **Verónica.**

1 (contar) Yo _____ dinero en un banco.

2 (lavar) Vosotros _____ autos en un lavadero de autos.

3 (cocinar) Uds. _____ en un restaurante de comida rápida.

4 (ayudar) Nosotros _____ en una farmacia.

5 (trabajar) Tú _____ en un hospital.

6 (tocar) Diego _____ el piano en un café.

You do the same thing for **-er** and **-ir** verbs that you did for **-ar** verbs: Drop the infinitive ending and add the following endings.

Subject	-er Verbs beber (to drink)	-ir Verbs recibir (to receive)
Yo	**beb*ía***	**recib*ía***
Tú	**beb*ías***	**recib*ías***
Él, ella, Ud.	**beb*ía***	**recib*ía***
Nosotros	**beb*íamos***	**recib*íamos***
Vosotros	**beb*íais***	**recib*íais***
Ellos, Ellas, Uds.	**beb*ían***	**recib*ían***

Here are more examples of the imperfect in action, using regular verbs:

Los monos comían cacahuetes. (*The monkeys were eating peanuts.*)

Los tigres preferían dormirse. (*The tigers preferred to go to sleep.*)

Use the imperfect to express what the following people were doing when a storm broke out.

Q. (comer) Dorotea _____ el almuerzo.

A. Dorotea *comía* el almuerzo. Drop the –**er** ending and add –**ía** for **Dorotea**.

7 (comer) Vosotros _____ el almuerzo.

8 (salir) Los alumnos _____ de la escuela.

9 (conducir) Nosotros _____ al centro.

10 (leer) Yo _____ una revista.

11 (volver) Raquel _____ a casa.

12 (escribir) Tú _____ tu tarea.

Forming the imperfect of irregular verbs

Want some good news? There are only three Spanish verbs that are irregular in the imperfect tense. They should be easy to commit to memory. Here they are:

Subject	Ir (to go)	Ser (to be)	Ver (to see)
yo	iba	era	veía
tú	ibas	eras	veías
él	iba	era	veía
nosotros	íbamos	éramos	veíamos
vosotros	ibais	erais	veíais
ellos	iban	eran	veían

Here are some sentences that use these irregular verbs:

> **Nosotros íbamos al restaurante.** (*We were going to the restaurant.*)

> **Él era feliz.** (*He was happy.*)

> **Ellas veían a sus amigos los viernes.** (*They saw their friends on Fridays.*)

In your journal, discuss what various people around you were doing during a blackout by using the imperfect tense. I include the infinitive of the verb and you must change it to the imperfect. Here's an example to get you started:

Q. nosotros/escuchar música

A. Nosotros escuchábamos música.

13 vosotros/dormir una siesta

_____

14 ellos/discutir con sus amigos

_____

15 tú/jugar al baloncesto

_____

16 Ana/hacer ejercicios

_____

17 yo/servir la comida

_____

18 nosotros/preparar la cena

_____

19 Pablo y José/mirar la televisión

_____

20 Geraldo/telefonear a su novia

_____

21 mis padres/limpiar la casa

_____

22 Ud./ir a la farmacia

_____

23 los niños/almorzar

_____

24 Diana/trae una amiga a casa

_____

PRACTICE

For Spanish homework, your teacher asked you to write a description of a photo. Use the imperfect tense to describe what was happening in the picture you chose. I provide the verb, and you provide its imperfect conjugation.

Q. (ser) _____ las dos de la tarde.

A. **Eran. Ser** is irregular in the imperfect. Use the plural because it was two o'clock.

(ser)_____ (25) la primavera. (hacer)_____ (26)
buen tiempo. No (haber)_____ (27) nubes en el cielo. La familia
Cortés (ir)_____ (28) al parque. Mi madre (empujar)
_____ (29) un cochecito mientras mi padre (hablar)_____
(30) con mi hermano mayor, Fernando. Fernando (tener)_____ (31)
un globo rojo en las manos. Él (estar)_____ (32) muy
contento. Una muchacha (mirar)_____ (33) a la familia.
Ella (llevar)_____ (34) un vestido amarillo y negro y (comer)
_____ (35) un helado. Ella (parecer)_____ (36)
como una abeja. (ser)_____ (37) evidente que (querer)
_____ (38) ver al bebé.

TIP

The imperfect expresses what the subject "would do" if *would* has the sense of *used to*:

Generalmente, me despertaba a las seis. (*Generally, I would wake up at six o'clock.*)

Comparing the Preterit and the Imperfect

The preterit tense (see Chapter 13) expresses an action that was completed at a specific time in the past. You could represent such an event or action by drawing a dot. Boom! The action took place and was completed, and that's the end of it.

The imperfect tense, on the other hand, expresses a past action that continued over an indefinite period of time. You could represent such an action or event with a wavy line: It just kept moving and moving without an end in sight. The action continued over a period of time in the past — it *was* happening, *used to* happen, or *would* (meaning "used to") happen.

To summarize, compare the preterit and the imperfect side by side.

Preterit	Imperfect
Expresses a completed action. **Ellos bailaron.** (*They danced.*)	Describes ongoing or continuous actions or events (what **was** happening) in the past (which may or may not have been completed). **Ellos bailaban.** (*They were dancing,*)
Expresses a specific action or event that occurred at a specific point in past time. **Yo salí anoche.** (*I went out last night.*)	Describes habitual or repeated actions in the past. **Yo salía cada noche.** (*I went out each night.*)
Expresses a specific action or event that was repeated a stated number of times. **Yo salí dos veces.** (*I went out three times.*)	Describes an action that continues for an unspecified period of time. **Vivíamos en México.** (*We lived in Mexico.*)
	Describes a person, place, thing, state of mind, time, day, weather. **Ella era optimista.** (*She was optimistic.*) **El viaje era agradable.** (*The trip was nice.*) **Esperaba ganar.** (*He was hoping to win.*) **Era la una.** (*It was one o'clock.*) **Era martes.** (*It was Tuesday.*) **Llovía.** (*It was raining.*)
	Describes actions that took place simultaneously: **Yo escuchaba la radio mientras mi amiga miraba la televisión.** (*I was listening to music while my friend was watching television.*)

REMEMBER

In some instances, either the preterit *or* the imperfect is acceptable as a past tense. The tense you use may depend on the meaning you want to convey. For instance, if you want to convey that the action was completed, you can say

   Ella estudió. (*She studied.*)

If you want to convey that the action was ongoing or continuous, you can say

   Ella estudiaba. (*She was studying.*)

PRACTICE

You recently wrote a composition for Spanish class in the present tense, but your teacher wanted it written in the past tense. Oops! Rewrite the composition, changing all the verbs in the present tense to the preterit or imperfect tense.

Q. **Estoy en casa.**

A. **Estaba en casa.** Use the imperfect to describe an action that continues for an unspecified period of time. Drop the **-ar** ending and add **-aba** for **yo.**

   Es _____ (39) sábado. **Hace** _____ (40) frío. **Está** _____ (41) nevando. El sol no **brilla** _____ (42) y **hay** _____ (43) muchas nubes en el cielo. Los pájaros no **cantan** _____ (44) No **tengo** _____ (45) nada que hacer en particular. De repente el teléfono **suena** _____ (46) y yo **contesto** _____ (47.) **Es** _____ (48) mi amigo, Manuel. Me **dice** _____ (49) que **se aburre** _____ (50) mirando la televisión. Me **pregunta** _____ (51) si **quiero** _____ (52) salir.

Yo creo _____ (53) que es _____ (54) una buena idea. Yo sugiero _____ (55): "Nosotros podemos _____ (56) construir un muñeco de nieve." A Manuel no le gusta _____ (57) esa idea. Él prefiere _____ (58) construir una fortaleza de niee. Yo acepto _____ (59) esa idea. Yo le pido _____ (60) permiso a mi madre para salir. Naturalmente, ella dice _____ (61) "Sí." inmediatamente: Nosotros decidimos _____ (62) reunirnos a la una y nosotros colgamos _____ (63) el teléfono. El día es (64) _____ maravilloso.

PRACTICE

You want to talk to a friend about why certain people acted in a particular way in the past by using the preterit and the imperfect tenses. I provide the infinitives and you provide the preterit of the first verb and the imperfect of the second verb.

Q. (ir/tener) Pablo _____ al dentista porque _____ un dolor de muelas.

A. **fue/tenía. Pablo fue al dentista porque tenía un dolor de muelas. Ir** is irregular in the preterit. Drop **-er** from **tener** and add **-ía** for *he*.

65 (comer/seguir) Yo no _____ chocolate porque _____ un régimen.

66 (quedarse/estar) Mi novio _____ en casa porque _____ enfermo.

67 (caerse/prestar) Tú _____ porque no _____ atención.

68 (comprar/querer) Los muchachos _____ billetes porque _____ ver el partido de fútbol.

69 (enviar/celebrar) Luisa _____ una carta a su amiga porque ella _____ su cumpleaños.

70 (sacar/hacer) Nosotros _____ un traje de baño porque _____ sol.

Finding Clues to the Preterit and the Imperfect

Certain words in Spanish act as clues that indicate whether you should use the preterit or the imperfect tense, because they show that an action occurred at a specific time or imply that an action was ongoing over a period of time. The sections that follow help you determine which past tense you should use in a given situation.

The preterit: Specifying a time period

You often use the preterit tense along with words and expressions that specify a time period. The following table presents many of these common words and expressions.

Spanish	Meaning
anoche	*last night*
anteayer	*day before yesterday*
ayer	*yesterday*
ayer por la noche	*last night*
de repente	*suddenly*
el año pasado	*last year*
el otro día	*the other day*
el verano pasado	*last summer*
finalmente	*finally*
la semana pasada	*last week*
por fin	*finally*
primero	*at first*
un día	*one day*
una vez	*one time*

Here are some example sentences that show how you use these words with the preterit:

Anoche me quedé en casa. (*Last night I stayed home.*)

De repente, oímos un ruido fuerte. (*Suddenly we heard a loud noise.*)

Finalmente, lo terminé. (*Finally, I finished it.*)

The imperfect: Implying habitual action or repetition

You often use the imperfect tense with words and expressions that imply habitual action or repetition in the past. The following table lists many of these words and expressions.

Spanish	Meaning
a menudo	*often*
a veces	*sometimes*
cada día	*each day, every day*
con frecuencia	*frequently*
de vez en cuando	*from time to time*
en general	*generally*
frecuentemente	*frequently*
generalmente	*generally*
habitualmente	*habitually*
normalmente	*normally*
siempre	*always*
todo el tiempo	*all the time*
todos los días	*every day*
usualmente	*usually*

Here are examples that show how you use the imperfect tense with some words and expressions from the previous table:

Normalmente regresaba a las seis. (*You normally returned home at six o'clock.*)

Siempre jugaban al tenis. (*They always played tennis.*)

PRACTICE

You are writing a composition for school about your friend, Eduardo, who received a sizable inheritance from his grandfather. Express what he did on one fine summer day by putting the verbs in parentheses in their proper tense: the preterit or the imperfect. Be on the lookout for the clue words.

Q. (llover) _____ No _____.

A. **llovía.** Use the third-person singular imperfect to describe the weather.

(ser) _____ (71) el verano. (hacer) _____ (72) buen tiempo. (ser) _____ (73) el mediodía. Ayer Eduardo (recibir) _____ (74) una herencia de su abuela y (ir) _____ (75) al banco con el cheque que (querer) _____ (76) depositar en su cuenta. (pasar) _____ (77) por una concesión de coches. (llegar) _____ (78) al banco pero desafortunadamente (estar) _____ (79) cerrado porque (ser) _____ (80) la hora de almorzar. No (haber) _____ (81) otra cosa que hacer. En ese momento Eduardo (regresar) _____ (82) a la concesión y (mirar) _____ (83) por los escaparates. Él (escoger) _____ (84) un coche gris que le (gustar) _____ (85) enormemente. Él (tener) _____ (86) mucha curiosidad. Él (entrar) _____ (87) y (empezar) _____ (88) a hablar con el vendedor. Él le (hacer) _____ (89) muchas preguntas. El vendedor le (contestar) _____ (90) con mucha paciencia. Él le (explicar) _____ (91) todo. Ese coche (ser) _____ (92) muy deportivo. Eduardo (desear) _____ (93) comprarlo. Él le (pedir) _____ (94) el precio al vendedor. (ser) _____ (95) veinte mil dólares. Eduardo (tener) _____ (96) suficiente dinero y (comprar) _____ (97) el coche. (estar) _____ (98) tan contento. Ese día, Eduardo no (ir) _____ (99) otra vez al banco. En vez de hacer eso, él (ir) _____ (100) al campo en su coche nuevo.

Answers to "Looking Back with the Imperfect" Practice Questions

1. **contaba.** Drop the **-ar** ending and add **-aba** for **Verónica.**

2. **lavabais.** Drop the **-ar** ending and add **-abais** for **vosostros.**

3. **cocinaban.** Drop the **-ar** ending and add **-aban** for **Uds.**

4. **ayudábamos.** Drop the **-ar** ending and add **-ábamos** for **nosotros.**

5. **trabajabas.** Drop the **-ar** ending and add **-abas** for **tú.**

6. **tocaba.** Drop the **-ar** ending and add **-aba** for **Diego.**

7. **bebíais.** Drop the **-er** ending and add **-íais** for **vosotros.**

8. **salían.** Drop the **-ir** ending and add **-ían** for **los alumnos.**

9. **conducíamos.** Drop the **-ir** ending and add **-íamos** for **nosotros.**

10. **leía.** Drop the **-er** ending and add **-ía** for **yo.**

11. **volvía.** Drop the **-er** ending and add **-ía** for **Raquel.**

12. **escribías.** Drop the **-ir** ending and add **-ías** for **tú.**

13. **Vosotros** *dormíais* **una siesta.** Drop the **-ir** ending and add **-íais** for **vosotros.**

14. **Ellos** *discutían* **con sus amigos.** Drop the **-ir** ending and add **-ían** for **ellos.**

15. **Tú** *jugabas* **al baloncesto.** Drop the **-ar** ending and add **-abas** for **tú.**

16. **Ana** *hacía* **ejercicios.** Drop the **-er** ending and add **-ía** for **Ana.**

17. **Yo** *servía* **la comida.** Drop the **-ir** ending and add **-ía** for **yo.**

18. **Nosotros** *preparábamos* **la cena.** Drop the **-ar** ending and add **-àbamos** for **nosotros.**

19. **Pablo y José** *miraban* **la televisión.** Drop the **-ar** ending and add **-aban** for **Pablo y José.**

20. **Geraldo** *telefoneaba* **a su novia.** Drop the **-ar** ending and add **-aba** for **Geraldo.**

21. **Mis padres** *limpiaban* **la casa.** Drop the **-ar** ending and add **-aban** for **mis padres.**

22. **Ud.** *iba* **a la farmacia. Ir** is irregular in the imperfect.

23. **Los niños** *almorzaban.* Drop the **-ar** ending and add **-aban** for **los niños.**

24. **Diana** *traía* **una amiga a casa.** Drop the **-er** ending and add **-ía** for **Diana.**

25. **era. Ser** is irregular in the imperfect. Use the third-person singular to describe the season.

26. **hacía.** Drop the **-er** ending and add **-ía** to describe the weather.

27. **había.** Drop the **-er** ending and add **-ía** for the description.

(28) **iba. Ir** is irregular in the imperfect. Use the third-person singular for **la familia.**

(29) **empujaba.** Drop the **-ar** ending and add **-aba** for **mi madre.**

(30) **hablaba.** Drop the **-ar** ending and add **-aba** for **mi padre.**

(31) **tenía.** Drop the **-er** ending and add **-ía** for **Fernando.**

(32) **estaba.** Drop the **-ar** ending and add **-aba** for **él.**

(33) **miraba.** Drop the **-ar** ending and add **-aba** for **una muchacha.**

(34) **llevaba.** Drop the **-ar** ending and add **-aba** for **ella.**

(35) **comía.** Drop the **-er** ending and add **-ía** for **ella.**

(36) **parecía.** Drop the **-er** ending and add **-ía** for **ella.**

(37) **era. Ser** is irregular in the imperfect.

(38) **quería. (Needs accent.)** Drop the **-er** ending and add **-ía** for **ella.**

(39) **era.** Use the imperfect to describe an action that continues for an unspecified period of time. **Ser** is irregular in the imperfect.

(40) **hacía.** Use the imperfect to describe the weather. Drop the **-er** ending and add **-ía** for the third-person singular.

(41) **estaba.** Use the imperfect to describe the weather. Drop the **-ar** ending and add **-aba** for the third-person singular.

(42) **brillaba.** Use the imperfect to describe the weather. Drop the **-ar** ending and add **-aba** for **ella.**

(43) **había.** Use the imperfect to describe the scene. Drop the **-er** ending and add **-ía** for the third-person singular.

(44) **cantaban.** Use the imperfect to describe what was happening. Drop the **-ar** ending and add **-aban** for **los pájaros.**

(45) **tenía.** Use the imperfect to describe something occurring over an unspecified period of time. Drop the **-er** ending and add **-ía** for the subject **yo.**

(46) **sonó.** Use the preterit to express a completed action. Drop the **-ar** ending and add **-ó** for **el teléfono.**

(47) **contesté.** Use the preterit to express a completed action. Drop the **-ar** ending and add **-é** for **yo.**

(48) **era.** Use the imperfect to describe a person. **Ser** is irregular in the imperfect.

(49) **dijo.** Use the preterit to express a completed action. **Decir** has a stem change from **-e** to **-i** and has a **-j** in its preterit stem. Drop the **-ir** ending and add **-o** for **Manuel.**

(50) **aburría.** Use the imperfect to describe a state of mind. Drop the **-er** ending and add **-ía** for the **Manuel.**

(51) **preguntó.** Use the preterit to express a completed action. Drop the **-ar** ending and add **-ó** for **Manuel.**

(52) **queria.** Use the imperfect to describe a state of mind. Drop the **-er** ending and add **-ía** for **yo.**

(53) **creía.** Use the imperfect to describe a state of mind. Drop the **-er** ending and add **-ía** for the subject **yo.**

(54) **era.** Use the imperfect to describe a thing. **Ser** is irregular in the imperfect.

(55) **sugerí.** Use the preterit to express a completed action. Drop the **-ir** ending and add **-í.**

(56) **podíamos.** Use the imperfect to describe a state of mind. Drop the **-er** ending and add **-íamos** for the **nosotros.**

(57) **gustaba.** Use the imperfect to describe a state of mind. Drop the **-ar** ending and add **-aba** for **esa idea.**

(58) **prefería.** Use the imperfect to describe a state of mind. Drop the **-er** ending and add **-ía** for **él.**

(59) **acepté.** Use the preterit to express a completed action. Drop the **-ar** ending and add **-é** for **yo.**

(60) **pedí.** Use the preterit to express a completed action. Drop the **-ir** ending and add **-í** for the **yo.**

(61) **dijo.** Use the preterit to express a completed action. **Decir** has a stem change from **-e** to **-i** and has a **-j** in its preterit stem. Drop the **-ir** ending and add **-o** for **ella.**

(62) **decidimos.** Use the preterit to express a completed action. Drop the **-ir** ending and add **-imos** for the **nosotros.**

(63) **colgamos.** Use the preterit to express a completed action. Drop the **-ar** ending and add **-amos** for the **nosotros.**

(64) **era.** Use the imperfect to describe a thing. **Ser** is irregular in the imperfect.

(65) **comí/seguía.** Drop the **-er** ending and add **-í.** Drop the **-ir** ending and add **-ía** for **yo.**

(66) **se quedó/estaba.** Drop the **-ar** ending and add **-ó** and the reflexive pronoun **se** for **mi novio.** Drop the **-ar** ending and add **-aba.**

(67) **te caíste/prestabas.** Drop the **-er** ending and add **-íste** for **tú. Caer** takes an accent on the **-i.** Drop the **-ar** ending and add **-abas** for **tú.**

(68) **compraron/querían.** Drop the **-ar** ending and add **-aron** for **los muchachos.** Drop the **-er** ending and add **-ían.**

(69) **envió/celebraba.** Drop the **-ar** ending and add **-ó** for **ella.** Drop the **-ar** ending and add **-aba** for **ella.**

(70) **sacamos/hacía.** Drop the **-ar** ending and add **-amos** for **nosotros.** Drop the **-er** ending and add **-ía** for the third-person singular.

(71) **era.** Use the imperfect to describe the season. **Ser** is irregular in the imperfect.

(72) **hacía.** Use the imperfect to describe the weather. Drop the **-er** ending and add **-ía** for the third-person singular.

(73) **era.** Use the imperfect to describe the time. **Ser** is irregular in the imperfect.

(74) **recibió.** Use the preterit to express a completed action at a specific time. Drop the **-ir** ending and add **ió** for **Eduardo.**

(75) **fue.** Use the preterit to express a completed action at a specific time. **Ir** is irregular in the preterit.

(76) **quería.** Use the imperfect to describe a state of mind. Drop the **-er** ending and add **-ía** for **Eduardo.**

(77) **pasó.** Use the preterit to express a completed action. Drop the **-ar** ending and add **-ó** for **él.**

(78) **llegó.** Use the preterit to express a completed action. Drop the **-ar** ending and add **-ó** for **él.**

(79) **estaba.** Use the imperfect to describe a thing. Drop the **-ar** ending and add **-aba** for **el banco.**

(80) **era.** Use the imperfect to describe a time. **Ser** is irregular in the imperfect.

(81) **había.** Use the imperfect to describe a thing. Drop the **-er** ending and add **-ía** for the third-person singular.

(82) **regresó.** Use the preterit to express a completed action. Drop the **-ar** ending and add **-ó** for **Eduardo.**

(83) **miró.** Use the preterit to express a completed action. Drop the **-ar** ending and add **-ó** for **él.**

(84) **escogió.** Use the preterit to express a completed action. Drop the **-er** ending and add **-ió** for **él.**

(85) **gustaba.** Use the imperfect to describe a state of mind. Drop the **-ar** ending and add **-aba** for **el coche.**

(86) **tenía.** Use the imperfect to describe a state of mind. Drop the **-er** ending and add **-ía** for **él.**

(87) **entró.** Use the preterit to express a completed action. Drop the **-ar** ending and add **-ó** for **él.**

(88) **empezó.** Use the preterit to express a completed action. Drop the **-ar** ending and add **-ó** for **él.**

(89) **hizo.** Use the preterit to express a completed action. **Hacer** is irregular in the third-person singular. Change **-c** to **-z.**

(90) **contestó.** Use the preterit to express a completed action. Drop the **-ar** ending and add **-ó** for **el vendedor**.

(91) **explicó.** Use the preterit to express a completed action. Drop the **-ar** ending and add **-ó** for **él.**

(92) **era.** Use the imperfect to describe a thing. **Ser** is irregular in the imperfect.

(93) **deseaba.** Use the imperfect to describe a state of mind. Drop the **-ar** ending and add **-aba** for **Eduardo.**

(94) **pidió.** Use the preterit to express a completed action. **Pedir** changes **-e** to **-i** in the third-person. Drop **-ir** and add **ió** for **él.**

(95) **era.** Use the imperfect to describe a thing. **Ser** is irregular in the imperfect.

(96) **tenía.** Use the imperfect to describe a thing. Drop the **-er** ending and add **-ía** for **Eduardo.**

(97) **compró.** Use the preterit to express a completed action. Drop the **-ar** ending and add **-ó** for **Eduardo.**

(98) **estaba.** Use the imperfect to describe a state of mind. Drop the **-ar** ending and add **-aba** for **Eduardo.**

(99) **fue.** Use the preterit to express a completed action. **Ir** is irregular in the preterit.

(100) **fue.** Use the preterit to express a completed action. **Ir** is irregular in the preterit.

IN THIS CHAPTER

» Using the present and ir + a to form the future

» Putting regular and irregular verbs into the future

» Reviewing the uses of the future

Chapter **15**

Seeing into the Future

At one time or another, every person thinks about the future and makes plans based on hopes and dreams. For some dreamers, "preparing for the future" means getting an education. For others, it means getting a job, saving money, and starting a family. And then there are those who, each week without fail, proceed to the nearest candy store to purchase lottery tickets with the fantasy of becoming an instant millionaire! What unites everyone is the fact that the future is a time you look toward. In Spanish, you have three different ways to express future actions. One of them, believe it or not, is using the present tense. Another is to state what you're "going to do." Finally, you can use the future tense, which expresses what you "will do."

This chapter covers these topics to allow you to look toward the future. You discover how to use the present tense to express a future action. You practice using the Spanish verb **ir** (*to go*) + the preposition **a** (*to*) to say what a subject is going to do. I also show you how to form the future of regular and irregular verbs. You'll like this tense because there are no verbs with spelling or stem changes! Finally, you practice this tense so that you can comfortably use it when you speak or write — in the future!

Forming and Expressing the Future

In Spanish, you can express the future in three ways. One way is to use the present. If that's your choice, look back to Chapter 5 for all the details on proper usage. Another way is to use the verb **ir** (*to go*) and the preposition **a** (*to, at*). You use this expression to say what the subject is going to do in the near future. For this, you need to know the present-tense conjugation of **ir** (see later in this section). Then I cover how to form the future tense, which requires some new stems and some new endings.

Discussing the future by using the present

You use the present tense to imply the future when asking for instructions or when the proposed action will take place in the not-so-distant or near future. Here are two examples of these usages:

¿Dejo de hablar? (*Shall I stop talking?*)

Salimos mañana para Boston. (*We're leaving for Boston tomorrow.*)

For all the details on proper usage, check out Chapter 5.

Using ir + a to express the near future

You use the present tense of the verb **ir** (*to go*) + the preposition **a** (*to, at*) + the infinitive of the verb to express an action that will take place rather soon or that's imminent. Here are some examples that allow you to express what the subject is going to do:

Voy a salir. (*I'm going to go out.*)

Vamos a esperarlos. (*We are going to wait for them.*)

The present tense of **ir** is irregular, and you conjugate as shown in the following table.

ir (to go)	
yo voy	nosotros vamos
tú vas	vosotros vais
él, ella, Ud. va	ellos, ellas, Uds. van

PRACTICE

The parents in a family have decided to assign chores for everyone so the house stays clean. In Spanish, write the chores they must execute by using **ir** + **a.** Here's an example:

Q. Marta/lavar la ropa

A. Marta va a lavar la ropa.

1 yo/pasar la aspiradora

_____

2 nosotros/preparar la comida

_____

3 Alejandro/arreglar su cuarto

_____

4 vosotros/limpiar el coche

_____

5 tú/cortar el césped

_____

6 Cristina y Blanca/quitar el polvo de los muebles

_____

Expressing the future tense

The future tense explains what a subject will do or what action or event will take place in future time. Want some good news? The future tense in Spanish is just about as easy to form as possible, because it has only one set of endings. *All* verbs — that's right, every single one of them: regular verbs, verbs with spelling and stem changes, and irregular verbs — have the same future endings. (Well, some verbs do have irregular future stems, but these are limited in number.)

Sending regular verbs to the future

To form the future tense of a regular verb, you add the appropriate future ending for each subject to the infinitive of the verb, as shown in the following table with the verbs **trabajar**, **vender**, and **discutir**.

Subject	-ar Verbs trabajar	-er Verbs vender	-ir Verbs discutir
yo	trabajaré	Venderé	discutiré
tú	trabajarás	venderás	discutirás
él, ella, Ud.	trabajará	venderá	discutirá
nosotros	trabajaremos	venderemos	discutiremos
vosotros	trabajaréis	venderéis	discutiréis
ellos, ellas, Uds.	trabajarán	venderán	discutirán

TIP

The future endings are the same for **-ar**, **-er**, and **-ir** verbs. That really makes life so much easier!

Now check out some example sentences using the future tense:

Yo no los invitaré a mi fiesta. (*I won't invite them to my party.*)

Ellos no beberán alcohol. (*They won't drink alcohol.*)

¿Abrirás una cuenta bancaria pronto? (*Will you open a bank account soon?*)

PRACTICE

In the following exercises, express what different students both will and won't do in a study-abroad program. The first section provides the subject. The second section provides the verb that states what the subject will do. The final section provides the verb that, when preceded by the word **no,** states what the subject won't do. Follow this example:

Q. Elena/escribir notas/jugar

A. Elena escribirá notas. No jugará. Add **-á** to the infinitives for **Elena.**

7   tú/estudiar/mirar la televisión

_____

8   Carolina/asistir a todas las clases/visitar a sus amigas

_____

9   Luz y yo/leer todos los libros/escuchar música

_____

10   vosotros/aprender el vocabulario/descansar

_____

11   yo/prestar atención/pensar en otras cosas

_____

12   Jaime y Luis/correr a las clases/andar por el parque

_____

Sending irregular verbs to the future

Certain Spanish verbs are irregular in the future tense. These verbs have irregular future stems, which always end in **-r** or **-rr** — an easy way to remember them! To form the future of these irregular verbs, you do one of three things:

» Drop **-e** from the infinitive ending before adding the proper future ending.

Infinitive	Meaning	Future Stem
caber	to fit	cabr-
haber	to have	habr-
poder	to be able	podr-
querer	to want	querr-
saber	to know	sabr-

Here are some example sentences:

- **¿Cabrá esa máquina en el gabinete?** (*Will that machine fit in the cabinet?*)
- **¿Habrán terminado a tiempo?** (*Will they have finished on time?*)
- **No podremos venir.** (*We will not be able to come.*)
- **Querré verlo.** (*I will want to see it.*)
- **¿Sabrá hacerlo?** (*Will he know how to do it?*)

» Drop **-e** or **-i** from the infinitive ending and replace the vowel with a **-d** before adding the proper future ending:

Infinitive	Meaning	Future Stem
poner	*to put*	**pondr-**
salir	*to leave*	**saldr-**
tener	*to have*	**tendr-**
valer	*to be worth*	**valdr-**
venir	*to come*	**vendr-**

These verbs are illustrated in the following example sentences:

- **Yo pondré los papeles en la mesa.** (*I will put the papers on the table.*)
- **¿Cuándo saldrán?** (*When will they leave?*)
- **Ella no tendrá bastante dinero.** (*She will not have enough money.*)
- **¿Cuánto valdrá ese coche?** (*How much will that car be worth?*)
- **¿No vendrás mañana?** (*Won't you be coming tomorrow?*)

» Memorize the irregular future stems of the only two high-frequency verbs in Spanish that you will need. Then add the proper future endings:

Infinitive	Meaning	Future Stem
decir	*to say*	**dir-**
hacer	*to make, to do*	**har-**

Observe these verbs in action:

- **Yo diré lo que pienso.** (*I will say what I think.*)
- **¿Qué harán para resolver el problema?** (*What will they do to solve the problem?*)

In the following exercise, use the future tense to express what will happen at the next business conference you attend.

PRACTICE

Q. (escuchar) Yo _____ atentamente.

A. Yo escucharé atentamente. (*I will listen attentively.*)

13. (valer)_____la pena asistir a la conferencia.
14. (querer) Todos _____ venir a la conferencia en tren.
15. (venir) Todos los participantes_____mañana.
16. (hacer) Nosotros _____ todo lo posible para todos.
17. (saber) Nosotros no_____con antelación si el presidente (venir)_____.
18. (poder) Nosotros_____ hospedar a todos.
19. (poner) Nosotros_____carros a las órdenes de todos.
20. (tener) Todos _____que reservar lo más antes posible.
21. (decir) Todo el mundo_____ que es una conferencia importante.
22. (salir) Todos_____contentos.

Write an email message to a friend. Express what may or will happen by using the future tense.

PRACTICE

Q. (ir) Nosotros _____ al cine.

A. **iremos.** Add the **nosotros** ending **-emos** to **ir**.

Ernesto me (decir) _____ (23) sus planes para mañana, por la tarde. Él (poder) _____ (24) estar en mi casa a las dos. Yo sé que tu familia y tú (querer) _____ (25) ir con nosotros al cine pero tantas personas no (caber) _____ (26) en su coche. Ernesto (tener) _____ (27) que hacer dos viajes pero los (hacer) _____ (28) sin quejarse. ¿(saber) _____ (29) tú como ir al cine? (valer) _____ (30) la pena llegar allí temprano porque (haber) _____ (31) mucha gente a esa hora. Yo te (ver) _____ (32) pronto.

Using the Future Tense to Foretell, Predict, and Wonder

The idea that you should use the future to express future time may seem obvious. However, you must be aware of other instances in Spanish when you may use the future, too. Keep in mind that you use the future in the following instances:

>> To express what will happen:

● **Yo te ayudaré.** (*I will help you.*)

>> To predict a future action or event:

● **Lloverá pronto.** (*It will rain soon.*)

>> To express wonder, probability, conjecture, or uncertainty in the present. The Spanish future, in this case, is the equivalent to the following English phrases: *I wonder, probably,* or *must be:*

- **¿Cuánto dinero tendrán?** (*I wonder how much money they have.*)

- **Serán las seis.** (*It's probably [It must be] six o'clock.*)

- **Alguien viene. ¿Quién será?** (*Someone is coming. I wonder who it is.*)

- **¿Será mi esposo?** (*I wonder if it's my husband.*)

- **¿Irá a darme un anillo mi novio?** (*I wonder if my boyfriend is going to give me a ring.*)

PRACTICE

It's your job to write Spanish horoscopes for your club's newsletter. Complete each prediction by giving the correct form of the verbs in parentheses in Spanish.

Q. ARIES (marzo 21–abril 19): (hablar) Ud. _____ con su mejor amigo. (revelar) Él le _____ un secreto.

A. Hablará con su mejor amigo. Le revelará un secreto.

33 ARIES (marzo 21–abril 19): (conocer) Ud. _____ a una persona importante. (dar) Él le _____ una oportunidad increíble.

34 TAURO (abril 20–mayo 20): (tener) Ud. _____ buena suerte. (comprar) Ud. _____ un billete de lotería y (ganar) _____ mucho dinero.

35 GEMINIS (mayo 21–junio 21): (recibir) Ud. _____ una carta importante en el correo (dar) Le _____ buenas noticias.

36 CANCER (junio 22–julio 21): (dar) Su amigo le _____ consejos. (escuchar) Ud. los _____ y (poder) _____ conseguir un mejor puesto.

37 LEO (julio 22–agosto 21): (hacer) Ud. _____ un viaje y (conocer) _____ a muchas personas influyentes.

38 VIRGO (agosto 22–septiembre 22): (valer) Pronto su casa _____ un millón de dólares. (vender) Ud. la _____ y (hacer) _____ un crucero por el mundo.

39 LIBRA (septiembre 23–octubre 22): (salir) Ud. _____ con un amigo y (divertirse) Uds. _____ mucho.

40 ESCORPION (octubre 23–noviembre 21): (perder) Ud. _____ documentos importantes. (devolver) Un desconocido se los _____ a Ud.

41 SAGITARIO (noviembre 22–diciembre 21): (mentir) Ud. _____ a un amigo. (perdonar) Su amigo le _____ a Ud.

42 CAPRICORNIO (diciembre 22–enero 20): (ganar) Ud. _____ mucho dinero. (poner) Ud. _____ ese dinero en el banco para el futuro.

43 ACUARIO (enero 21–febrero 19): (ir) Ud. _____ en España y (aprender) _____ a hablar español con fluidez.

44 PISCIS (febrero 20–marzo 20): (salir) Ud. _____ de su oficina y (encontrar) _____ un billete de cien dólares en la calle.

Answers to "Seeing into the Future" Practice Questions

1. **Yo voy a pasar la aspiradora.** Conjugate **ir** to agree with **yo**. Add **a** and follow it with the infinitive.

2. **Nosotros vamos a preparar la comida.** Conjugate **ir** to agree with **nosotros**. Add **a** and follow it with the infinitive.

3. **Alejandro va a arreglar su cuarto.** Conjugate **ir** to agree with **Alejandro**. Add **a** and follow it with the infinitive.

4. **Vosotros vais a limpiar el coche.** Conjugate **ir** to agree with **vosotros**. Add **a** and follow it with the infinitive.

5. **Tú vas a cortar el césped.** Conjugate **ir** to agree with **tú**. Add **a** and follow it with the infinitive.

6. **Cristina y Blanca van a quitar el polvo de los muebles.** Conjugate **ir** to agree with **Cristina y Blanca**. Add **a** and follow it with the infinitive.

7. **Tú estudiarás. No mirarás la televisión.** Add **-ás** to the infinitives for **tú**.

8. **Carolina asisitirá a todas las clases. No visitará a sus amigas.** Add **-á** to the infinitives for **Carolina**.

9. **Luz y yo leeremos todos los libros. No escucharemos música.** Add **-emos** to the infinitives for **Luz y yo**.

10. **Vosotros aprenderéis el vocabulario. No descansaréis.** Add **-éis** to the infinitives for **vosotros**.

11. **Yo prestaré atención. No pensaré en otras cosas.** Add **-é** to the infinitives for **yo**.

12. **Jaime y Luis correrán a las clases. No andarán por el parque.** Add **-án** to the infinitives for **Jaime y Luis**.

13. **Valdrá la pena asistir a la conferencia.** Drop the **-e** from the infinitive ending and add **-d** in its place. Add **-á** for the third-person singular to express *it will be worth*.

14. **Todos querrán venir a la conferencia en tren.** Drop the **-e** from the from the infinitive ending and add **-án** for **todos**.

15. **Todos los participantes vendrán mañana.** Drop the **-i** from the infinitive ending and add **-d** in its place. Add **-án** for **todos los participantes**.

16. **Nosotros haremos todo lo posible para todos.** **Hacer** is irregular. Use **har-** as the future stem. Add **-emos** for **nosotros**.

17. **Nosotros no sabremos con antelación si el presidente vendrá.** Drop the **-e** from the infinitive ending and add **-emos** for **nosotros**. Drop the **-i** from the infinitive ending and add **-d** in its place. Add **-á** for **el presidente**.

18. **Nosotros podremos hospedar a todos.** Drop the **-e** from the infinitive ending and add **-emos** for **nosotros**.

(19) **Nosotros pondremos carros a los órdenes de todos.** Drop the **-e** from the infinitive ending and add **-d** in its place. Add **-emos** for **nosotros.**

(20) **Todos tendrán que reservar lo más antes posible.** Drop the **-e** from the infinitive ending and add **-d** in its place. Add **-án** for **todos.**

(21) **Todo el mundo dirá que es una conferencia importante. Decir** is irregular. Use **dir-** as the future stem. Add **-á** for **todo el mundo.**

(22) **Todos saldrán contentos.** Drop the **-i** from the infinitive ending and add **-d** in its place. Add **-án** for **todos.**

(23) **dirá. Decir** is irregular. Use **dir-** as the future stem. Add **-á** for **Ernesto.**

(24) **podrá.** Drop the **-e** from the infinitive ending and add **-d** in its place. Add **-á** for **Él.**

(25) **querréis.** Drop the **-e** from the infinitive ending and add **-éis** for **vosotros.**

(26) **cabrán.** Drop the **-e** from the infinitive ending and add **-án** for **nosotros.**

(27) **tendrá.** Drop the **-e** from the infinitive ending and add **-d** in its place. Add **-á** for **Él.**

(28) **hará. Hacer** is irregular. Use **har-** as the future stem. Add **-á** for **él.**

(29) **sabrás.** Drop the **-e** from the infinitive ending and add **-ás** for **tú.**

(30) **valdrá.** Drop the **-e** from the infinitive ending and add **-d** in its place. Add **-á** for the third-person singular to express *it will be worth.*

(31) **habrá.** Drop the **-e** from the infinitive ending and add **-á** for the third person singular to express *there will be.*

(32) **veré. Ver** is regular in the future. Add **-é** to the infinitive for **yo.**

(33) **Conocerá a una persona importante. Le dará una oportunidad increíble.** Add **-á** to the infinitive for both verbs that are regular in the future.

(34) **Tendrá buena suerte. Comprará un billete de lotería y ganará mucho dinero. For tener** drop the **-e** from the infinitive ending and add **-d** in its place. Add **-á** for **Ud.** Add **-á** to **comprar** and **ganar.**

(35) **Recibirá una carta importante en el correo. Le dará buenas noticias.** Add **-á** to the infinitive for both verbs that are regular in the future.

(36) **Su amigo le dará consejos. Los escuchará y podrá conseguir un mejor puesto.** Add **-á** to **dar** to form the future. Drop the **-e** from **poder** and add **-á** for both third-person subjects**.**

(37) **Hará un viaje y conocerá a muchas personas influyentes. Hacer** is irregular. Use **har-** as the future stem. Add **-á** for **Ud.** Add **-á** to **conocer.**

(38) **Pronto su casa valdrá un millón de dólares. La venderá y hará un crucero por el mundo.** For **valer:** drop the **-e** from the infinitive ending and add **-d** in its place. Add **-á** for **su casa.** Add **-á** to **vender. Hacer** is irregular. Use **har-** as the future stem. Add **-á** for **Ud.**

(39) **Saldrá con un amigo y se divertirán mucho.** For **salir:** drop the **-i** from the infinitive ending and add **-d** in its place. Add **-á** for **Ud.** Add **-án** to **divertir** for **Uds.**

(40) **Perderá documentos importantes. Un desconocido se los devolverá a Ud.** Add **-á** to the infinitive for both verbs that are regular in the future.

(41) **Mentirá a un amigo. Su amigo le perdonará a Ud.** (*You will lie to a friend. Your friend will forgive you.*) Add **-á** to the infinitive for both verbs that are regular in the future.

(42) **Ganará mucho dinero. Pondrá este dinero en el banco para el futuro.** (*You will earn a lot of money. You will put that money in the bank for the future.*) For **ganar:** add **-á** to the infinitive. For **poner:** drop the **-e** from the infinitive ending and add **-d** in its place. Add **-á** for **Ud.**

(43) **Irá en España y aprenderá a hablar español con fluidez.** (*You will go to Spain and you will learn to speak Spanish fluently.*) Add **-á** to the infinitive for both verbs that are regular in the future.

(44) **Saldrá de su oficina y encontrará un billete de cien dólares en la calle.** (*You will leave your office and you will find a $100 bill in the street.*) For **salir:** drop the **-i** from the infinitive ending and add **-d** in its place. Add **-á** for **Ud.** Add **-á** to **encontrar.**

5

The Part of Tens

Chapter **16**

Ten Most Common Mistakes in Spanish

Learning a second language is certainly a challenge. Mastering your native language was difficult enough, with all its rules and exceptions, but when you want to acquire a second language — especially after you've already reached the ripe old age of 12 or 13, when the rules of your first language are deeply rooted into your subconscious — you really have to work *hard* at memorizing and internalizing a whole new set of sounds, vocabulary, structures, and rules. This is quite a daunting task; I commend you for undertaking it!

As a token of my admiration, allow me to attempt to help you perfect your Spanish. In this chapter, I present the ten most common mistakes people make when learning Spanish. You'll want to avoid these if you want to sound authentic.

Confusing Gender Differences

In English, a noun is a noun and an adjective is an adjective. In Spanish, however, every noun — no matter who or what it is — is either masculine or feminine. The gender of the noun determines whether you must use a masculine or feminine adjective to describe that noun. Also, if the noun is singular, the adjective you use to describe it must also be singular. Likewise for plural nouns: They require plural adjectives. To complicate matters further, unlike in English, Spanish adjectives generally follow the nouns they describe.

Make sure your adjectives agree with your nouns and that they're in the right position (see Chapter 4). Here's an example sentence:

Los vestidos rojos son bonitos. (*The red dresses are pretty.*)

Insisting on Word-for-Word Translations

Whatever you do, don't try to translate your English thoughts word for word into Spanish. It simply won't work, and you may sound quite foolish if you make an unwise word selection.

Every language has its own set of idiomatic phrases that just don't translate well. Imagine how impossible it would be to translate and capture the true flavor of this English sentence: "She fell head over heels for him." Here's a Spanish example: **Él se ahogó en un vaso de agua.** The literal translation is *He drowned in a glass of water.* The Spanish idiomatic expression **Ahogarse en un vaso de agua** means *To make a mountain out of a molehill.* A computer language translator or even the best bilingual dictionary won't help you write Spanish properly unless you take idioms into consideration.

Forgetting the Personal "A"

English has no equivalent for the Spanish personal **a**; it's something so foreign and so unusual to English speakers that many of us tend to forget all about it when communicating in Spanish. No doubt, if you omit the personal **a**, you'll be marked as a foreigner! Do not despair! Even if you forget the personal **a**, you will certainly be able to get your point across and be understood by a native speaker.

REMEMBER

Use the personal **a** when the direct object in a sentence refers to a person. And don't forget that the preposition **a** contracts with the definite article **el** to become **al** before a masculine singular noun (see Chapter 3). Here are some examples: (Note that in the first example the personal **a** is not needed because you are referring to books and not to a person.)

Busco los libros. (*I'm looking for the books.*)

Busco a Ana. (*I'm looking for Ana.*)

Busco al muchacho. (*I'm looking for the boy.*)

Busco a las muchachas. (*I'm looking for the girls.*)

Using the Indefinite Article with an Unqualified Profession

"What do you do for a living?" "Well, I'm a teacher and my husband is an artist." In English, you use the indefinite article *a* or *an* when referring to a person's profession. In Spanish, the only time you use the indefinite article with a career is when the career is qualified or described with the help of an adjective. If you're mentioning only the profession, omit the indefinite article:

> **Es ingeniero y su esposa es dentista.** (*He's an engineer and his wife is a dentist.*)

> **Es un buen ingeniero y su esposa es una dentista popular.** (*He's a good engineer and his wife is a popular dentist.*)

Being Confused about Time

Spanish has three different words for *time:* **vez** (time in a series), **hora** (the time of day), and **tiempo** (time, in general). Here are examples that show the difference:

> **Vi esa película una vez (dos veces).** (*I saw that film one time [two times].*)

> **¿Qué hora es?** (*What time is it?*)

> **No tengo tiempo para mirar la televisión.** (*I don't have time to watch television.*)

Avoiding Double Negatives

In English, using a double negative is definitely a no-no because it's seen as being contradictory. In Spanish, however, double negatives are common and necessary. Sometimes, even triple negatives may appear in a sentence. That's because negative words in Spanish are used to reinforce the negative meaning. Consider the following examples:

> **No dije eso.** (*I didn't say that.*)

> **No dije nada.** (*I didn't say anything.*)

> **No dije nada a nadie.** (*I didn't say anything to anybody.*)

Misusing Gustar

English speakers often misuse **gustar** (*like*) because they forget that in the **gustar** construction, an indirect object precedes the verb and the subject follows the verb. Because a verb must agree with its subject, **gustar** must agree with the noun that comes *after* it. In most instances, you use only the third-person singular form (**gusta**) and the third-person plural form (**gustan**). Only the **gusta** form may be used before infinitives. The following examples highlight these points:

> **Me gusta el postre.** (*I like the dessert.*)
>
> **Me gustan las frutas.** (*I like fruits.*)
>
> **Me gusta bailar.** (*I like to sing.*)
>
> **Me gusta bailar y cantar.** (*I like to sing and dance.*)

Forgetting about Idioms with Tener

Although **tener** literally means *to have*, in certain very commonly used idiomatic expressions, **tener** means *to be* or may have another, unexpected meaning. Be careful not to use the verbs **ser** or **estar** (*to be*) in these idiomatic expressions. Improper verb selection for common phrases will mark you as a novice. These idiomatic expressions include the following:

tener calor (*to be warm, hot*)	**tener sed** (*to be thirsty*)
tener frío (*to be cool, cold*)	**tener lugar** (*to take place*)
tener celos de . . . (*to be jealous of*)	**tener miedo de** (*to be afraid of*)
tener cuidado (*to be careful*)	**tener prisa** (*to be in a hurry*)
tener dolor de . . . (*to have a . . . ache*)	**tener razón** (*to be right*)
tener éxito (*to succeed*)	**tener sueño** (*to be sleepy*)
tener ganas de . . . (*to feel like*)	**tener suerte** (*to be lucky*)
tener hambre (*to be hungry*)	

Here are some examples:

> **Tienes mucha suerte.** (*You are very lucky.*)
>
> **Yo tengo hambre.** (*I'm hungry.*)
>
> **Ella tiene ganas de bailar.** (*She feels like dancing.*)

Using the Incorrect Past Tense (Preterit or the Imperfect)

The fact that Spanish has two past tenses — one to state a completed action and one to describe what was happening in the past — confuses English speakers and causes a tremendous number of mistakes. Time and again, I've had students perfectly memorize the uses of the preterit and the imperfect only to use them improperly when they had to write compositions. (See Chapter 13.)

When communicating in the past, always consider the following:

» Am I referring to a completed action at a particular moment in the past? If so, then I must use the preterit.

» Am I describing a scene or expressing what *used to be* or *was* happening? If so, then I must use the imperfect.

Certain verbs that describe a state of mind — such as **querer** (*to want*), **poder** (*to be able to*), **saber** (*to know*), **pensar** (*to think*), and so on — are generally, but not always, used in the imperfect. The correct tense often depends on whether the writer perceives the action as completed at a specific time.

Ignoring the Subjunctive

Because English speakers are so unaware of the use of the subjunctive in English, we tend to have difficulty with its use in Spanish. If, however, you want to communicate like a native Spanish speaker, and if you want to do more than create simple, one-clause sentences, you must have a good command of the subjunctive. The subjunctive helps you express, among other things, your wishes, emotions, needs, and doubts.

Using the subjunctive properly will help you avoid the common mistakes associated with word-for-word translations. Here's an example:

I want you to go to the supermarket. (**Quiero que vayas al supermercado**.)

Although the English "I want you to go" is perfectly acceptable, in Spanish you can't say "I want you . . ." without being very fresh, if you know what I mean. You must join your two thoughts with **que** and you must put your dependent clause (the one following the clause showing the wishing, emotion, doubt, need, and so on) in the subjunctive. I cover the subjunctive in detail in Chapter 6.

Chapter **17**

Ten Important Verb Distinctions

H ave you used a thesaurus lately? A thesaurus is a wonderful tool that helps you write and speak without having to constantly repeat words. When your vocabulary varies, your prose tends to flow instead of dragging along. In some instances, if you're lucky, you'll find a word that has the exact meaning you're looking for. More often than not, however, the words you must choose from are very close in meaning to the word you want to replace, but don't communicate the precise idea you want to get across. You make your selection by trying to preserve, as much as possible, the thought or idea you want to express.

Just like in English, you can describe actions or situations in Spanish by using different verbs, depending on the exact meaning you want to convey. When you're learning a foreign language, picking up a good bilingual dictionary and reading the examples that show the subtle nuances in meaning will ensure that you select the verbs best suited to your needs. In this chapter, I present 20 verbs in Spanish but only 10 English meanings. These verbs are often misused because they have the same English meanings but different English connotations. But not to worry. I explain how you can determine which to use in any given situation.

Ser versus Estar

The verbs **ser** and **estar** always cause considerable confusion, because both verbs mean *to be*. You use each of these verbs differently, however.

You use **ser** to express the following:

›› An inherent characteristic or quality (one that probably won't change any time soon):

- **Mi abuela es vieja.** (*My grandmother is old.*)

›› The identity of the subject:

- **Mi padre es abogado.** (*My father is a lawyer.*)

›› The date, time, or place of an event:

- **Es jueves.** (*It's Thursday.*)
- **Son las once.** (*It's eleven o'clock.*)
- **¿Dónde es el concierto?** (*Where is the concert?*)

›› Origin and nationality:

- **Ella es de Cuba.** (*She is from Cuba.*)
- **Ella es cubana.** (*She is Cuban.*)

›› Ownership:

- **Es mi perro.** (*It's my dog.*)

›› Material:

- **Es de oro.** (*It's made of gold.*)

›› An impersonal idea:

- **Es fácil escribir en español.** (*It's easy to write in Spanish.*)

On the other hand, you use **estar** to express:

›› Health:

- **¿Cómo estás? Estoy bien.** (*How are you? I'm fine.*)

›› Location, situation, or position:

- **El diccionario está en la mesa.** (*The dictionary is on the table.*)

›› Temporary conditions or states:

- **Ella está ocupada.** (*She is busy.*)

›› The progressive tense (see Chapter 5):

- **El niño está durmiendo.** (*The child is sleeping.*)

Saber versus Conocer

Both **saber** and **conocer** mean *to know.* **Saber** expresses knowing how to do something or knowing a fact. **Conocer** expresses knowing in the sense of being acquainted with a person, place, thing, or idea. Note the differences in the following examples:

Yo sé hablar español. (*I know how to speak Spanish.*)

Ella sabe mi nombre. (*She knows my name.*)

Sabemos el poema. (*We know the poem [by heart].*)

Yo conozco al señor López. (*I know Mr. López.*)

¿Conoces este libro? (*Do you know [Are you acquainted with] this book?*)

Conocemos el poema. (*We know [are acquainted with] the poem.*)

Deber versus Tener Que

You use both **deber** and **tener que** to express what a subject *must* or *has* to do. You generally use **deber** to express a moral obligation, whereas **tener que** expresses what *has to be done*:

Debes pedir permiso antes de salir. (*You must ask for permission before going out.*)

Tengo que ir al dentista porque tengo un dolor de las muelas. (*I have to go to the dentist because I have a toothache.*)

Preguntar versus Pedir

Preguntar and **pedir** both mean *to ask*. You use **preguntar** to show that the subject is asking a question or inquiring about someone or something. You use **pedir** to show that the subject is asking for or requesting something in particular:

Quiero preguntarle si quiere acompañarme. (*I want to ask him if he wants to go with me.*)

¿Van a pedirles permiso? (*Are you going to ask them permission?*)

Yo le pregunté por qué me pidió tu dirección. (*I asked him why he asked me for your address.*)

Jugar versus Tocar

Jugar and **tocar** both mean *to play*. You use **jugar** when the subject is engaging in a sport or game. You use **tocar** when the subject is playing a musical instrument:

Ellos jugaban a los naipes mientras yo tocaba el piano. (*They were playing cards while I was playing the piano.*)

Gastar versus Pasar

If you're into *spending,* **gastar** and **pasar** are the verbs you need to discuss your passions. Those of us who love to spend money use **gastar,** while people who spend time engaging in an activity should use **pasar:**

> **Gasté mucho dinero allí.** (*I spent a lot of money there.*)
>
> **Pasé dos semanas en México.** (*I spent two weeks in Mexico.*)

Dejar versus Salir

Dejar expresses the idea that the subject has left something behind, whereas **salir** expresses that the subject has left a place:

> **Yo dejé mis gafas en casa.** (*I left my glasses home.*)
>
> **Ella no puede salir sin ellos.** (*She can't leave without them.*)

Volver versus Devolver

Volver(-ue) and **devolver(-ue)** both have the same meaning — *to return* — and you conjugate them in the same way. Use **volver** when the subject is physically returning to a place. Use **devolver** when the subject is returning an item to its owner:

> **Siempre le devuelvo a ella sus llaves cuando vuelve a casa.** (*I always return her keys to her when she returns home.*)

Tomar versus Llevar

Determining the correct usage for **tomar** and **llevar** can be a bit tricky. Both verbs mean *to take.* You use **tomar** when the subject picks up something in their hands to physically carry it to another location. You use **llevar** when the subject is taking or leading a person/thing somewhere (to a place) or is carrying or transporting an item.

TIP

In most instances, if you can substitute the word *lead* or *carry* for *take,* you should use the verb **llevar.** If you can't substitute one of those words, you should use **tomar.**

Here are some examples to help clarify:

> **Tomo tu lápiz.** (*I'm taking your pencil.*)
>
> **Tomó al niño de la mano.** (*He took the child by the hand.*)

Llevo a mi hermano a la playa. (*I'm taking my brother to the beach.*)

Llevaron su coche al garaje. (*They took their car to the garage.*)

You can compare the two verbs at work in this example sentence:

Tomé mi libro y lo llevé a la escuela. (*I took my book and I brought it to school.*)

Poder versus Saber

Poder and **saber** can be a tricky pair of verbs. Here's how they differ: **Poder** shows that the subject has the ability to perform an action, and **saber** shows that the subject actually knows how to perform the action.

TIP

If you can substitute the words *knows how to* for *can*, you should use **saber**. Otherwise, use **poder.** Here are some examples:

Yo puedo cocinar. (*I can cook.*) Here you're saying that you have the ability to cook, but that doesn't necessarily mean that you know *how* to cook.

Yo sé cocinar. (*I can cook.*) Now you're saying that, yes, you know how to cook!

6

Appendixes

Appendix A
Verb Charts

Regular Verbs

The three families of Spanish verbs are those that end in **-ar, -er,** and **-ir.** Regular verbs within those categories all follow the same rules for conjugation no matter what the tense (present, past, future) or mood (imperative, subjunctive). The regular verbs listed below drop their respective infinitive ending (**-ar, -er,** or **-ir**) and add endings the endings highlighted below.

-ar Verbs

hablar (to work)

Gerund: habl**ando**

Commands: ¡Habl**e** Ud.! ¡Habl**en** Uds.! ¡Habl**emos!** ¡Habl**a** tú! ¡No habl**es** tú! ¡Habl**ad** vosotros! ¡Habl**éis** vosotros!

Present	Preterit	Imperfect	Future	Subjunctive
habl**o**	habl**é**	habl**aba**	hablar**é**	habl**e**
habl**as**	habl**aste**	habl**abas**	hablar**ás**	habl**es**
habl**a**	habl**ó**	habl**aba**	hablar**á**	habl**e**
habl**amos**	habl**amos**	habl**ábamos**	hablar**emos**	habl**emos**
habl**áis**	habl**asteis**	habl**ábais**	hablar**éis**	habl**éis**
habl**an**	habl**aron**	habl**aban**	hablar**án**	habl**en**

-er Verbs

comer (to eat)

Gerund: com**iendo**

Commands: ¡Com**a** Ud.! ¡Com**an** Uds.! ¡Com**amos**! ¡Com**e** tú! ¡No com**as** tú! ¡Com**ed** vosotros! ¡No com**áis** vosotros!

Present	Preterit	Imperfect	Future	Subjunctive
com**o**	com**í**	com**ía**	comer**é**	com**a**
com**es**	com**iste**	com**erías**	com**eras**	com**as**
com**e**	com**ió**	com**ía**	com**erá**	com**a**
com**emos**	com**imos**	com**íamos**	comer**emos**	com**amos**
com**éis**	com**isteis**	com**íais**	comer**éis**	com**áis**
com**en**	com**ieron**	com**ían**	comer**án**	com**an**

-ir Verbs

abrir (to open)

Gerund: abr**iendo**

Commands: ¡Abr**a** Ud.! ¡Abr**an** Uds.! ¡Abr**amos**! ¡Abr**e** tú! ¡No abr**as** tú! ¡Abr**id** vosotros! No abr**áis** vosotros!

Present	Preterit	Imperfect	Future	Subjunctive
abr**o**	abr**í**	abr**ía**	abrir**é**	abr**a**
abr**es**	abr**iste**	abr**ías**	abrir**ás**	abr**as**
abr**e**	abr**ió**	abr**ía**	abrir**á**	abr**a**
abr**imos**	abr**imos**	abr**íamos**	abrir**emos**	abr**amos**
abr**ís**	abr**isteis**	abr**íais**	abrir**éis**	abr**áis**
abr**en**	abr**ieron**	abr**ían**	abrir**án**	abr**an**

Stem-Changing Verbs

Stem-changing verbs require an internal change in the stem vowel (the vowel before the **-ar**, **-er**, or **-ir** infinitive ending) in the **yo, tú, él, (ella, Ud.)**, and **ellos (ellas, Uds.)** forms of certain tenses. In all other tenses, stem-changing verbs don't require any change and follow the examples given in the previous section on regular verbs according to their infinitive ending.

-ar Verbs

pensar (e to ie; to think)

Present: pienso, piensas, piensa, pensamos, penséis, piensan

Subjunctive: piense, pienses, piense, pensemos, penséis, piensen

Other verbs like **pensar** include **cerrar** (*to close*), **comenzar** (*to begin*), **despertarse** (*to wake up*), **empezar** (*to begin*), and **sentarse** (*to sit down*).

mostrar (o to ue; to show)

Present: muestro, muestras, muestra, mostramos, mostráis, muestran

Subjunctive: muestre, muestres, muestre, mostremos, mostréis, muestren

Other verbs like **mostrar** include **acordarse de** (*to remember*), **almorzar** (*to eat lunch*), **acostarse** (*to go to bed*), **contar** (*to tell*), **costar** (*to cost*), **encontrar** (*to find*), **probar** (*to prove, to try*), and **recordar** (*to remember*).

jugar (u to ue; to play [a sport or game])

Present: juego, juegas, juega, jugamos, jugáis, juegan

Subjunctive: juegue, juegues, juegue, juguemos, juguéis, jueguen

-er Verbs

querer (e to ie; to wish, want)

Present: quiero, quieres, quiere, queremos, queréis, quieren

Subjunctive: quiera, quieras, quiera, queramos, queráis, quieran

Other verbs like **querer** include **defender** (*to defend, to forbid*), **descender** (*to descend*), **entender** (*to understand, to hear*), and **perder** (*to lose*)

volver (o to ue; to return)

Present: vuelvo, vuelves, vuelve, volvemos, volvéis, vuelven

Subjunctive: vuelva, vuelvas, vuelva, volvamos, volváis, vuelvan

Other verbs like **volver** include **devolver** (*to return*), **envolver** (*to wrap*), **llover** (*to rain*), **morder** (*to bite*), **mover** (*to move*), and **poder** (*to be able to, can*).

-ir Verbs

pedir (e to i; to ask)

Gerund: pidiendo

Present: pido, pides, pide, pedimos, pedís, piden

Preterit: pedí, pediste, pidió, pedimos, pedisteis, pidieron

Subjunctive: pida, pidas, pida, pidamos, pidáis, pidan

Other verbs like **pedir** include **impedir** (*to prevent*), **medir** (*to measure*), **repetir** (*to repeat*), and **servir** (*to serve*).

sentir (e to ie/i; to feel)

Gerund: sintiendo

Present: siento sientes, siente, sentimos, sentís, sienten

Preterit: sentí, sentiste, sintió, sentimos, sentisteis, sintieron

Subjunctive: sienta, sientas, sienta, sintamos, sintáis, sientan

Other verbs like **sentir** include **advertir** (*to warn, to notify*), **consentir** (*to consent*), **mentir** (*to lie*), **preferir** (*to prefer*), and **referir** (*to refer*).

dormir (o to ue/u; to sleep)

Gerund: durmiendo

Present: duermo, duermes, duerme, dormimos, dormís, duermen

Preterit: dormí, dormiste, durmió, dormimos, dormisteis, durmieron

Subjunctive: duerma, duermas, duerma, durmamos, durmáis, duerman

Another verb like **dormir** is **morir** (*to die*).

-uir Verbs (except -guir)

construir (y; to construct, build)

Gerund: construyendo

Present: construyo, construyes, construye, construimos, construís, construyen

Preterit: construí, construiste, construyó, construimos, construisteis, construyeron

Subjunctive: construya, construyas, construya, construyamos, construyáis, construyan

Other verbs like **construir** include **concluir** (*to conclude*), **contribuir** (*to contribute*), **destruir** (*to destroy*), **incluir** (*to include*), and **sustituir** (*to substitue*).

-eer Verbs

creer (i to y; to believe)

> Preterit: creí, creíste, cre**y**ó, creímos, creísteis, cre**y**eron

Other verbs like **creer** include **leer** (*to read*) and **poseer** (*to possess*), and **proveer** (*to provide*).

-iar Verbs

guiar (i to í; to guide)

> Present: guío, guías, guía, guiamos, guiáis, guían

> Subjunctive: guíe, guíes, guíe, guiemos, guiéis, guíen

Other verbs like **guiar** include **confiar + en** (*to confide in*), **enviar** (*to send*), **esquiar** (*to ski*), and **variar** (*to vary*).

-uar Verbs

continuar (u to ú; to continue)

> Present: contin**ú**o, contin**ú**as, contin**ú**a, continuamos, continuáis, contin**ú**an

> Subjunctive: contin**ú**e, contin**ú**es, contin**ú**e, continuemos, continuéis, contin**ú**en

Another verb like **continuar** is **actuar** (*to act*).

Spelling-Change Verbs

Some verbs require a spelling change in certain tenses to preserve proper pronunciation. In all tenses not listed in this section, verbs with spelling changes don't require the change and follow the examples given in the "Regular Verbs" section, according to their infinitive ending.

-car Verbs

buscar (c to qu; to look for)

> Preterit: bus**qu**é, buscaste, buscó, buscamos, buscasteis, buscaron

> Subjunctive: bus**qu**e, bus**qu**es, bus**qu**e, bus**qu**emos, bus**qu**éis, bus**qu**en

Other verbs like **buscar** include **acercar** (*to bring near*), **aplicar** (*to apply*), **criticar** (*to criticize*), **educar** (*to educate*), **explicar** (*to explain*), **identificar** (*to identify*), **pescar** (*to fish*), **practicar** (*to practice*), **sacar** (*to take out*), and **significar** (*to mean*).

-gar Verbs

llegar (g to gu; to arrive)

> Preterit: lle**gu**é, llegaste, llegó, llegamos, llegasteis, llegaron
>
> Subjunctive: lle**gu**e, lle**gu**es, lle**gu**e, lle**gu**emos, lle**gu**éis, lle**gu**en

Other verbs like **llegar** include **apagar** (*to extinguish*), **castigar** (*to punish*), **jugar** (*to play*) and **pagar** (*to pay*).

-zar Verbs

lanzar (z to c; to throw)

> Preterit: lan**c**é, lanzaste, lanzó, lanzamos, lanzasteis, lanzaron
>
> Subjunctive: lan**c**e, lan**c**es, lan**c**e, lan**c**emos, lan**c**éis, lan**c**en

Other verbs like **lanzar** include **avanzar** (*to advance*), **gozar** (*to enjoy*), **memorizar** (*to memorize*), **organizar** (*to organize*), and **utilizar** (*to use*).

Consonant + -cer or -cir Verbs

ejercer (c to z; to exercise)

> Present: ejer**z**o, ejerces, ejerce, ejercemos, ejercéis, ejercen
>
> Subjunctive: ejer**z**a, ejer**z**as, ejer**z**a, ejer**z**amos, ejer**z**áis, ejer**z**an

Other verbs like **ejercer** include **convencer** (*to convince*) and **vencer** (*to conquer*).

esparcir (c to z; to spread out)

> Present: espar**z**o, esparces, esparce, esparcimos, esparcéis, esparcen
>
> Subjunctive: espar**z**a, espar**z**as, espar**z**a, espar**z**amos, espar**z**áis, espar**z**an

Vowel + -cer or -cir Verbs

conocer (c to zc; to know)

> Present: cono**zc**o, conoces, conoce, conocemos, conocéis, conocen
>
> Subjunctive: cono**zc**a, cono**zc**as, cono**zc**a, cono**zc**amos, cono**zc**áis, cono**zc**an

Other verbs like **conocer** include **crecer** (*to grow*), **desobedecer** (*to disobey*), **desaparacer** (*to disappear*), **establecer** (*to establish*), **obedecer** (*to obey*), **ofrecer** (*to offer*), and **parecer** (*to seem*).

traducir (c to zc; to translate)

Present: tradu**zc**o, traduces, traduce, traducimos, traducéis, traducen

Subjunctive: tradu**zc**a, tradu**zc**as, tradu**zc**a, tradu**zc**amos, tradu**zc**áis, tradu**zc**an

Other verbs like **traducir** include **conducir** (*to drive*) and **deducir** (*to deduce*).

-ger or -gir Verbs

escoger (g to j; to choose)

Present: esco**j**o, escoges, escoge, escogimos, escogéis, escogen

Subjunctive: esco**j**a, esco**j**as, esco**j**a, esco**j**amos, esco**j**áis, esco**j**an

Other verbs like **escoger** include **coger** (*to take, to pick up*), **proteger** (*to protect*), and **recoger** (*to pick up*).

dirigir (g to j; to direct)

Present: diri**j**o, diriges, dirige, dirigimos, dirigís, dirigen

Subjunctive: diri**j**a, diri**j**as, diri**j**a, diri**j**amos, diri**j**áis, diri**j**an

Another verb like **dirigir** is **exigir** (*to demand*).

-uir Verbs

distinguir (gu to g; to distinguish)

Present: distin**g**o, distingues, distingue, distinguimos, distinguís, distinguen

Subjunctive: distin**g**a, distin**g**as, distin**g**a, distin**g**amos, distin**g**áis, distin**g**an

Irregular Verbs

Irregular verbs may have changes in some or all tenses and moods and for some or all subjects. Irregular forms must be memorized because they follow no specific rules. In all tenses not listed in this section, the irregular verb follows the examples given in the "Regular Verbs" section, according to its infinitive ending.

dar (to give)

Present: **doy,** das, da, damos, dáis, dan

Preterit: **di, diste, dió, dimos, disteis, dieron**

Subjunctive: **dé,** des, **dé,** demos, déis, den

decir (to say, tell)

Gerund: **diciendo**

Affirmative Familiar Singular Command: **di**

Present: **digo**, **dices**, **dice**, decimos, decís, **dicen**

Preterit: **dije, dijiste, dijo, dijimos, dijisteis, dijeron**

Future: **diré, dirás, dirá, diremos, diréis, dirán**

Subjunctive: **diga, digas, diga, digamos, digáis, digan**

estar (to be)

Present: **estoy, estás, está**, estamos, estáis, **están**

Preterit: **estuve, estuviste, estuvo, estuvimos, estuvisteis, estuvieron**

Subjunctive: **esté, estés, esté**, estemos, estéis, **estén**

hacer (to make, do)

Affirmative Familiar Singular Command: **haz**

Present: **hago,** haces, hace, hacemos, hacéis, hacen

Preterit: **hice, hiciste, hizo, hicimos, hicisteis, hicieron**

Future: **haré, harás, hará, haremos, haréis, harán**

Subjunctive: **haga, hagas, haga, hagamos, hagáis, hagan**

ir (to go)

Gerund: *yendo*

Affirmative Familiar Command: **ve**

Present: **voy, vas, va, vamos, vais, van**

Preterit: **fui, fuiste, fue, fuimos, fuisteis, fueron**

Subjunctive: **vaya, vayas, vaya, vayamos, vayáis, vayan**

oír (to hear)

Gerund: **oyendo**

Affirmative Informal Singular Command: **oye**

Affirmative Informal Plural Command: **oíd**

Present: **oigo, oyes, oye**, oímos, oís, **oyen**

Preterit: oí, oíste, **oyó**, oímos, oísteis, **oyeron**

Subjunctive: **oiga, oigas, oiga, oigamos, oigáis, oigan**

poder (o to ue; to be able to, can)

Gerund: **pudiendo**

Present: **puedo, puedes, puede,** podemos, podéis, **pueden**

Preterit: pude, pudiste, pudo, pudimos, pudisteis, pudieron

Future: **podré, podrás, podrá, podremos, podréis, podrán**

Subjunctive: **pueda, puedas, pueda**, podamos, podáis, **puedan**

poner (to put)

Affirmative Familiar Singular Command: **pon**

Present: **pongo,** pones, pone, ponemos, ponéis, ponen

Preterit: **puse, pusiste, puso, pusimos, pusisteis, pusieron**

Future: **pondré, pondrás, pondrá, pondremos, pondréis, pondrán**

Subjunctive: **ponga, pongas, ponga, pongamos, pongáis, pongan**

querer (to want, wish)

Present: **quiero, quieres, quiere**, queremos, queréis, **quieren**

Preterit: **quise, quisiste, quiso, quisimos, quisisteis, quisieron**

Future: **querré, querrás, querrá, querremos, querréis, querrán**

Subjunctive: quiera, **quieras, quiera**, queramos, **queráis, quieran**

saber (to know)

Present: **sé,** sabes, sabe, sabemos, sabéis, saben

Preterit: **supe, supiste, supo, supimos, supisteis, supieron**

Future: **sabré, sabrás, sabrá, sabremos, sabréis, sabrán**

Subjunctive: **sepa, sepas, sepa, sepamos, sepáis, sepan**

salir (to go out, leave)

Affirmative Familiar Singular Command: **sal**

Present: **salgo,** sales, sale, salimos, salís, salen

Future: **saldré, saldrás, saldrá, saldremos, saldréis, saldrán**

Subjunctive: **salga, salgas, salga, salgamos, salgáis, salgan**

ser (to be)

Affirmative Familiar Singular Command: **sé**

Present: **soy, eres, es, somos, sois, son**

Preterit: **fui, fuiste, fue, fuimos, fuisteis, fueron**

Imperfect: **era, eras, era, éramos, erais, eran**

Subjunctive: **sea, seas, sea, seamos, seáis, sean**

tener (to have)

Affirmative Familiar Singular Command: **ten**

Present: **tengo, tienes, tiene**, tenemos, tenéis, **tienen**

Preterit: **tuve, tuviste, tuvo, tuvimos, tuvisteis, tuvieron**

Future: **tendré, tendrás, tendrá, tendremos, tendréis, tendrán**

Subjunctive: **tenga, tengas, tenga, tengamos, tengáis, tenga**

traer (to bring)

Gerund: **trayendo**

Present: **traigo**, traes, trae, traemos, traéis, traen

Preterit: **traje, trajiste, trajo, trajimos, trajisteis, trajeron**

Subjunctive: **traiga, traigas, traiga, traigamos, traigáis, traigan**

venir (to come)

Gerund: **viniendo**

Affirmative Familiar Singular Command: **ven**

Present: **vengo, vienes, viene**, venimos, venís, **vienen**

Preterit: **vine, viniste, vino, vinimos, vinisteis, vinieron**

Future: **vendré, vendrás, vendrá, vendremos, vendréis, vendrán**

Subjunctive: **venga, vengas, venga, vengamos, vengáis, vengan**

ver (to see)

Present: **veo,** ves, ve, vemos, veis, ven

Preterit: **vi,** viste, **vio,** vimos, visteis, vieron

Imperfect: **veía, veías, veía, veíamos, veíais, veían**

Subjunctive: **vea, veas, vea, veamos, veáis, vean**

Appendix B

Thematic Vocabulary

EDUCATION

The Classroom

alumno (-a): *student*
asignatura: *subject*
bandera: *flag*
boletín (m.): *report card*
bolígrafo: *ballpoint pen*
borrador (m.): *chalkboard eraser*
cafeteria: *cafeteria*
calculadora: *calculator*
carpeta: *looseleaf binder*
cesto (de papeles): *wastepaper basket*
cinta: *tape*
clase (f.): *class*
consejero (-a): *counselor*
cuaderno: *notebook*
diccionario: *dictionary*
director (-a): *principal*
ejercicio: *exercise*
escritorio: *desk*
escuela: *school*
estudiante (m./f.): *student*
examen (m.): *test, exam*
goma: *pencil eraser*

horario: *schedule*
lapicero: *pencil case*
lápiz (m.): *pencil*
lección (f.): *lesson*
libro: *book*
maestro (-a): *teacher*
mapa (m.): *map*
marcador: *felt-tipped marker*
materia: *subject*
mochila: *backpack*
nota: *grade, mark*
página: *page*
palabra: *word*
papel (m.): *paper*
permiso: *pass (bathroom)*
pizarra: *chalkboard*
pluma: *pen*
profesor (-a): (a) *teacher*
prueba: *quiz, test*
pupitre (m.): *student's desk*
regla: *rule, ruler*
reloj (m.): *clock*
ropero: *locker*
sala de clase: *classroom*

tarea: *homework*
tijeras: *scissors*
timbre (m.): *bell*
tiza: *chalk*
vocabulario: *vocabulary*

Subjects

álgebra: *algebra*
arte (m.): *art*
artes industriales (f. pl.): *shop*
biología: *biology*
ciencias: *sciences*
coro: *chorus*
educación física (f.): *gym*
español (m.): *Spanish*
física: *physics*
francés (m.): *French*

geografía: *geography*
geometría: *geometry*
historia: *history*
informática: *computer science*
inglés (m.): *English*
matemáticas: *math*
música: *music*
química: *chemistry*
recreo: *recess*

Activities

banda: *band*
club (m.): *club*
cuadro de honor: *honor roll*
equipo: *team*
orquesta: *orchestra*

PERSONAL INFORMATION

Nationalities

americano (-a): *American*
canadiense: (m./f.): *Canadian*
chino (-a): (-a): *Chinese*
coreano (-a): (-a) *Korean*
cubano (-a): (-a) *Cuban*
francés/francesa: *French*
griego (-a): (-a) *Greek*
inglés/: inglesa: *English*
irlandés/: irlandesa: *Irish*
italiano (-a): (-a) *Italian*
japonés/japonesa: *Japanese*
mexicano;mejicano (-a): *Mexican No dash*
portugués/portguesa: *Portuguese*
puertorriqueño (-a): *Puerto Rican*
ruso (-a): (-a) *Russian*

Physical Characteristics

alto (-a): *tall*
bajo (-a): *short*
bonito (-a): *pretty*
calvo (-a): *bald*
delgado (-a): *thin*
feo (-a): *ugly*

gordo (-a): *fat*
grande: *big*
guapo (-a): *handsome*
joven: *young*
lindo (-a): *pretty*
moreno (-a): *dark-haired, dark-skinned*
pelirrojo (-a): *redheaded*
pequeño (-a): *small*
rubio(-a): *blond*
trigueño (-a): *dark-skinned*
viejo (-a): *old*

Personality Characteristics and Feelings

aburrido (-a): *boring*
agradable: *pleasant, nice, likable*
alegre: *happy*
amable: *courteous, nice*
amistoso (-a): *friendly*
antipático (-a): *unpleasant*
bueno (-a): *good*
cariñoso (-a): *affectionate*
cómico (-a): *funny*
confiado (-a): *trusting*
cortés: *courteous*

crudo (-a): *rude*
desagradable: *disagreeable*
descortés: discourteous
discreto (-a): *discreet*
divertido (-a): *fun*
educado (-a): *well-mannered, polite*
egoísta: *selfish*
encantador (a): *charming*
generoso(-a): *generous*
grosero (-a): *rude*
honrado (-a): *honorable*
impaciente: *impatient*
independiente: *independent*
indiscreto (-a): *indiscreet*
insociable: *unsociable*
inteligente: *intelligent*
interesante: *interesting*

irresponsable: *irresponsible*
listo (-a): clever, *sharp*
mal educado (-a): *impolite*
malo (-a): *bad*
optimista: *optimistic*
paciente: *patient*
pesimista: *pessimistic*
popular: *popular*
prudente: wise, *sensible*
respetuoso: *respectful*
responsable: *responsible*
serio (-a): *serious*
simpático (-a): *nice, friendly, likable*
sociable: *sociable*
tacaño (-a): *stingy*
tímido (-a): *shy*
trabajador (a): *hardworking*

EARNING A LIVING

Professions

abogado (-a): (-a) *lawyer*
actor: *actor*
actriz: *actress*
arquitecto (-a): (-a) *architect*
artista (m./f.): *artist*
auxiliar de vuelo: *flight attendant*
banquero (-a): *banker*
bibliotecario (-a): *librarian*
bombero (-a): *firefighter*
camarero (-a): *server*
carnicero (-a): *butcher*
carpintero (-a): *carpenter*
cartero (-a): *letter carrier*
científico (-a): *scientist*
cirujano (-a): *surgeon*
cocinero (-a): *cook*
comerciante (m./f.): *merchant*
consejero (-a): *counselor*
contable: : (m./f.) (Sp.): *accountant*
contador (a):(L.Am.) *accountant*
dentista: (m./f.): *dentist*
dependiente (m./f.): *salesperson*
director (a): *director, manager*
doctor (a): *doctor*
electricista: (m./f.): *electrician*

enfermero (-a): *nurse*
farmacéutico (-a): *pharmacist*
fotógrafo (-a): *photographer*
gerente (m./f.): *manager*
hombre de negocios: *businessman*
ingeniero (-a): *engineer*
investigador (-a): researcher No dash
jardinero (-a): *gardener*
jefe/jefa: boss, supervisor
joyero (-a): *jeweler*
juez (m./f.): *judge*
maestro (-a): *teacher*
mecánico (-a): *mechanic*
médico (-a): *doctor*
mesero (-a): *server*
mujer de negocios (f.): *businesswoman*
músico (-a): *musician*
oficinista: (m./f.): *office worker*
panadero (-a): *baker*
peluquero (-a): *hairdresser*
periodista: (m./f.): *journalist*
piloto (-a): *pilot*
policía (m./f.): *police officer*
profesor (a): *teacher*
programador (-a): *programmer*
psicólogo (-a): *psychologist*
veterinario (-a): *veterinarian*

Work Places

aeropuerto: *airport*
almacén: (m.): *warehouse*
banco: *bank*
casa: *home*
centro comercial: *mall*
comisaría: *police station*
consultorio: *doctor's office*
corte (m.): *court*

cuartel (m.) de bomberos: *firehouse*
escuela: *school*
fábrica: *factory, plant*
hospital (m.): *hospital*
laboratorio: *laboratory*
oficina: *office*
restaurante (m.): *restaurant*
taller (m.): *workshop*
tienda: *store*
universidad (f.): *university*

LEISURE ACTIVITIES

Sports

baloncesto: *basketball*
béisbol (m.): *baseball*
bolos (m. pl.): *bowling*
boxeo: *boxing*
buceo: *diving*
caza: *hunting*
ciclismo: *cycling*
ejercicios aeróbicos: *aerobics*
esquí (m.): *skiing*
footing (m.): *jogging*
fútbol (m.): *soccer*
fútbol americano: *football*
hockey (m.): *hockey*
lucha libre: *wrestling*
navegación (f.): *sailing*
patinaje (m.) sobre hielo: *ice skating*
patinaje (m.) sobre ruedas: *roller skating*
pesquería: *fishing*
tenis (m.): *tennis*
voleibol (m.): *volleyball*

Pastimes and Hobbies

andar en bicicleta: *to bike ride*
bailar: *to dance*
cantar: *to sing*
hacer yoga: *to practice yoga*
jugar a las damas: *to play checkers*
jugar a los naipes: *to play cards*
jugar al ajedrez: *to play chess*
levantar pesas: *to lift weights*
nadar: *to swim*
patinar: *to skate*
sacar fotos: *to take pictures*
viajar: *to travel*

Leisure Activities

ballet (m.): *ballet*
cine (m.): *movies*
concierto: *concert*
ópera: *opera*
playa: *beach*
teatro: *theater*

THE FAMILY

abuela: *grandmother*
abuelo: *grandfather*
abuelos: grandfathers, grandparents
esposa: *wife*
esposo: *husband*
familia: *family*

hermana: *sister*
hermanastra: *stepsister*
hermanastro: *stepbrother*
hermano: *brother*
hermanos: *brothers, brothers and sisters*
hija: *daughter*

hijastra: *stepdaughter*
hijastro: *stepson*
hijo: *son*
hijos: *children*
madrasta: *stepmother*
madre (f.): *mother*
nieta: *granddaughter*
nieto: *grandson*
niña: *girl*
niño: *boy*
niños: *children*

padastro: *stepfather*
padre: *father*
padres: *parents*
pariente (m.): *relative*
primo (-a): *cousin*
sobrina: *niece*
sobrino: *nephew*
tía: *aunt*
tío: *uncle*
tíos: *uncles, aunts and uncles*

MEALS, FOODS, BEVERAGES, AND QUANTITIES

Meals

almuerzo: *lunch*
cena: *supper, dinner*
comida: *meal, food*
desayuno: *breakfast*

Foods

alimento: *food*
apio: *celery*
atún (m.): *tuna*
azúcar (m.): *sugar*
brécol (m.): *broccoli*
brócoli (m.): *broccoli*
camarones (m. pl.): *shrimp*
carne (f.): *meat*
carne de cerdo (f.): *pork*
carne de vaca (f.): *beef*
cebolla (f.): *onion*
cereza: *cherry*
champiñón (m.): *mushroom*
chocolate (m.): *chocolate*
coliflor (f.): *cauliflower*
postre (m.): *dessert*
ensalada: *salad*
espárragos: *asparagus*
espinaca: *spinach*
filete (m.): *steak*
fresa: *strawberry*
fruta: *fruit*
gaseosa: *soda*
guisantes (m. pl.): *peas*

hamburguesa: *hamburger*
helado: *ice cream*
huevo: *egg*
jamón (m.): *ham*
judías: *beans*
langosta: *lobster*
lechuga: *lettuce*
legumbre (f.): *vegetable*
limón (m.): *lemon*
maíz (m.): *corn*
mantequilla: *butter*
manzana: *apple*
melocotón (m.): *peach*
naranja: *orange*
pan (m.): *bread*
papa: *potato*
pasa: *raisin*
pastel (m.): *pie, pastry*
patata: *potato*
pavo: *turkey*
pera: *pear*
pescado: *fish*
pimienta: *pepper (spice)*
pimiento: *pepper (vegetable)*
piña: *pineapple*
plátano: *banana*
pollo: *chicken*
refresco: *refreshment, soda*
sal (f.): *salt*
salchicha: *sausage*
sopa: *soup*
tocino: *bacon*
tomate (m.): *tomato*

uva: *grape*
ternera (carne de) (f.): *veal*
veneras: *scallops*
verdura: *vegetable*
zanahoria: *carrot*

Beverages

agua (el agua mineral): *(mineral) water*
café (m.): *coffee*
cerveza: *beer*
jugo: *juice*
leche (f.): *milk*
limonada: *lemonade*
sidra: *cider*
té (m.): *tea*
vino: *wine*
zumo: *juice*

Quantities

una botella de: *a bottle of*
una caja de: *a box of*
una copa de: *a glass of (wine)*
una docena de: *a dozen*
un frasco de: *a jar of*
un jarro de: *a pitcher of*

una lata de: *a can of*
un litro de: *a liter of*
un paquete de: *a package of*
una rebanada: *a slice of*
un saco de: *a bag of, a sack of*
una tableta de: *a bar of*
una taza de: *a cup of*
un tubo de: *a tube of*
un vaso de: *a glass of*

Table Setting

bol (m.): *bowl*
botella: *bottle*
copa: *wine glass*
cubierto: *silverware*
cuchara: *spoon*
cuchara: *soup spoon*
cuchillo: *knife*
mantel (m.): *tablecloth*
platillo: *saucer*
plato: *plate*
servilleta: *napkin*
taza: *cup*
tenedor (m.): *fork*
vaso: *glass*

APPAREL

Clothing

abrigo: *coat*
bata: *robe*
blazer (m.): *blazer*
blusa: *blouse*
bolsa: *pocketbook*
botas: *boots*
bufanda: *scarf*
calcetines (m. pl.): *socks*
camisa: *shirt*
camiseta: *T-shirt*
cartera: *wallet*
chal (m.): *shawl*
chaleco: *vest*
chaqueta: *jacket*

cinturón (m.): *belt*
corbata: *tie*
falda: *skirt*
gorro: *cap*
guantes (m. pl.): *gloves*
impermeable (m.): *raincoat*
jeans (m. pl.) (vaqueros): *jeans*
medias: *stockings*
pantalón (m.) de chándal: *sweatpants*
pantalones (m. pl.): *pants*
pantalones cortos (m. pl.): *shorts*
paraguas (m.): *umbrella*
pijamas (m. pl.): *pajamas*
ropa interior: *underwear*
sandalias: *sandals*
sombrero: *hat*

sudadera: *sweatshirt*
sudadera con capucha: *hoodie*
suéter: *sweater*
traje (m.): *suit (man's)*
traje (m.) de baño: *bathing suit*
traje (m.) sastre: *suit (woman's)*
vestido: *dress*
zapatillas: *slippers*
zapatillas deportivas: *sneakers*
zapatos: *shoes*

Colors

amarillo (-a): *yellow*
anaranjado (-a): *orange*
azul: *blue*
beige: *beige*
blanco (-a): *white*
gris: *gray*
marrón: *brown*

morado (-a): *purple*
negro (-a): *black*
pardo (-a): *brown*
rojo (-a): *red*
rosado (-a): *pink*
verde: *green*

Jewelry

anillo: *ring*
aretes (m. pl.): *earrings*
brazalete (m.): *bracelet*
cadena: *chain*
collar (m.): *necklace*
dije (m.): *charm*
pendientes (m. pl.): *earrings*
pulsera: *bracelet*
reloj (m.): *watch*
sortija: *ring*

HEALTH

Parts of the Body

boca: *mouth*
brazo: *arm*
cabello: *hair*
cabeza: *head*
cara: *face*
cerebro: *brain*
codo: *elbow*
corazón (m.): *heart*
cuello: *neck*
cuerpo: *body*
dedo: *finger*
dedo del pie: *toe*
diente (m.): *tooth*
espalda: *back*
estómago: *stomach*
frente (f.): *forehead*
garganta: *throat*

hombro: *shoulder*
labio: *lip*
lengua: *tongue*
mano: *hand*
mejilla: *cheek*
mentón (m.): *chin*
muñeca: *wrist*
nariz (f.): *nose*
ojo: *eye*
oreja: *ear*
pecho: *chest*
pelo: *hair*
pie (m.): *foot*
piel (f.): *skin*
pierna: *leg*
pulmón (m.): *lung*
rodilla: *knee*
tobillo: *ankle*
uña: fingernail

HOUSE AND HOME

House

apartamento: *apartment*
ascensor (m.): *elevator*
balcón (m.): *balcony*
baño: *bathroom*
casa: *house*
césped (m.): *lawn*
chimenea: *fireplace*
clóset (m.): *closet*
cocina: *kitchen*
comedor (m.): *dining room*
cuarto: *room*
despensa: *pantry*
desván (m.): *attic*
dormitorio: *bedroom*
ducha: *shower*
escalera: *stairs*
estudio: *study, den*
fregadero: *kitchen sink*
jardín (m.): *yard*
garaje (m.): *garage*
habitación (f.): *bedroom*
jardín (m.): *garden*
lavabo: *bathroom sink*
lavandería: *laundry room*
oficina: *office*
pared (f.): *wall*
pasillo: *corridor, hall*
patio: *courtyard*
patio trasero: *backyard*
piscina: *swimming pool*
piso: *floor, story*
porche (m.): *porch*
puerta: *door*
sala: *living room*
sala de estar: *family room, den*
sótano: *basement*
suelo: *floor, ground*
techo: *ceiling, roof*
terraza: *terrace*
ventana: *window*
vestíbulo: *foyer*

Furniture

alfombra: *rug*
armario: *wardrobe*
banca: *bench*
cama: *bed*
cómoda: *dresser*
cortina: *curtain*
escritorio: *desk*
espejo: *mirror*
estante (m.): *bookcase*
lámpara: *lamp*
librero: *bookcase*
mesa: *table*
mesita de noche: *night table*
moqueta: *carpet*
muebles (m. pl.): *furniture*
piano: *piano*
pintura: *picture*
reloj (m.): *clock*
silla: *chair*
sillón (m.): *armchair*
sofá: *sofa*

Chores

cargar (descargar) el lavaplatos: *load (unload) the dishwasher*
cocinar: *cook*
cortar el césped: *mow the lawn*
cuidar a los niños: *watch the children*
hacer la cama: *make the bed*
hacer las tareas domésticas: *do the housework*
ir de compras: *go shopping*
lavar el coche: *wash the car*
lavar la ropa: *do the laundry*
lavar los platos: *do the dishes*
limpiar la casa: *clean the house*
limpiar la mesa: *clear the table*
ordenar la sala: *tidy the living room*
pasar la aspiradora: *vacuum*
planchar la ropa: *iron the clothes*
poner la mesa: *set the table*
quitar el polvo: *dust*
quitar la mesa: *clear the table*
sacar la basura: *take out the garbage*
sacudir los muebles: *dust*

TRAVEL

aduana: *customs*
aeropuerto: *airport*
asiento: *seat*
autobús (m.): *bus*
automóvil (m.): *car*
avión (m.): *airplane*
barco: *boat*
bicicleta: *bicycle*
billete (m.): *ticket*
buque (m.): *ship*
camino: *road*
camión (m.): *truck*
carreterra: *highway*
carro: *car*
coche (m.): *car*
crucero: *cruise*
entrada: *entrance*
equipaje (m.): *baggage*
estación (f.): *station*
ferrocarril (m.): *railroad*
maleta: *suitcase*

mapa (m.): *map*
metro: *subway*
motocicleta: *motorcycle*
muelle (m.): *pier*
parada: *stop*
pasajero (-a): *passenger*
peaje (m.): *toll*
puerta: *gate*
ruta: *route*
salida: *exit*
tarifa: *fare*
taxi (m.): *taxi*
transporte (m.): *transportation*
tranvía (m.): *trolley*
tren (m.): *train*
vapor (m.): *steamship*
ventanilla: *ticket window*
viaje (m.): *trip*
viaje (m.) compartido: *ride share*
viajero (-a): *traveler*
vuelo: *flight*

THE NEIGHBORHOOD, THE COMMUNITY, AND THE ENVIRONMENT

Buildings

acuario: *aquarium*
aeropuerto: *airport*
ayuntamiento: *town hall*
banco: *bank*
biblioteca: *library*
café (m.): *coffee shop*
casa: *house*
castillo: *castle*
catedral (f.): *cathedral*
centro communal: *community center*
cine (m.): *movies*
comisaría: *police station*
correo: *post office*
edificio: *building*
escuela: *school*
estadio: *stadium*
hospital (m.): *hospital*

hotel (m.): *hotel*
iglesia: *church*
kiosco de diarios: *newsstand*
museo: *museum*
palacio: *palace*
puesto de diarios: *newsstand*
plaza: *square*
puente (m.): *bridge*
restaurante (m.): *restaurant*
sala de conciertos: *concert hall*
teatro: *theater*
templo: *temple*
tienda: *store*
torre (m.): *tower*

Areas and Directions

avenida: *avenue*
barrio: neighborhood

barrio residencial: *suburbs*
calle (f.): *street*
campo: *countryside*
centro: *downtown*
ciudad (f.): *city*
este (m.): *east*
fuente (f.): *fountain*
norte (m.): *north*
oeste (m.): *west*
parque (m.): *park*
pueblo: *town*
sur (m.): south
vecindario: *neighborhood*

Stores

almacén (m.): *department store*
bodega: *grocery store*
carnicería: *butcher shop*
centro: *commercial mall*
droguería: *drugstore*

dulcería: *candy store*
farmacia: *pharmacy, drug store*
floristería: *florist shop*
frutería: *fruit store*
joyería: *jewelry store*
juguetería: *toy store*
lechería: *dairy store*
librería: *bookstore*
marroquinería: *leather goods store*
mercado: *market*
mueblería: *furniture store*
panadería: *bakery*
papelería: *stationery store*
pastelería: *pastry shop*
peluquería: *hair salon*
pescadería: *fish store*
salón de belleza (m.): *beauty salon*
supermercado: *supermarket*
tabaquería: *tobacco shop*
tienda: *store*
tienda de ropa: *clothing store*
zapatería: *shoe store*

THE PHYSICAL ENVIRONMENT

Nature

aire (m.): *air*
árbol (m.): *tree*
arroyo: *stream*
bosque (m.): *forest*
campo: *country, field*
cielo: *sky*
desierto: *desert*
estrella: *star*
flor (f.): *flower*
hierba: *grass*
hoja: *leaf*
jardín (m.): *garden*
lago: *lake*
luna: *moon*
mar (m.): *sea*
montaña: *mountain*
naturaleza: *nature*
nube (f.): *cloud*
océano: *ocean*
planta: *plant*
playa: *beach*

río: *river*
sol (m.): *sun*
tierra: *earth, land*
viento: *wind*

Animals and Insects

abeja: *bee*
araña: *spider*
ballena: *whale*
caballo: *horse*
cabra: *goat*
canguro: *kangaroo*
cebra: *zebra*
cerdo: *pig*
ciervo: *deer*
cisne (m.): *swan*
cochino: *pig*
conejo: *rabbit*
cordero: *lamb*
elefante (m.): *elephant*
gallina: *hen*

gallo: *rooster*
gato: *cat*
jirafa: *giraffe*
león (m.): *lion*
leopardo: *leopard*
lobo: *wolf*
mono: *monkey*
mosca: *fly*
oso: *bear*
oveja: *sheep*
pájaro: *bird*
pantera: *panther*
pato: *duck*

pavo: *turkey*
perro: *dog*
pez (m.): *fish*
pollo: *chicken*
ratón (m.): *mouse*
serpiente (f.): *snake*
tiburón (m.): *shark*
tigre (m.): *tiger*
toro: *bull*
tortuga: *turtle*
vaca: *cow*
zorro: *fox*

TECHNOLOGY AND COMMUNICATION

adjunto: *attachment*
aplicación (f.): *app*
archivo: *file*
basura: *trash*
blog (m.): *blog*
buscador (m.): *search engine*
carpeta: *folder*
cartucho: *cartridge*
cibercafé (m.): *Internet cafe*
computadora: *computer*
correo basura: *junk mail, spam*
correo electrónico: *email*
cortafuegos (m. s.): *firewall*
cursor (m.): *cursor*
documento: *document*
enlace (m.): *link*
escritorio: *desktop*
favorito: *bookmark*
gráficos: *graphics*
hoja de cálculo: *spreadsheet*
ícono: *icon*
impresora: *printer*
informática: *computer science*
memoria: *memory*
memoria flash : *thumb drive*

mensaje (m.): *message*
navegador (m.): *browser*
ordenador (m.): *computer*
página: *page*
página principal: *home page*
pantalla: *monitor*
pirata (m./f.): *hacker*
portapapeles (m. s.): *clipboard*
portátil (m.): *laptop*
procesador (m.) de texto: *word processor*
programa (m.): *program*
programa (m.) antivirus: *antivirus software*
ratón (m.): *mouse*
red (f.): *network*
servidor (m.): *server*
símbolo: *symbol*
sitio: *site*
tecla: *key*
teclado: *keyboard*
tesauro: *thesaurus*
tinta: *ink*
tweet (m.): *tweet*
ventana: *window*
verificador (m.) de gramática: *grammar check*
verificador (m.) de ortografía: *spell-check*

MUSIC

Musical Instruments

acordeón (m.): *accordeon*
arpa (f.) (el arpa): *harp*
bajo eléctrico: *bass guitar*
batería: *drums*
clarinete (m.): *clarinet*
contrabajo: *bass*
corno francés: *French horn*
fagot (m.): *bassoon*
flauta: *flute*
flautín (m.): *piccolo*
guitarra: *guitar*
guitarra eléctrica: *electric guitar*

oboe (m.): *oboe*
órgano: *organ*
pandereta: *tambourine*
piano: *piano*
saxofón (m.): *saxophone*
tambor (m.): *drum*
trombón (m.): *trombone*
trompeta: *trumpet*
tuba: *tuba*
viola: *viola*
violín (m.): *violin*
violonchelo: *cello*
xilófono: *xylophone*

Appendix C

English-Spanish Dictionary

The English-Spanish Dictionary includes words that are needed to complete the English-Spanish exercises contained in this book. Where gender isn't obvious, (m.) or (f.) indicate masculine or feminine, respectively. Feminine and/or plural forms of adjectives are shown in parenthesis by a bolded (-a) or (-s) respectively. A bolded (se) at the end of a verb indicates that the verb may or may not be used reflexively. Stem changes (ie, ue, and so on) are shown in parentheses in bold after verbs that require them. For further information on the tenses that require stem changes, see Appendix A.

advice: **consejos**
after: **después**
afternoon (p.m.): **tarde**
all: **todo (-a)(-s)**
almost: **casi**
April: **abril**
around: **alrededor de**
arrive, to: **llegar**
ask, to: **pedir, preguntar**
August: **agosto**
autumn: **otoño**
bad: **mal (-o)(-a)**
be, to: **ser, estar**

beach: **playa**
because: **porque**
best: **mejor**
better: **mejor**
bill: **billete (m.)/cuenta /factura**
book: **libro**
box: **caja**
bring: **traer, llevar**
brother: **hermano**
but: **pero**
call, to: **llamar, telefonear**
candy: **dulces (m. pl.)**
Christmas: **Navidad (f.)**

chicken: **pollo**
come, to: **venir**
correct, to: **corregir**
cruise: **crucero**
date: **fecha**
day: **día**
December: **diciembre**
deserve, to: **merecer**
dinner: **cena**
do, to: **hacer**
document: **documento**
downtown: **centro**
dress oneself, to: **vestirse (i)**
drive, to: **conducir**
dry oneself, to: **secarse**
early: **temprano**
earn, to: **ganar**
eat breakfast, to: **desayunar**
eat, to: **comer**
eight: **ocho**
eighteen: **dieciocho (diez y ocho)**
eighty: **ochenta**
every: **cada**
everybody: **todo el mundo**
family: **familia**
fast: **rápido (-a)**
February: **febrero**
fifteen: **quince**
fifty: **cincuenta**
film: **película**
find, to: **encontrar (ue)**
first: **primero**
five: **cinco**
fluently: **con fluidez**
follow: **seguir (i)**
for: **por, para**
forgive, to: **perdonar**
forty: **cuarenta**
four: **cuatro**
fourteen: **catorce**
Friday: **viernes (m.)**
friend: **amigo**
fun, to have: **divertirse (ie)**
get, to: **conseguir/obtener**
get up, to: **levantarse**
gift: **regalo**
give, to: **dar**
go, to: **ir**
go out, to: **salir**
gold: **oro**

good: **buen (-o) (-a)**
he: **él**
help (to): **ayudar**
her: **su (-s)**
here: **aquí**
his: **su (-s)**
home: **casa**
how: **¿cómo?**
immediately: **inmediatamente**
important: **importante**
in: **en**
in front of: **enfrente de**
insist, to: **insistir (en)**
January: **enero**
job: **puesto/trabajo**
July: **julio**
June: **junio**
kiss, to: **besar**
know, to: **conocer, saber**
learn, to: **aprender**
leave, to: **salir (de)**
less: **menos**
letter: **carta**
lie, to: **mentir (ie)**
listen (to), to: **escuchar**
little: **poco**
lose, to: **perder**
lot, a: **mucho**
luck: **suerte (f.)**
lucky, to be: **tener suerte**
magazine: **revista**
March: **marzo**
May: **mayo**
mail: **correo**
me: **me, mí**
meal: **comida**
meet, to: **encontrar (ue)**
merchant: **comerciante (m./f.)**
midnight: **medianoche (f.)**
mistake: **error (m.), falta**
Monday: **lunes (m.)**
money: **dinero**
more: **más**
morning (a.m.): **mañana**
movies: **cine (m.)**
much: **mucho**
my: **mi (-s)**
neither . . . nor: **ni . . . ni**
news: **noticias**
nine: **nueve**

nineteen: **diecinueve (diez y nueve)**
ninety: **noventa**
nobody: **nadie**
noon: **mediodía (m.)**
November: **noviembre**
October: **octubre**
of: **de**
of course: **por supuesto**
office: **oficina**
one: **un (-o), una**
open, to: **abrir**
opportunity: **oportunidad (f.)**
other: **otro (-a)**
our: **nuestro (-a)(-s)**
park: **parque (m.)**
person: **persona**
please, to: **gustar**
prepare, to: **preparar**
present: **regalo**
put, to: **poner**
question: **pregunta**
quickly: **rápidamente**
receive, to: **recibir**
remain, to: **quedar (-se)**
repeat, to: **repetir (i)**
restaurant: **restaurante (m.)**
return, to: **regresar, volver (ue), devolver (ue)**
run, to: **correr**
salesperson: **dependiente (m./f.)**
Saturday: **sábado**
say, to: **decir**
school: **escuela**
sell, to: **vender**
September: **septiembre**
serve, to: **servir (i)**
seven: **siete**
seventeen: **diecisiete (diez y siete)**
seventy: **setenta**
she: **ella**
sister: **hermana**
some: **algunos (-as)**
soon: **pronto**
Spain: **España**
speak, to: **hablar**
spring: **primavera**
street: **calle (f.)**
study, to: **estudiar**
summer: **verano**

Sunday: **domingo**
sweater: **suéter (m.)**
take, to: **tomar**
take a trip, to: **hacer un viaje (m.)**
tell, to: **decir**
ten: **diez**
theater: **teatro**
their: **su (-s)**
there is (are): **hay**
they: **ellos, ellas**
thirteen: **trece**
thirty: **treinta**
thousand: **mil**
three: **tres**
through: **por**
Thursday: **jueves (m.)**
ticket: **billete (m.), boleto**
time: **hora, tiempo, vez (f.)**
trip: **viaje (m.)**
Tuesday: **martes (m.)**
twelve: **doce**
twenty: **veinte**
two: **dos**
until: **hasta**
us: **nosotros**
very: **muy**
walk, to: **andar**
want, to: **querer (ie)**
watch, to: **mirar**
we: **nosotros**
Wednesday: **miércoles (m.)**
well: **bien**
what: **¿qué?, ¿cuál?**
when: **¿cuándo?**
where: **¿dónde?**
while: **mientras**
who: **¿quién (-es)?**
why: **¿por qué?**
win, to: **ganar**
winter: **invierno**
with: **con**
without: **sin**
worth, to be: **valer**
word: **palabra**
work, to: **trabajar**
write, to: **escribir**
you: **tú, Ud., vosotros, Uds.**
your: **tu (-s), su (-s), vuestro (-a)(-s)**

Appendix D

Spanish-English Dictionary

The Spanish-English Dictionary includes words that are needed to complete the Spanish-English exercises contained in this book. Where gender isn't obvious, **(m.)** or **(f.)** indicate masculine or feminine, respectively. Feminine and/or plural forms of adjectives are shown in parenthesis by a bolded **(-a)** or **(-s)**, respectively. A bolded **(se)** at the end of a verb indicates that the verb may or may not be used reflexively. Stem changes (**ie, ue,** and so on) are shown in parentheses in bold after verbs that require them. For further information on the tenses that require stem changes, see Appendix A.

a: *to, at*
abeja: *bee*
abrigo: *coat*
abrazar: *to hug*
aburrir: *to bore*
acabar de: *to have just*
afeitar: *to shave*
afuera: *outside*
ahora: *now*
alamacén (m.): *department stores*
algún (alguno [-a]): *some, any*
allá: *there*
allí: *there*
almorzar: *to eat lunch*

amarillo (-a): *yellow*
andar: *to walk*
antelación, con: *in advance, beforehand*
añadir: *to add*
año: *year*
apagar: *to turn off*
aparecer: *to appear*
aprender: *to learn*
aquí: *here*
arreglar: *to tidy, fix up*
asistir: *to attend*
aspiradora: *vacuum*
asustado (-a): *afraid*
aterrizar: *to land*

avergonzado (-a): *embarrassed, ashamed*
ayer: *yesterday*
ayudar: *to help*
bailar: *to dance*
baloncesto: *basketball*
bañera: *bathtub*
barco: *boat*
bastante: *quite, rather, enough*
basura: *garbage*
beber: *to drink*
besar: *to kiss*
biblioteca: *library*
billete (m.): *ticket, bill*
bolsillo (m.): *pocket*
brillar: *to shine*
broma: *joke*
bronceador (m.): *suntan lotion*
broncearse: *to tan*
burlarse (de): *to make fun of*
caber: *to fit*
cada: *each, every*
caer: *to fall*
caja: *box*
calle (f.): *street*
cama: *bed*
camarote (m.): *cabin*
cambiar: *to change/to exchange*
camisa: *shirt*
campo: *countryside*
canción (f.): *song*
cansado (-a): *tired*
cariño: *affection*
carta: *letter/card*
cartel (m.): *sign*
cartera: *wallet/purse*
casarse: *to get married*
casi: *almost*
cena: *dinner*
cerrar (ie): *to close*
césped (m.): *lawn*
chiste (m.): *joke*
chófer (m.): *driver*
cielo: *sky*
cita: *appointment, date*
ciudad (f.): *city*
coche (m.): *car*
cocinar: *to cook*
coger: *to catch, grab*
colgar (ue): *to hang (up)*
colocar: *to place (something)*

comer: *to eat*
como: *like, as*
cómo: *how*
compartir: *to share*
comportamiento: *behavior*
comprar: *to buy*
con: *with*
conocer: *to know (to be acquainted with)*
conseguir (i): *to get, obtain*
consejo: *advice*
contar (ue): *to tell*
contestar: *to answer*
corregir (i): *to correct*
correo: *mail*
correr: *to run*
cortar: *to cut*
cosa: *thing*
crucero: *cruise*
cuál (-es): *which, what*
cuándo: *when*
cuánto (-a)(-s): *how much, many*
cuarto: *room*
cuenta (de ahorros): *account (savings account)*
cumpleaños (m.): *birthday*
dar: *to give*
dar un paseo: *to take a walk*
de: *of, from, by*
deber: *to have to (v.)/duty (n.)*
decir: *to tell, say*
dejar: *to leave, allow*
delante (de): *in front of*
demás, los: *the others*
demasiado: *too much*
dentro (de): *inside (of)*
deporte (m.): *sport*
deportivo (-a): *sporty*
derecha: *right*
derramar: *to spill*
desconocido (-a): *stranger*
desde: *from, since*
desear: *to desire, to wish, to want*
desfile (m.): *parade;* **(de moda)** *fashion show*
despacio: *slowly*
despertar (-se) (ie): *to wake up*
después: *after*
desvestir (-se) (i): *to undress*
devolver (ue): *to return*
dinero: *money*
divertir (-se) (i): *to amuse*
dolor (m.): *pain*

dónde: *where*
dormir (ue): *to sleep*
ducharse: *to take a shower*
duda: *doubt*
edificio: *building*
ejercicio: *exercise*
empezar (ie): *to begin, start*
empleado (-a): *employee, worker*
empujar: *to push*
encontrar (ue): *to meet, find*
enfadar: *to anger, irritate*
enfermo (-a): *sick*
engañar: *to deceive*
enojarse: *to become angry*
enseñar: *to teach, show*
entender (ie): *to understand*
entonces: *then*
entre: *between*
entrenador (-a): *coach*
entrevista: *interview*
equipaje (m.): *baggage*
equivocarse: *to make a mistake, to be mistaken*
escaparate (m): *store window*
escoger: *to choose*
esconder: *to hide (something)*
escribir: *to write*
escuchar: *to listen to*
esfuerzo: *effort*
esparcir: *to spread out*
esperar: *to hope, to wait for*
estadio: *stadium*
estar: *to be*
estómago: *stomach*
estrecho (-a): *narrow*
exigir: *to require, to demand*
extranjero (-a): *foreign*
extraño (-a): *strange*
fe (f.): *faith*
fecha: *date*
fiel: *loyal*
fijarse (en): *to notice*
firmar: *to sign*
folleto: *brochure, pamphlet*
ganar: *to earn, win*
ganga: *bargain*
gastar: *to spend (money)*
gato: *cat*
gente (f.): *people*
gerente (m./f.): *manager*
globo: *balloon*

gris: *gray*
guantera: *glove compartment*
guía (m./f.): *guide*
guisantes (m. pl.): *peas*
gustar: *to please*
hacer: *to make, to do*
hacer frío: *to be cold*
hambre (f.): *hunger*
hay: *there is, are*
herencia: *inheritance*
hora: *hour, time*
hospedar: *to house*
idioma (m.): *language*
impuesto: *tax*
increíble: *incredible*
ir: *to go*
jefa, jefe (m.): *boss*
jugar (ue) [a las damas]: *to play[checkers]*
jugo: *juice*
juguete (m.): *toy*
largo (-a): *wide/long*
lástima: *pity*
lavar (-se): *to wash (oneself)*
leer: *to read*
lejos: *far*
levantar (-se): *to raise*
libra: *pound*
ligero (-a): *light*
limpiar: *to clean*
llamar: *to call*
llave (f.): *key*
llegar: *to arrive*
llevar: *to take, wear*
llover: *to rain*
lodo: *mud*
luz (f.): *light*
maleta: *suitcase*
maletín (m.): *briefcase*
mandar: *to command, to order, to send*
maquillarse: *to put on makeup*
marcharse: *to go away*
más: *more*
medir (i): *to measure*
mejor: *better, best*
menos: *less*
mentir (ie): *to lie*
merecer: *to deserve, merit*
mezclar: *to mix*
mesa: *table*
mientras: *while*

mirar: *to look at*
mismo (-a): *same*
modo: *style*
mojado (-a): *wet*
mostaza: *mustard*
mostrar (ue): *to show*
muebles (m. pl.): *furniture*
mujer (f.): *woman*
muñeco (-a): *doll*
nada: *nothing*
naipe (m.): *playing card*
negar (ie): *to deny*
ningún (ninguno [-a]): *none*
nota: *grade*
noticias: *news*
nube (m.): *cloud*
nunca: *never*
oír: *to hear*
olvidarse (de): *to forget*
orgulloso (-a): *proud*
otro (-a): *other, another*
país (m.): *country*
pájaro: *bird*
palabra: *word*
palomitas de maíz: *popcorn*
pantalla: *screen*
papel (m.): *paper, role*
para: *for, in order to*
parecer: *to seem*
partido: *match*
pasar: *to spend (money)*
pastel (f.): *cake*
pedir (i): *to ask for*
pelear: *to fight*
película: *film, movie*
peligroso (-a): *dangerous*
pena (valer la): *trouble (to be worth the effort)*
pensar (ie): *to think*
perder (ie): *to lose*
perezoso (-a): *lazy*
pero: *but*
perro: *dog*
peso: *weight*
pierna: *leg*
piso: *floor*
planchar: *to iron*
playa: *beach*
poder (ue): *to be able to, can*
polvo: *dust*
poner: *to put*

por: *for, by, through, out (of)*
por supuesto: *of course*
postre (m.): *dessert*
pregunta: *question*
preguntar: *to ask*
prestar: *to borrow*
prestar atención: *to pay attention*
primavera: *spring*
probar (ue): *to try (on)*
pronto: *soon*
puerta: *door*
puesto: *job*
qué: *what*
quedar (-se): *to remain*
quejarse (de): *to complain*
quemadura: *burn*
querer (ie): *to wish, want*
quién (-es): *who, whom*
quitar (-se): *to remove, to take off*
rascacielos (m.): *skyscraper*
rato: *while*
rebanada: *slice, piece*
receta: *recipe*
régimen (m.): *diet*
refresco: *soft drink*
regalo: *gift*
regar (ie): *to water*
regla: *rule*
regresar: *to return*
reír: *to laugh*
relajar (-se): *to relax*
relámpagos: *lightning*
retraso, de: *late*
reunirse: *to meet*
romper: *to break*
ropa: *clothing*
ruido: *noise*
ruta: *road, route*
saber: *to know*
sacudir: *to dust*
sagaz: *astute, wise*
sala: *living room*
salir: *to go out*
saludable: *healthy*
secar (-se): *to dry (oneself)*
seguir (i): *to follow*
selva: *rainforest/jungle*
sentir (ie): *to be sorry, to regret*
ser: to *be*
siempre: *always*

sin: *without*
sol (m.): *sun*
sonar (ue): *to ring*
sorprendido (-a): *surprised*
sucio (-a): *dirty*
suelo: *ground, floor*
suerte (f.): *luck*
sugerir (ie): *to suggest*
tal vez: *perhaps*
también: *also, too*
tampoco: *either*
tanto (-a): *so much*
tantos (-as): *so many*
tarde: *late*
tarea (f.): *homework*
tarjeta: *card*
temprano: *early*
tener (ie): *to have*
tener cuidado: *to be careful*
tener hambre: *to be hungry*
tener miedo: *to be afraid*
tener que: *to have to*
tener sueño: *to be sleepy*
tiempo: *time*

tienda: *store*
timbre (m.): *bell*
tocar: *to play (an instrument)*
traer: *to bring*
traje (m.) [de baño]: *suit [bathing suit]*
tratar de: *to try to*
tren (m.): *train*
trueno: *thunder*
uva: *grape*
vaciar: *to empty*
valer: to be worth
venir: *to come*
ventana: *window*
ver: *to see*
verduras (f. pl.): *vegetables*
verdad (f.): *truth*
vestir (i): *to clothe, to dress*
vez (f.): *time;* **(de vez en cuando)** *from time to time*
viajar: *to travel*
viaje (m.): *trip*
volver (ue): *to return*
voz (f.): *voice*
ya: *already*
zanahoria: *carrot*

Index

F

false friends, 44–45

family, thematic vocabulary for, 322–323

feeling, present subjunctive after adjectives for, 139–140

first person, subject pronoun, 10

foods, thematic vocabulary for, 323–324

formal command, 218–223

friend, expression, greeting, salutation for, 8

furniture, thematic vocabulary for, 326

future tense, 283, 284, 285––289

G

-gar verb, 258–259, 314

gastar (to spend), 304

gender
  of adjectives, 74–78
  considerations regarding, 51
  definite article, 51–54
  with indefinite articles, 54–56
  mistakes regarding, 295–296
  of nouns, 34–35, 51, 59–61, 295–296
  sensitivity regarding, 78

gender neutral pronoun, 12–13. See also pronoun

-ger verb, 315

gerund, 114–115, 196, 212, 213

"Getting a Jump Start" practice question answers, 27–29

"Getting Answers with the Right Questions" practice question answers, 182–184

"Getting Attention with Commands" practice question answers, 234–238

-gir verb, 315

grande (adjective), 82

greeting, 7–10

guiar (to guide), 313

gustar (to please), 198–199, 297–298

H

habitual action, imperfect tense for, 277–278

hablar (to work), 309

hacer (to make, do), 112, 262, 316

hasta (until), 242

hay (there is/are?), 177, 179–180

health, thematic vocabulary for, 325

hobby, thematic vocabulary for, 322

house/home, thematic vocabulary for, 326

I

-iar verb, 106, 129, 313

idiomatic phrase, 34

imperative mood, 217

imperfect tense, 269–276, 277–278, 298–299

indefinite adjective, 36. See also adjective

indefinite article, 54–56, 297

indicative verb, present subjunctive for, 138. See also verb

indirect object noun, 189, 192–193. See also noun

indirect object pronoun, 35, 189–197, 198–199. See also pronoun

inequality, comparisons using, 156

infinitive, of the verb, 36, 196, 244–248. See also verb

informal command, 223–232. See also command

information, asking for, 171–177

insect, thematic vocabulary for, 328–329

interrogative adjective, 36, 171–172. See also adjective

interrogative adverb, 173–174. See also adverb

interrogative pronoun, 35, 174–177. See also pronoun

intonation, within yes/no questions, 166

inversion, of yes/no questions, 167–168

inverted exclamation mark (¡), within commands, 218

ir (to go), 264, 284–285, 316

-ir verb
  abrir (to open), 310
  conjugation of, 98–100, 256–257
  construir (to construct, build), 312
  dirigir (to direct), 315
  distinguir (to distinguish), 315
  dormir (to sleep), 312
  future tense for, 285–286
  gerund from, 114–115
  imperfect tense of, 270
  infinitive, 260
  pedir (to ask), 303, 312
  practice, 99, 124
  present subjunctive of, 124
  present tense of, 98–100
  preterit tense of, 256–257
  sentir (to feel), 312
  stem changes of, 104–105, 128–129, 312
  traducir (to translate), 315

irregular verb
  command with, 218–220, 222–223
  completely, 109–111
  dar (to give), 111–112, 264, 315

About the Author

Gail Stein, MA, is a retired language instructor who taught in New York City public junior and senior high schools for more than 33 years. She has authored several French and Spanish books, including *CliffsQuickReview French I* and *CliffsQuickReview French II*, *CliffsStudySolver Spanish I* and *CliffsStudySolver Spanish II*, *575+ French Verbs*, *Webster's Spanish Grammar Handbook*, *Working Spanish for Homeowners*, *Working Spanish for Teachers and Educational Professionals*, *Spanish Essentials For Dummies*, *Spanish All-in-One For Dummies*, and *Intermediate Spanish For Dummies*. Gail is a multiple-time honoree in *Who's Who Among America's Teachers*.

Dedication

This book is dedicated to my husband, Douglas, for his love and patience; and to my best friend, "Willy," for being so over-the-top supportive and excited for me, and for promising to promote this book in a rather unique and creative fashion.

Author's Acknowledgments

Many thanks to Lindsay Lefevere, my acquisitions editor, who was so helpful in getting this book off the ground. To Paul Levesque, my project editor, and Jennette ElNaggar, my copy editor, whose excellent editing skills and suggestions made this book a reality. To Maribel Campoy, whose technical expertise and input were invaluable. And to all the other people at Wiley for their patience and help.

Publisher's Acknowledgments

Acquisitions Editor: Lindsay Lefevere

Senior Project Editor: Paul Levesque

Copy Editor: Jennette ElNaggar

Tech Editor: Maribel Campoy

Production Editor: Saikarthick Kumarasamy

Cover Image: © Davide Angelini/Adobe Stock Photos